INFRASTRUCTURE FOUNDATIONS

This book, along with any associated content or subsequent updates, can be accessed at https://hdl.handle.net/10986/44671.

Reproducible Research Repository

https://reproducibility.worldbank.org

A reproducibility package is available for this book in the Reproducible Research Repository at https://reproducibility.worldbank.org/catalog/536.

Scan to see all titles in the series.

SUSTAINABLE INFRASTRUCTURE SERIES

INFRASTRUCTURE FOUNDATIONS

FROM CURRENT ASSETS TO FUTURE GROWTH

Stéphane Straub, He He, Yue Li, Xinxin Lyu, Jevgenijs Steinbuks, Estefanía Vergara Cobos, Christopher Dann, Manuel García-Santana, and Harris Selod

Contents

Part 1

Chapter 1 A Framework to Assess Infrastructure Capital Investment 3

Chapter 2 A World of Unequal Endowments 17

Chapter 3 Social Rates of Return and Efficiency Ratios 33

Boxes

Figures

Maps

Tables

Foreword

Infrastructure lies at the heart of development. Reliable energy systems, efficient transportation networks, and robust digital connectivity are essential for economic growth, job creation, social inclusion, and resilience. They connect people to employment clusters and markets, enable firms to compete and innovate, and allow societies to deliver basic services—from health and education to water and sanitation—at scale. Across much of the developing world, however, large gaps in infrastructure access and quality persist, even as fiscal space remains constrained and investment needs continue to grow.

This report, *Infrastructure Foundations: From Current Assets to Future Growth*, responds to a fundamental policy challenge: how to make better infrastructure investment decisions when resources are scarce and the stakes are high. Governments and development partners face difficult trade-offs, because large unmet needs coexist with tight financing conditions and rising costs. In this context, improving the effectiveness and prioritization of infrastructure spending is as important as mobilizing additional resources.

The report's core contribution is twofold. First, it brings together, for virtually the entire world, systematic and internally consistent data sets on infrastructure assets, unit costs, and capital stocks across the energy, transportation, and digital sectors. This effort provides an unprecedented global picture of existing infrastructure endowments—their scale, composition, and value—grounded in harmonized data that can be compared across countries and over time. Second, the report builds on this empirical foundation to develop a coherent analytical framework to assess where additional infrastructure investment can deliver the greatest social benefits. By combining detailed information on assets and replacement costs with evidence on growth impacts, financing conditions, and depreciation, it moves beyond measuring needs alone and offers a structured approach to prioritizing investments based on their expected returns to society.

The analysis highlights a central message: although infrastructure is indispensable for development, not all investments are equally productive. Returns vary widely across sectors, countries, and stages of development, reflecting differences in existing capital stocks, construction costs, and the broader economic environment. The report shows that high social rates of return often coincide with severe service gaps, particularly in low- and middle-income countries, but that realizing these opportunities also depends on borrowing costs, implementation efficiency, and institutional capacity. Addressing these constraints is, therefore, integral to translating investment opportunities into tangible development outcomes.

The findings underscore both urgency and opportunity. In many countries, especially those facing the largest infrastructure deficits, well-chosen investments in the energy, transportation, and digital sectors can yield substantial economic and social gains. At the same time, the evidence points to the importance of balanced investment strategies and sectoral complementarities, because infrastructure systems deliver the greatest value when they are developed in a coordinated manner.

This report is intended as a practical tool for governments, development practitioners, and finance institutions seeking to translate infrastructure spending into sustained growth and shared prosperity. By grounding investment choices in transparent data and comparable metrics, it aims to support better prioritization, foster more informed policy dialogue, and help countries turn existing infrastructure assets into durable foundations for future development.

<table>
<tr><td>Valerie Levkov</td><td align="right">Guangzhe Chen</td></tr>
<tr><td>Vice President, Infrastructure</td><td align="right">Vice President, Planet</td></tr>
<tr><td>World Bank Group</td><td align="right">World Bank Group</td></tr>
</table>

Acknowledgments

This report was prepared by a World Bank Group team led by Stéphane Straub. The core team comprised He He (transportation), Yue Li (overall coordination, energy, transportation), Xinxin Lyu (data coordination, energy), Jevgenijs Steinbuks (energy), Estefanía Vergara Cobos (digital), Christopher Dann (transportation), Manuel García-Santana (framework), and Harris Selod (transportation). Jisoo An, Ayse Battal, Mats Brouwer, Soyun Choi, Petrus Gerrits, Yujin Gum, Brian Heo, Dhruv Jain, Grace Kim, Minsuk Kim, Seojin Kim, Jaeeun Lee, Xuerong Lei, Ruoyi Li, Hansol Yoon, and Yawen Zheng served as research assistants. Pariwash Gouhari provided administrative support.

The report was sponsored by the Infrastructure Vice Presidency of the World Bank Group. Guangzhe Chen, former Vice President of Infrastructure and current head of the Planet Vice Presidency, and Indermit S. Gill, Senior Vice President and Chief Economist of the World Bank Group, provided overall guidance.

The team is grateful for the comments provided by Vivien Foster of Imperial College London, Peter Blair Henry from Stanford University, and Richard Damania, Pablo Fajnzylber, Aart Kraay, Somik V. Lall, Franziska Lieselotte Ohnsorge, Mark Roberts, and Ming Zhang of the World Bank Group during the World Bank Group–wide review process. The team also thanks other World Bank colleagues who offered comments at various stages of the report's preparation.

The team also received suggestions, inputs, and support from Andrea Barone, Erik Berglof, Henri Blas, Matteo Bobba, Geoff Cooper, Ariel Alberto Coremberg, Nicolas De Leon De Maria, Gilles Duranton, Marianne Fay, Stephane Hallegatte, Javier Inõn, Sangbu Kim, Eric R. Lancelot, Martha Lawrence, Yan Liu, Elitza Mileva, Sebastian Molineus, Lars Christian Moller, Anders Pedersen, Nicolas Peltier, Matthias Plavec, Christine Zhenwei Qiang, Wenxin Qiao, Martin Raiser, Martin Rama, Binyam Reja, Idah Pswarayi Riddihough, Dan Rogger, Julie Rozenberg, Renaud Seligman, Sharada Srinivasan, Clara Stinshoff, Mortaza Syed, Jang Ping Thia, Casey Torgusson, Matt Turner, Yi Wu, and Jing Xiong.

The report greatly benefited from feedback received in presentations at different stages of its realization, including from the World Bank Infrastructure leadership management team during the retreat before the 2025 Infrastructure for Development conference in Guangzhou; from World Bank Group regional teams and colleagues in Argentina, Brazil, China, Kenya, Singapore, and Uruguay; from the World Bank East Asia and

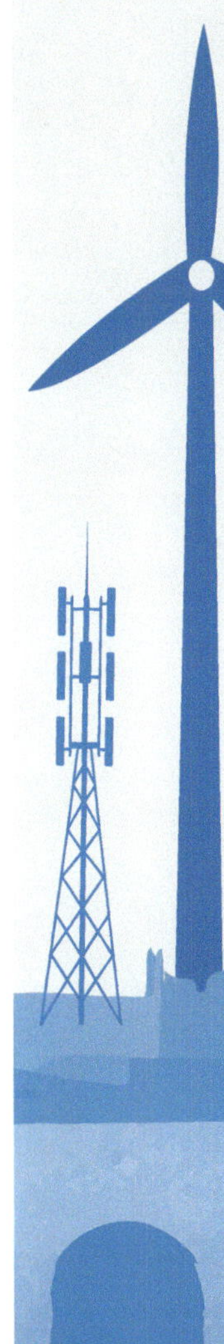

Pacific Infrastructure team; from participants in the January 2026 Tokyo LEADS [Learn. Adapt. Scale] workshop; and from the Instituto Nacional de Estadística y Censos team in Argentina, the New Zealand Infrastructure Commission–Te Waihanga, and the National Infrastructure and Service Transformation Authority in the United Kingdom. The team thanks colleagues at various World Bank country offices who assisted with logistics and stakeholder engagements.

The team also extends a special thanks to the Japan International Cooperation Agency and Asian Development Bank in Japan; the Asian Infrastructure Investment Bank in Beijing; the Inter-American Development Bank in Washington, DC; and KPMG in Singapore for organizing and hosting presentations and discussions in their offices with academics, policy makers, and private sector stakeholders.

The communications and engagement strategy was led by a team comprising Erin Scronce and John Mackedon. Special thanks are extended to Mark Elliot McClure for coordinating and overseeing the production of the report. Editing was carried out by Honora Mara, and proofreading was done by Ann O'Malley. The cover design was developed by Estefanía Vergara Cobos, with support from Betsega Girma Teklegiorgis. Thanks are also extended to the World Bank's formal publishing program, including Cindy Fisher, Patricia Katayama, and Jewel McFadden. Deborah Appel-Barker managed the printing and electronic conversion of the report and its ancillary products. Brenan Andre and Patricia Janer of the Cartography team reviewed the report's maps. Datapage provided typesetting services. Maria Torre and the Reproducibility team led the verification of reproducibility. Ivonne Georgina Rivas Cardona and Anca Chitic Patapievici provided the team with resource management support.

Despite efforts to be comprehensive, the team apologizes to any individuals or organizations inadvertently omitted from this list and expresses its gratitude to all who contributed to this report.

About the Authors

Christopher Dann is a PhD candidate at Stanford University. His research focuses on the political economy of large-scale infrastructure investments and how it shapes the social contract, alongside broader development outcomes. He was previously a predoctoral fellow at the London School of Economics's Suntory and Toyota International Centres for Economics and Related Disciplines, where he worked for Professor Sir Tim Besley. He has collaborated closely with the World Bank's Office of the Chief Economist for Infrastructure and previously engaged with the Asian Infrastructure Investment Bank. He holds a BSc from the London School of Economics and an MSc from the University of Oxford.

Manuel García-Santana is a tenured associate professor at Universitat Pompeu Fabra and a researcher affiliated with the Barcelona School of Economics and Centre de Recerca en Economia Internacional. His research focuses on macroeconomics, international trade, and economic growth, with an emphasis on firm dynamics, public sector policies, and productivity. He has published in leading journals such as the *American Economic Review*, *Econometrica*, and the *Journal of Financial Economics* and currently serves as associate editor for the *Journal of International Economics* and *SERIEs*. Before his current role, he was a senior economist at the World Bank and held academic positions at Princeton University and Université Libre de Bruxelles. His work has been recognized with multiple awards and grants, including an ERC Consolidator Grant and the Hicks-Tinbergen Medal. He holds a PhD in economics from Centro de Estudios Monetarios y Financieros in Madrid.

He He is an economist in the Office of the Chief Economist for Infrastructure at the World Bank Group. He is a transportation economist and urban modeler, working to build more sustainable and efficient cities, and leads the team's transportation portfolio. His work is at the forefront of the field, exploring topics such as transportation sector decarbonization, the wider economic benefits of transportation and accessibility, and applied urban models. He holds a PhD in transportation from the Massachusetts Institute of Technology and a BASc in engineering science (infrastructure) from the University of Toronto.

Yue Li is a senior economist in the Office of the Chief Economist for Infrastructure at the World Bank Group, where she began her career in 2010 through the Young Professionals

Program and has since held various roles. Her research encompasses international economics, firm dynamics, economic geography, and urban economics. Her work has been published in the *Journal of Development Economics*, *Journal of International Economics*, and *Journal of Urban Economics*. From 2021 to 2024, she also served as a senior economist and head of research and development impact at the Asian Infrastructure Investment Bank. She holds a PhD in economics from Rutgers University, master's degrees in economics and political science from Syracuse University, and a bachelor's degree from Peking University.

Xinxin Lyu is an economist and data scientist in the Office of the Chief Economist for Infrastructure at the World Bank Group, where she works on infrastructure, development, and applied quantitative analysis. Her research spans public investment, inequality, and institutional design in developing countries. Her work focuses on policy-relevant questions related to incentives, cooperation, and the effectiveness of development interventions. She also serves as the focal point for the Infrastructure Vice Presidency in Data360, where she coordinates data needs and supports data integration across teams. Before her current role, she worked as a research analyst in the World Bank's Poverty Global Practice. She holds a PhD in economics from Purdue University, specializing in game theory, agent-based modeling, and experimental economics.

Harris Selod is a senior economist in the World Bank Group's research department, where his work centers on urban development, transportation infrastructure, and land markets. Within the World Bank, he has held multiple roles over the years—including visiting scholar, land policy expert seconded by the French government, and staff member—and chaired the Land Policy and Administration thematic group from 2011 to 2013. Before joining the World Bank in 2007, he was a tenured researcher at the French National Institute for Agricultural Research and an associate professor at the Paris School of Economics, where he taught microeconomic theory and urban studies. He has published numerous academic journal papers in urban economics, economic geography, public economics, and development economics. He has also taught economics at various French institutions, including the Ecole Polytechnique and École nationale de la statistique et de l'administration économique de Paris (ENSAE). He holds a PhD in economics from Sorbonne University, a BSc/MSc in statistics from ENSAE, and a BBA/MBA from the École Supérieure de Commerce de Paris Business School.

Jevgenijs Steinbuks is a senior economist in the Office of the Chief Economist for Infrastructure at the World Bank Group. His areas of expertise are economic development, energy and extractives, and urban and regional development. His current knowledge and operational work focus on sustainable resource use, electric power, and infrastructure and economic development. He has extensive experience in academia, the public sector, and international institutions. He holds a PhD in economics from George Washington University.

Stéphane Straub is the World Bank Group chief economist for Infrastructure. Previously, he was a professor at the Toulouse School of Economics, where he remains an associate member, and president of the European Development Network. He has held academic and teaching positions in France, Latin America, the United States, and the United Kingdom.

He has worked as a consultant for several international institutions and published extensively on infrastructure topics, including infrastructure's social and economic impact, public-private partnerships, procurement, and institutional issues in developing countries. He holds a PhD in economics from the University of Toulouse.

Estefanía Vergara Cobos is an economist in the Office of the Chief Economist for Infrastructure at the World Bank Group, where she leads research on digital transformation. She has held academic positions teaching economics at various universities in Ecuador and the United States and is a published author of research at the frontier of digitalization, including work on cybersecurity economics, artificial intelligence infrastructure, and the economics of digital systems. She holds a PhD in economics and a master's degree in game theory from Stony Brook University, as well as advanced studies in computer science.

Key Messages

Infrastructure is the foundation upon which economies grow, societies thrive, and development opportunities are created. For many low- and middle-income countries, however, vast infrastructure gaps persist alongside severely constrained fiscal resources—making every investment dollar count more than ever. This report offers a comprehensive, evidence-based framework for understanding the value of global infrastructure stocks, measuring the economic returns of infrastructure investments, and guiding policy makers toward smarter, more targeted decisions. It introduces two powerful diagnostic tools—the *social rate of return* and the *infrastructure efficiency ratio*—to help governments identify where infrastructure investment can generate the greatest economic and social impact relative to its cost.

To measure infrastructure investment and its impacts, the report draws on a pioneering geolocated data set that systematically maps physical infrastructure assets across the energy, transportation, and digital sectors in nearly every country in the world. Going beyond simple physical counts, it derives the economic value of these stocks by applying country-specific unit replacement costs—the estimated cost to build 1 kilometer of paved road, 1 megawatt of generating capacity, or 1 kilometer of transmission line. These capital values, adjusted for depreciation, provide an unprecedented empirical foundation for cross-country comparison and investment analysis, resulting in the following key findings.

Infrastructure assets and their value evolve along the development ladder. Although physical infrastructure stocks per capita generally rise with income, the composition of these stocks shifts markedly as countries develop. In the poorest countries, transportation infrastructure accounts for only about 27 percent of total infrastructure capital; in the richest, this share rises to 75 percent. Energy and digital stocks, by contrast, tend to remain stable or decline as a share of gross domestic product as countries grow wealthier. These patterns reflect the changing nature of development needs and underscore the importance of tailoring investment strategies to a country's specific stage of development.

Significant untapped investment opportunities exist worldwide. The report's infrastructure efficiency ratio—which compares the social rate of return on infrastructure to the cost of financing it—reveals that worthwhile investment opportunities are far from exhausted. In the vast majority of countries, efficiency ratios exceed 1 (meaning that social benefits outweigh costs). This finding carries an important message: even in a high-borrowing-cost environment, considerable scope exists for net-positive infrastructure investments that governments and development partners can and should act upon.

The returns to infrastructure vary significantly by sector and income level. Social rates of return are not uniform—they reflect a country's existing stock of infrastructure, its stage of development, and the fundamentals of the sector in question. Transportation investments yield higher returns in lower-income countries, where physical networks are sparse and the marginal value of connectivity is high. Energy investments, by contrast, generate relatively consistent returns across income levels, reflecting universal demand—from expanding access in poorer nations to supporting quality upgrades and clean energy transitions in wealthier ones. Digital infrastructure exhibits a network effect, with higher payoffs in better-connected, higher-income economies where a larger user base can leverage digital services.

Balanced, cross-sectoral investment strategies amplify returns. Infrastructure does not deliver its full impact in isolation. The report finds that the colocation of complementary infrastructure—such as roads connecting communities to energy-powered logistics hubs, or digital connectivity enhancing the productivity of transportation networks—generates returns greater than the sum of individual sectoral investments. Countries that pursue coordinated, multisector investment strategies are better positioned to unlock these synergies and achieve more efficient development outcomes.

High construction costs are a policy challenge that can be addressed. Unit construction costs vary enormously across countries; where costs are high, the economic returns on investment are correspondingly eroded. In some cases, elevated costs reflect factors beyond immediate control—geography, conflict, or natural disasters. In many instances, however, high costs are attributable to limited competition in upstream sectors such as concrete and steel production, to weak procurement practices, or to governance deficiencies. These factors are remediable. Targeted reforms of market structure, procurement frameworks, and institutional capacity can meaningfully lower costs and improve the viability of infrastructure investment.

Optimal investment strategies must be tailored to country and regional context. No one-size-fits-all approach to infrastructure investment exists. For nearly half of countries in Europe and Central Asia, the data suggest that a focus on energy investment is most beneficial. In Sub-Saharan Africa, approximately half of countries would gain the most from strategies weighted heavily toward transportation, reflecting the critical importance of physical connectivity for economic integration. In countries with mature infrastructure networks and lower efficiency ratios, such as Brazil, the social payoff from maintaining and upgrading existing assets may exceed that of constructing new large-scale networks. These differentiated findings highlight the value of evidence-based, context-specific planning over generic spending targets.

Subnational disparities demand targeted investment. National averages often mask stark local inequalities that are critical for policy. The report's subnational disaggregation—reaching down to the local administrative level—reveals profound geographic disparities within countries. In Nigeria, for example, energy generation capacity is heavily concentrated in the south, leaving northern regions vastly underserved and generating exceptionally high potential returns for localized investment. Effective infrastructure planning must go beyond national totals to identify and address these subnational gaps.

Concessional finance and risk mitigation are essential to unlocking investment. Many countries with compelling investment opportunities are constrained not by a lack of worthwhile projects but by high borrowing costs and elevated risk premiums that render even socially beneficial projects fiscally unviable. Concessional finance, guarantees, and other risk-mitigation instruments are not merely supplementary tools—they are essential enablers that can bridge the gap between social and financial returns and unlock investment that would otherwise stall. Development partners have a pivotal role to play in deploying these instruments where they are most needed.

Executive Summary

Infrastructure is crucial for successful development. Energy, transportation, digital, water, sanitation, and services related to these sectors enable people to access jobs, economic opportunities, and basic services such as health and education. They also enhance the affordability and availability of goods and services. Ultimately, when available, of good quality, and affordable, infrastructure boosts productivity and economic growth and plays a crucial role in reducing poverty.

This report and the accompanying data sets are designed to help governments, practitioners, and development finance experts prioritize infrastructure investments and maximize the value people derive from them. The report does so first by thoroughly mapping infrastructure assets in approximately 200 countries and determining the value of these infrastructure stocks. It then derives two key measures: the social rates of return of infrastructure investments and the infrastructure efficiency ratio. These measures tell us the total return to society of a given investment in terms of added gross domestic product (GDP), the cost of mobilizing resources to finance it, and the relationship between the two. Finally, it compares these returns across sectors to determine an optimal investment mix.

Broadly, the report seeks to answer several important questions:

- How much infrastructure capital do countries have?

- How much does it cost to build more, and what drives that cost?

- How does the composition of the overall infrastructure stock evolve over the development path?

- What are the implied social rates of return of additional investments?

- Is there evidence of supply gaps, and where should countries prioritize investment given the constraints they face?

The report is structured as follows. Chapters 1–3 in Part 1 present the data and related resources developed as part of this work and then review and discuss the main findings that they support. Readers interested in learning about the facts, available data sets

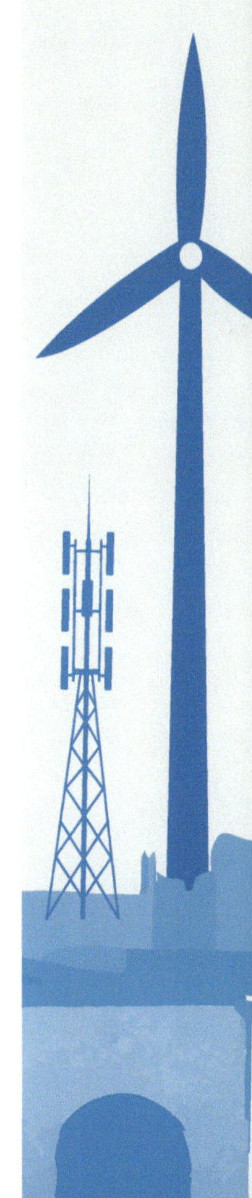

A reproducibility package is available for this book in the Reproducible Research Repository at https://reproducibility.worldbank.org/catalog/536.

and tools provided by this report, and research and policy conclusions can focus on this part. The detailed presentation of the methodology underlying the data collection and curation, as well as the models used to produce the results, can be found in Part 2, chapters 4–7. This information will be of interest to colleagues in the Work Bank Group, the broader policy community, and academic circles, and broadly to anyone interested in the technical aspects of the work. The rest of this executive summary focuses mostly on the main narrative of the report as presented in Part 1, with only cursory references to the methodology available in Part 2.

THE INFRASTRUCTURE POLICY CHALLENGE

The infrastructure policy challenge can be summarized with three main facts.

First, there will be no development without infrastructure. A large fraction of the populations of low- and middle-income countries still lacks access to the basic infrastructure that is essential to lift them out of poverty. According to the latest available figures, 685 million people, most of them in Sub-Saharan Africa, lack electricity access, 1 billion live more than 2 kilometers (km) away from an all-season road, only about half of the world's urban population has convenient access to public transportation, and 2.6 billion people still do not use the internet.

Second, there can, however, be infrastructure without development. Despite broad evidence that infrastructure investments help sustain growth and job creation, the impact of projects varies widely. Some projects generate high returns, whereas others have less impact. To produce the returns that society expects, investments need to be well targeted and implemented, which is possible only if adequate information is available.

Third, available resources to address infrastructure needs are constrained, especially in countries that have the highest needs. Overall public and concessional funds are limited, and developing countries face borrowing costs that often include significant country risk premiums. With few exceptions, these countries struggle to attract significant amounts of private financing for infrastructure projects.

Together, these three facts make up what we call the *infrastructure return imperative:* given the large infrastructure gaps and their welfare implications, scarce resources must be channeled to where they have the biggest impact.

A UNIQUE DATA SET OF INFRASTRUCTURE COSTS AND STOCKS

This report presents the results of an extensive data collection effort. It introduces original databases covering, for most countries of the world, physical infrastructure assets in the following subsectors:

- Energy generation capacity, in megawatts (MW), for all major technologies;

- Energy transmission and distribution lines, in km;

- Road and railroad networks, in km; and

- Digital assets, including data centers, radio access networks (or cell towers), internet exchange points, fiber-optic cables, and submarine cables.

For most assets, the coverage is nearly exhaustive. Also, with a few exceptions, assets are geolocated and can be disaggregated down to the local administrative level (that is, municipalities, districts, or counties) and merged spatially with other sources of data to support relevant economic analysis. Many of these subsector data also include time series going back about 10 years.

The data set reveals that, as countries gain wealth, they accumulate more infrastructure physical assets (km of roads, MW of energy generation capacity, number of cell towers, and so on) per person. Figure ES.1 shows this trend for some of the main items covered in the report.

FIGURE ES.1 **Physical infrastructure stocks per capita versus GDP per capita, by type of infrastructure**

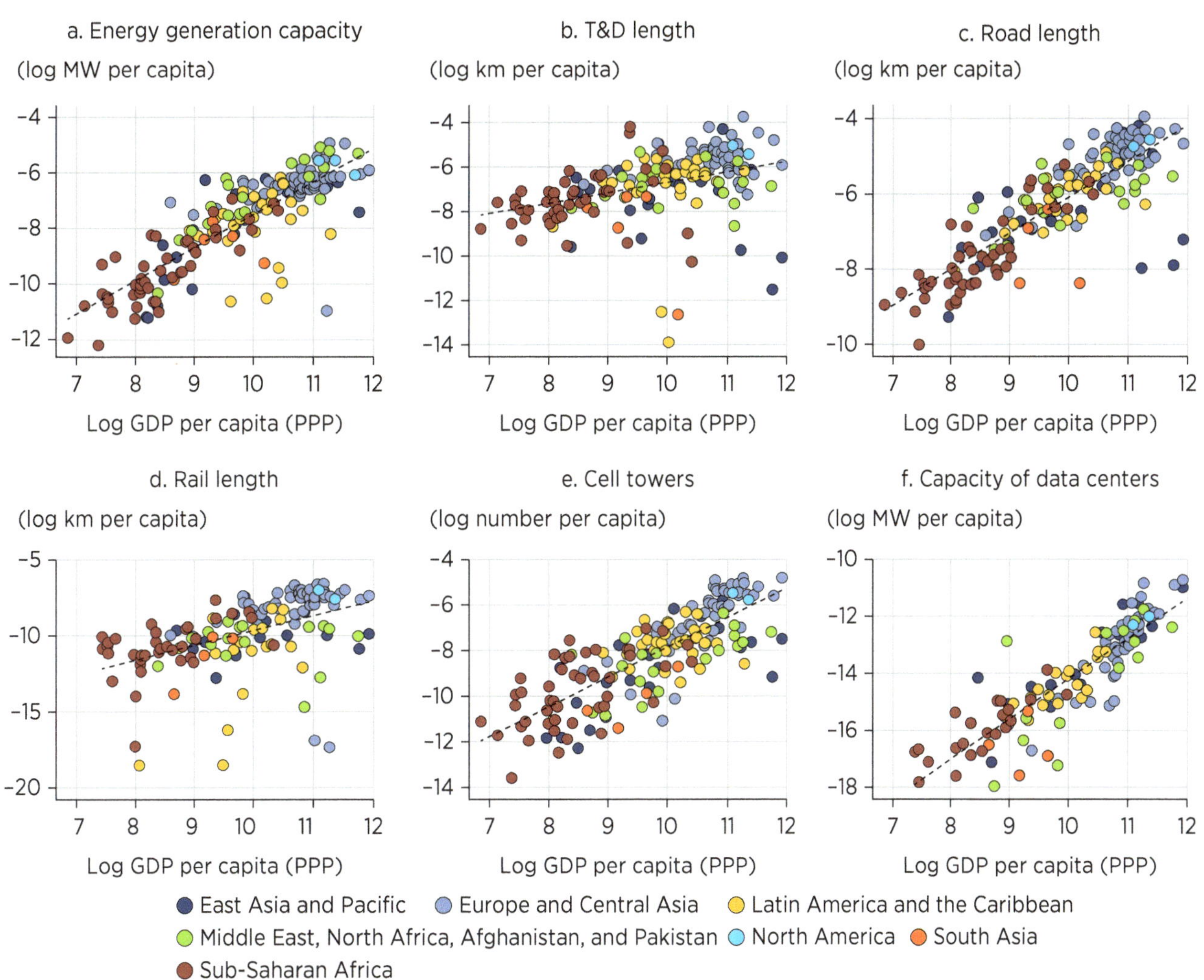

Source: Original figure for this publication.
Note: Although this figure focuses on the six major classes of assets, the pattern is similar for the other three not represented here (terrestrial fiber-optic cables, submarine cables, and internet exchange points). The data are for 2024. GDP = gross domestic product; km = kilometer; MW = megawatt; PPP = purchasing power parity; T&D = transmission and distribution.

Zooming in on the spatial distribution of assets shows where the main coverage gaps are. Maps ES.1 and ES.2 contrast the local distribution of energy generation assets in Brazil and Nigeria, respectively. Despite roughly similar populations in the two countries, Brazil has much more coverage than Nigeria. The difference in subnational coverage is striking, compounding the fact that Brazil has 14 times the total generation capacity as Nigeria.

MAP ES.1 Subnational generation capacity (MW), Brazil

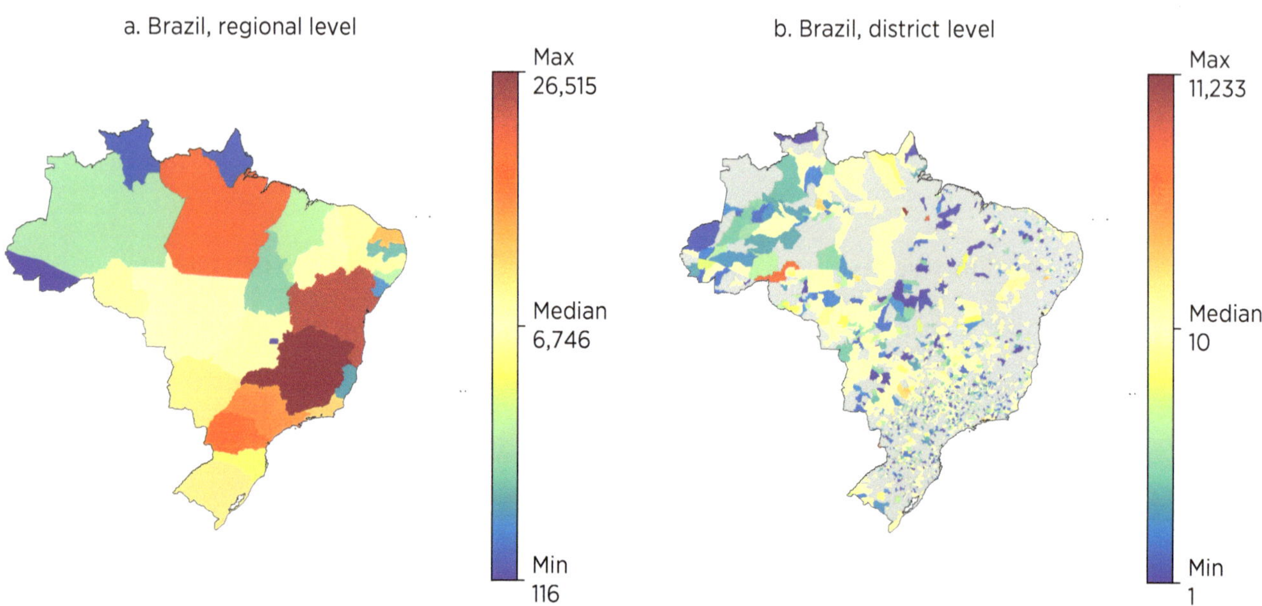

Source: Original map for this publication.
Note: The map shows total generation capacity, excluding some power plants without spatial information. The data are for 2024. MW = megawatt.

MAP ES.2 Subnational generation capacity (MW), Nigeria

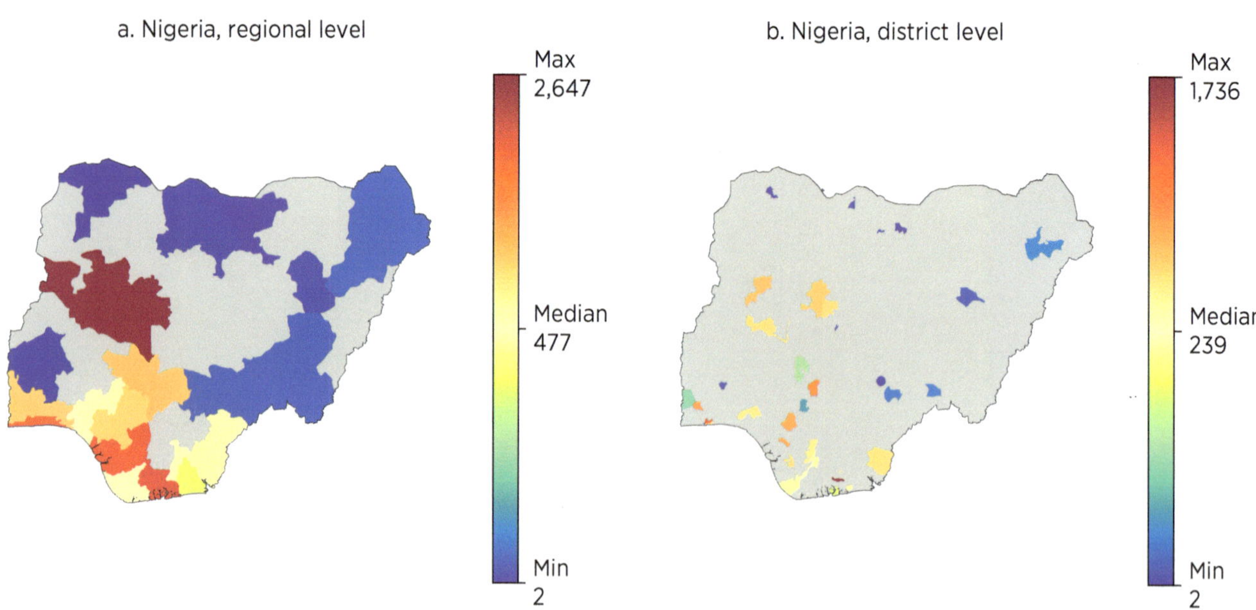

Source: Original map for this publication.
Note: The map shows total generation capacity, excluding some power plants without spatial information. The data are for 2024.
MW = megawatt.

MAP ES.3 Total transportation capital stock, by country

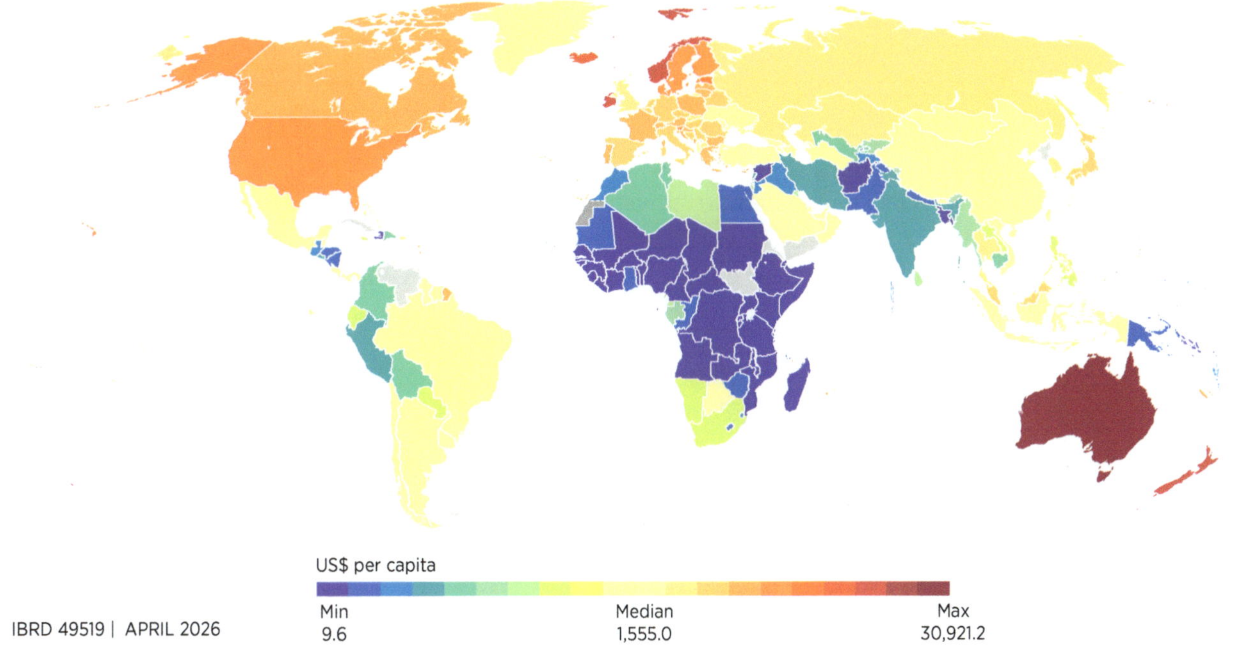

IBRD 49519 | APRIL 2026

Source: Original map for this publication.
Note: The data are for 2024.

Next, the report assesses how much it costs, in each country, to build these physical assets—that is, 1 km of paved road or railroad, 1 km of energy transmission line, 1 MW of storage in a data center, and so on. It does so by using several project databases, as well as engineering tables and other sources, to develop country-sector-level unit replacement costs for all the subsectors listed previously.

Combined with the information on physical assets, and with appropriate adjustments for depreciation, this cost assessment leads to complete characterizations of the total value of all subsectors' infrastructure capital stocks. Map ES.3 presents the results for transportation (roads and railroads), normalizing by countries' population, clearly showing much smaller capital stocks in most developing regions, especially the Middle East, North Africa, Afghanistan, and Pakistan; South Asia; and Sub-Saharan Africa.

INFRASTRUCTURE ALONG THE DEVELOPMENT PATH

Although low- and middle-income countries have significantly lower infrastructure stocks than higher-income countries when measured in physical units per person, the picture becomes more complex when looking at the value of countries' infrastructure capital relative to their overall economic weight as measured by GDP. Levels of infrastructure stocks as a percentage of GDP (the capital-output ratio) appear to hold roughly stable or to decrease slightly along the development ladder for energy and digital. By contrast, levels increase sharply for transportation, meaning that countries and regions that have developed and reached high-income status have accumulated capital in the transportation sector at a faster pace than that of economic growth.

In richer countries, transportation makes up a much larger share of infrastructure investment—75 percent in the richest countries compared to 27 percent in the poorest (figure ES.2). Of course, modern transportation services also mean more energy consumption, dominated by fossil fuels, which points to a key complementarity between transportation and energy: the increases in total energy consumption along the development path are, in fact, possible only if countries accumulate transportation infrastructure capital.

Transportation plays a critical role in economic development. Modern road and railroad corridors, ports, and airports enable the integration of countries in international value chains. They link producers and consumers in domestic regions and markets, potentially generating large welfare gains. Efficient urban transportation infrastructure is key to modern well-functioning cities, which, in turn, become major engines of growth and sources of innovation through agglomeration externalities. The patterns in figures ES.2 and ES.3 show that these mechanisms lie at the heart of the development process.

FIGURE ES.2 **Shares of total infrastructure capital, by sector and income decile**

Average share of total infrastructure capital

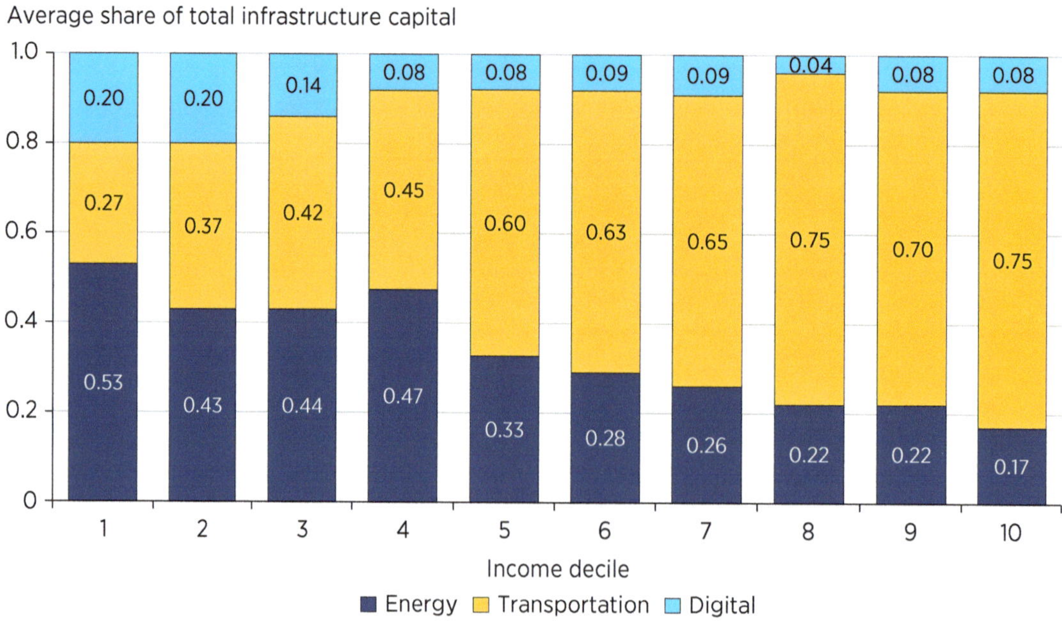

Source: Original figure for this publication.
Note: The data are for 2024.

FIGURE ES.3 Total infrastructure stocks over GDP, by sector and region

Average infrastructure capital-output ratio as a share of GDP

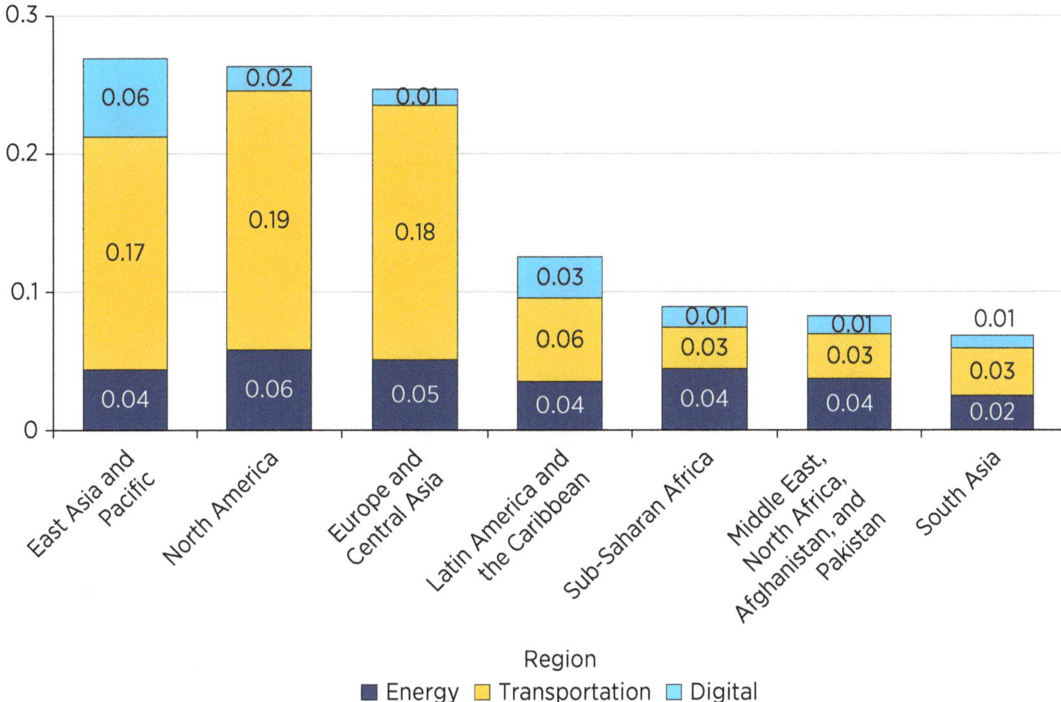

Source: Original figure for this publication.
Note: The data are for 2024.

Regions appear to have navigated this process in very different ways when it comes to the accumulation of transportation capital. Figure ES.3 shows the composition of the infrastructure capital stock across regions. Simple cross-country comparisons show that the four regions on the right-hand side—Latin America and the Caribbean; Sub-Saharan Africa; the Middle East, North Africa, Afghanistan, and Pakistan; and South Asia—have less infrastructure capital than their level of income would predict. By contrast, East Asia and Pacific and Europe and Central Asia, on average, punch above their weight.

THE CONTRIBUTION OF INFRASTRUCTURE TO GROWTH

The information in the preceding section allows for measurement of how expanding infrastructure stocks and services affect economic growth and social returns from new investments. The report does so by leveraging the results from a large-scale meta-analysis of the literature on infrastructure to provide systematic values of this impact, the so-called output elasticity.

The findings differ across sectors.

- *Transportation.* Investments have a bigger payoff in developing countries than in rich ones, likely because poorer countries still have major gaps (roads, ports, and transit), so each new project makes a big difference. As countries build more infrastructure, the benefits of adding yet another road or railway tend to decrease (diminishing returns to capital).

- *Energy.* The benefits of investing in energy (power generation, grids, and so on) are about the same everywhere, whether a country is poor or rich. This similarity may capture the returns from new connections in places where access gaps remain, as well as the benefits from quality improvement and the energy transition in more developed places.

- *Digital.* Digital investments have a bigger payoff in richer and more developed countries. Why? Because digital technologies work better when lots of people and businesses are already connected: the more users on the network, the more valuable the service becomes (the network effect).

SOCIAL RATES OF RETURN AND INFRASTRUCTURE EFFICIENCY RATIOS

The report then derives systematic country-sector-level measures of the social rates of return and infrastructure efficiency ratios (the relation between these returns and the cost of mobilizing resources to finance the investments) for about 150 countries and the three sectors (energy, digital, and transportation). It generally finds a higher social rate of return to transportation investments in developing countries, because of both the higher impact of the investments and the smaller capital stocks in these countries, but it finds the reverse in energy. This is, of course, only a broad pattern, with important variability at the specific country level.

In addition, higher social rates of return do not mean that these investments are systematically warranted: they must be compared to the cost of financing the services, which comes down to the rate at which countries or utilities borrow plus the depreciation rate. Combining the social rates of return with country-level borrowing cost measures and country-sector-level depreciation rates, the report derives an *infrastructure efficiency ratio* that indicates whether the potential benefits of investments exceed their cost at current market conditions.

An infrastructure efficiency ratio above 1 implies that additional investments are warranted, because they pass a basic benefit-cost threshold. It could also be taken to reveal a situation in which countries fail to act on investment opportunities that have potential social benefits, possibly because of market failures such as credit constraints or lack of information. A ratio below 1, by contrast, would indicate that costs exceed social benefits, a situation that might be due to a combination of overaccumulation of infrastructure assets, unfavorable construction costs, and excessive borrowing costs. Figures ES.4 and ES.5 plot these ratios for energy and transportation, respectively.

FIGURE ES.4 **Energy infrastructure efficiency ratio versus GDP per capita, by region**

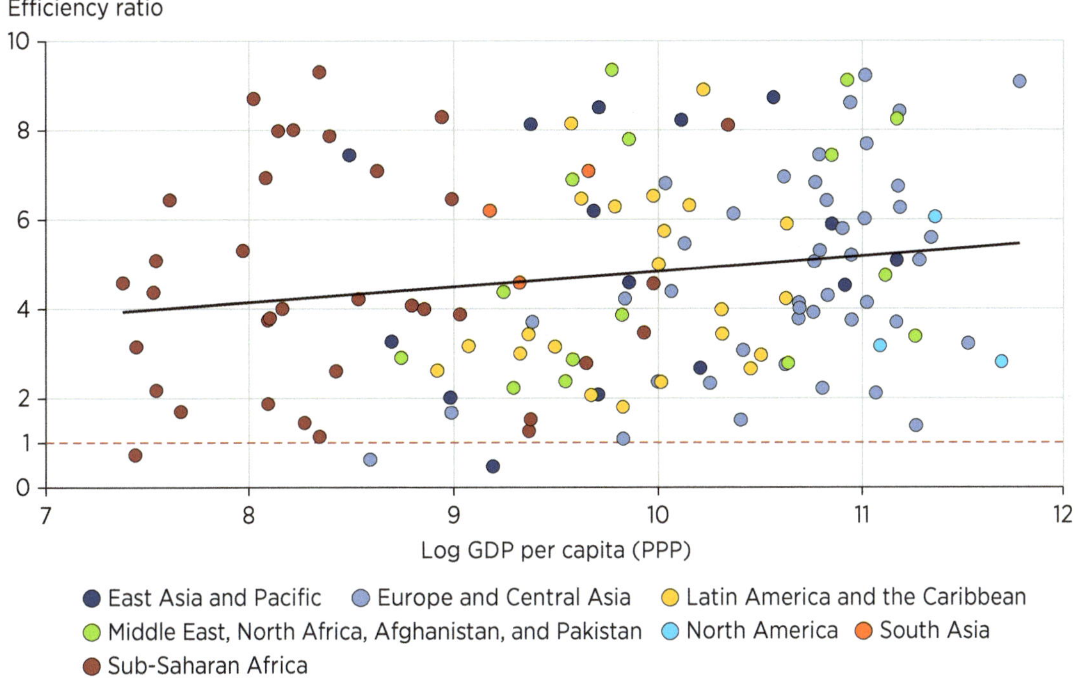

Source: Original figure for this publication.
Note: PPP = purchasing power parity.

FIGURE ES.5 **Transportation infrastructure efficiency ratio versus GDP per capita, by region**

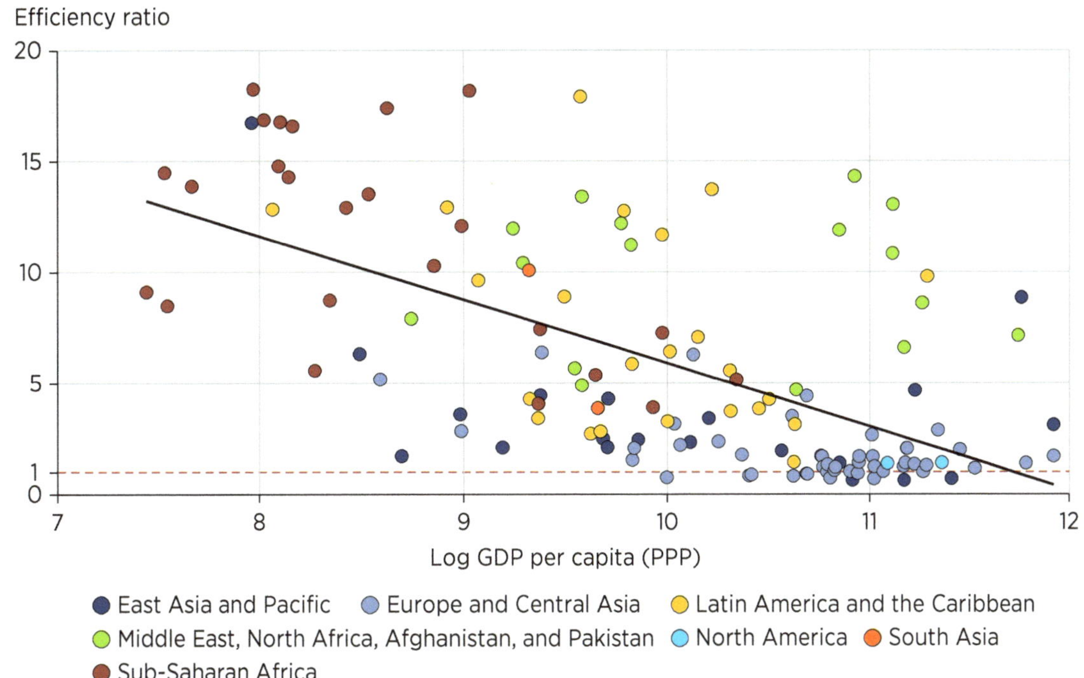

Source: Original figure for this publication.
Note: PPP = purchasing power parity.

A few key patterns emerge from the analysis. Most strikingly, efficiency ratios are overwhelmingly above 1 (92 percent of countries in transportation and 98 percent in energy), suggesting significant untapped investment opportunities. The dispersion of ratios across countries is large even at similar income levels, driven mainly by differences in existing capital stocks and, to a lesser extent, replacement costs. Energy and transportation, however, display very different patterns: low energy ratios occur mostly in countries facing high borrowing and replacement costs, pointing to clear policy interventions that could ease these constraints; by contrast, low transportation ratios are concentrated in low-borrowing-cost countries that have likely overaccumulated basic transportation networks.

Regionally, energy efficiency ratios are consistently high, especially in Sub-Saharan Africa, although a few countries there show low returns and require careful policy calibration. Transportation ratios vary much more, with Sub-Saharan Africa again standing out as having exceptionally high returns. Richer regions—including North America and much of Europe and Central Asia—show very low transportation ratios.

Finally, some caution is needed regarding the findings for the digital sector. The basic results indicate very high efficiency ratios, but the report discusses potential caveats, for example those linked to the lack of impact evaluation reflecting the recent evolution of the sector and to the need to consider the complementarity between energy and digital.

COUNTRY-LEVEL IMPLICATIONS

Consider again Brazil and Nigeria, which offer a striking contrast in infrastructure development despite similar population sizes. Brazil's energy network is mature and geographically extensive, enabling resilience and universal electricity access. In contrast, Nigeria's energy capacity is concentrated in a few southern states, leaving vast northern regions underserved. This disparity is reflected in capital stocks: Brazil's energy assets amount to 8.1 percent of GDP, nearly 10 times Nigeria's 0.9 percent, and replacement costs are significantly higher in Brazil.

These structural differences shape investment returns, and in both countries, the results signal that energy infrastructure stocks are still below their optimal levels. Nigeria's large service gaps translate into exceptionally high social rates of return and efficiency ratios—18 for energy and 32 for transportation—underscoring the urgency of investment. Yet fiscal constraints and market failures have stalled progress, leaving rural electrification below 30 percent and road access severely limited. Brazil, although at a more advanced stage, still faces challenges. Efficiency ratios remain positive but lower (2.4 for energy and 6.4 for transportation), signaling that targeted investments—particularly in transportation and quality improvements in energy, for example, through maintenance—could yield benefits. However, Brazil's high debt burden constrains its ability to scale up infrastructure spending.

Beyond the use of baseline efficiency ratios, the report advocates for using the information to inform a discussion of how the trade-offs might change under different policy interventions, such as lowering the borrowing cost through concessional finance or the provision of guarantees, lowering the cost of construction by introducing competition on upstream sectors and better procurement practices, or boosting benefits by providing complementary investments. By allowing for benchmarking of the different components involved in the computation of social rates of returns, it also provides a way to identify the main bottlenecks facing countries when it comes to maximizing the benefits from infrastructure investments.

Consider, for example, Honduras's generation costs, which are among the world's highest (US$2.2 million/MW), eroding returns and leaving the energy efficiency ratio at just 2.57. Heavy fossil fuel dependence, oil price swings, drought risks, and investment delays drive this costly structure. Aligning with Panama (US$1.7 million/MW) or the average for Latin America and the Caribbean (US$1.59 million/MW) could lift efficiency to 3.16–3.36, showcasing the potential of simple policy interventions to improve investment prospects.

A PRIORITIZATION FRAMEWORK

A key question raised by these findings is what they imply in terms of the optimal mix of investments. The report's findings suggest that pursuing joint investment strategies can exploit complementarities between the sectors. A clear case exists for countries not to put all their eggs in one basket. In fact, except for extreme cases with a very high efficiency ratio in one sector, for example, and a ratio below 1 in another, a balanced strategy is always going to be optimal. Importantly, the terms of the social rate of return and the efficiency ratio can be used to determine the optimal budget allocation across sectors.

Figure ES.6 shows, for countries in this report's data set, the optimal allocation of an investment of 10 percent of GDP between energy and transportation. For most countries, the optimal strategy involves investing in both energy and transportation, but important variations occur both within and across regions, with developing regions generally displaying a mix slightly more biased toward transportation. For almost half of the countries in Europe and Central Asia, an exclusive focus on energy appears optimal; the reverse is true for a significant number of Sub-Saharan African countries, with about half of them having optimal shares of transportation investment over 75 percent.

The fact that balanced investment strategies dominate can be thought of as a case of complementarity, which operates through two main channels: (1) a *diminishing returns component*, whereby diversifying investment generally outperforms a single sector approach because of diminishing returns in each single sector, and (2) a *colocation component*, whereby combined investments generate returns greater than the sum of individual sector gains. This synergy arises because infrastructure works best when interconnected: roads linking active economic hubs enhance productivity, and energy powering factories connected to logistics networks facilitate market access.

FIGURE ES.6 Optimal allocation of 10 percent of GDP investment between energy and transportation, by region and level of energy investment

Energy investment share

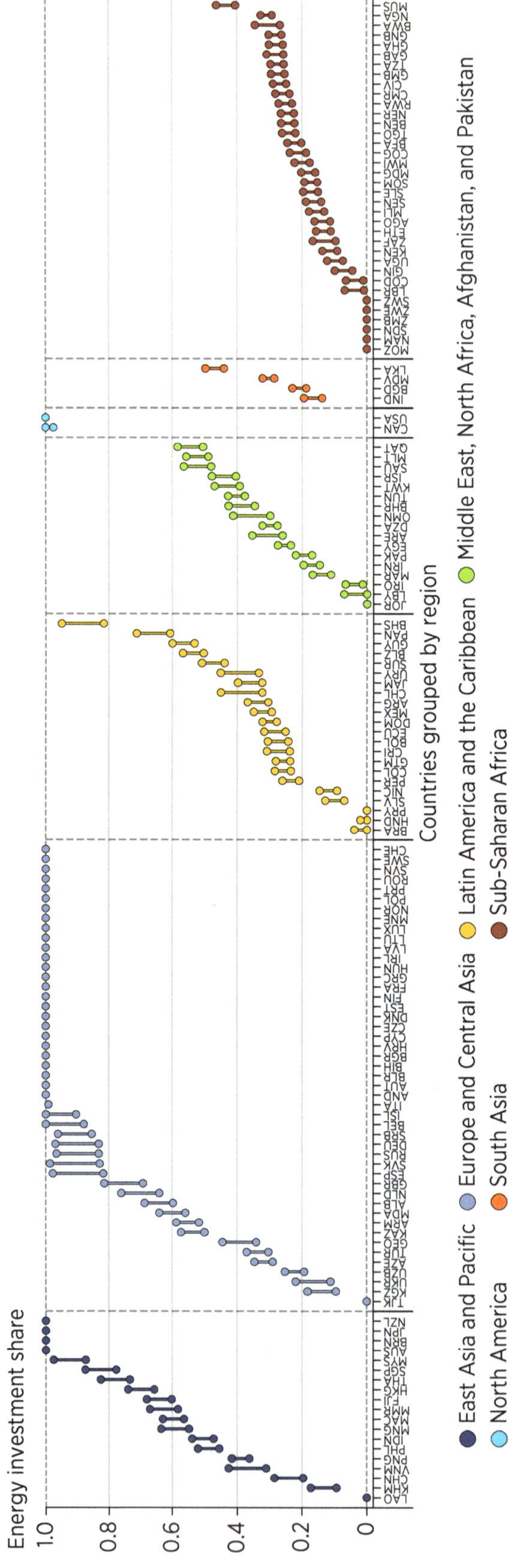

Source: Original figure for this publication.

Note: Economies are ordered within their regions by increasing shares of energy investment. For each country, the figure provides a range, represented by the vertical bar, based on the use of different elasticities (refer to chapter 7 for discussion).

FUTURE WORK

The social rate of return estimates presented here are an initial step toward a comprehensive prioritization framework for World Bank Group projects. A key dimension is to provide tools to prioritize across sectors and identify synergies and complementarities. This work can be done using spatially detailed data, as well as at a more aggregate level.

In addition, social return estimates should be compared with alternative investment opportunities to guide public prioritization and assess how returns and some of the broader social benefits can be appropriated in order to boost private sector attractiveness. The potential environmental impact of large-scale infrastructure works should also be factored in. Finally, large-scale infrastructure investments also have macrofiscal implications, requiring a better understanding of how macro conditions interact with social rates of return, especially in fiscally constrained countries.

Several activities are intended following the publication of this report, including development of an online tool to support the simulation of the potential optimal investment mix, based on choices of parameters regarding the different aspects listed previously. Information on physical assets, unit costs, and stock values will be made available as a global public good through World Bank Group data repositories. On the data side, additional assets—such as ports and airports—will be added to the framework. Work is already under way to assess costs and stocks for water and sanitation infrastructure. The water sector, however, requires improved treatment of environmental externalities when estimating social benefits.

Finally, this report aims to be a tool and a living source of information that can be updated as countries and sectors develop. To this end, it will be operationalized through online user-friendly platforms through which users can access the underlying data.

Abbreviations

2G	second generation
AI	artificial intelligence
ATT	average treatment effect on the treated
CCGT	combined cycle gas turbine
CCS	carbon capture and storage
CDS	credit default swap
CHP	combined heat and power
CRP	country risk premium
CT	cell tower
DC	data center
DSL	digital subscriber line
EAP	East Asia and Pacific
ECA	Europe and Central Asia
EPC	engineering, procurement, and construction
EPM	Electricity Planning Model
EVI	Enhanced Vegetation Index
FAAT	Funnel Asymmetry Test
FOC	fiber-optic cable
FY	fiscal year
GDP	gross domestic product
GPRS	general packet radio service
GQ	Golden Quadrilateral
GSM	Global System for Global Communications
GW	gigawatt
HH	household
HIC	high income country
HV	high voltage
IBRD	International Bank for Reconstruction and Development
ICT	information and communication technology

IDA	International Development Association
IEA	International Energy Agency
IGC	International Growth Center
IGCC	integrated gasification combined cycle
IP	internet protocol
IRENA	International Renewable Energy Agency
IXP	internet exchange point
km	kilometer
kV	kilovolt
kW	kilowatt
kWh	kilowatt-hour
LAC	Latin America and the Caribbean
LTE	Long-Term Evolution
m	meter
Mbps	megabits per second
MENAAP	Middle East, North Africa, Afghanistan, and Pakistan
MW	megawatt
NA	North America
OLS	ordinary least squares
OSM	OpenStreetMap
PC	personal computer
PCA	principal component analysis
PEESE	Precision-Effect Estimate with Standard Error
PET	Precision-Effect Test
PPP	purchasing power parity
PRS	Political Risk Services
PV	photovoltaic
RAN	radio access network
SA	South Asia
SDID	synthetic difference in differences
SMB	small and medium business
SMC	submarine cable
SSA	Sub-Saharan Africa
SSR	social rate of return
T&D	transmission and distribution
TFP	total factor productivity
TFPR	total factor productivity revenue
TowerXchange	Independent Community for Tower Professionals
UHV	ultra-high voltage
VoLL	Value of Lost Load

PART 1

1

A Framework to Assess Infrastructure Capital Investment

KEY MESSAGES

Infrastructure is essential for development, but not all infrastructure investments deliver development gains. Large access gaps persist across the energy, transportation, and digital sectors, yet empirical evidence shows wide variation in returns to investments, including a nonnegligible share of low- or negative-impact projects.

Scarce resources make prioritization a central policy challenge. Financial constraints, especially for public and concessional funds, mean that misallocating infrastructure spending carries high opportunity costs, increasing the need to target investments with the highest social returns.

The report develops a framework to benchmark social returns against financing costs across countries and sectors. By comparing the social rate of return of infrastructure capital to borrowing costs net of depreciation, the report introduces an efficiency ratio that signals under- or overinvestment and highlights drivers of returns.

New global data make systematic, comparative infrastructure prioritization feasible. The report assembles unprecedented data on physical assets, replacement costs, capital stocks, benefit elasticities, and borrowing costs across the energy, transportation, and digital sectors, enabling evidence-based prioritization and policy experimentation at scale.

A reproducibility package is available for this book in the Reproducible Research Repository at https://reproducibility.worldbank.org/catalog/536.

INTRODUCTION

The world faces a development challenge reflecting three realities:

1. There will be no development without infrastructure. A large fraction of the population of low- and middle-income countries still lacks access to the basic infrastructure that is essential to exit poverty and enjoy higher levels of prosperity.

2. There can, however, be infrastructure without development. Evidence shows that, in general, infrastructure investments do generate development dividends but have significant heterogeneity, with both very high-return projects and low- or even negative-return ones.

3. Available resources to address infrastructure needs are constrained, especially in the countries that have the highest needs.

These three intertwined facts mean that, although infrastructure policies such as fostering electrification and improving connectivity through better transportation options and digitization should be high on the agenda of policy makers, it is crucial that they direct the scarce resources available to the highest-return projects from a social point of view. The framework driving infrastructure choices and investments should, in turn, move from a resource-gap approach to a priority-based one.

Such a prioritization exercise needs to be grounded in two main components:

1. It requires a clear framework that allows for the understanding of how the returns of different investment options vary across places and sectors.

2. It must be informed by systematic and reliable data to put that framework to use.

This report takes seriously the need to make that shift and proposes such a framework. It then presents the outcome of extensive empirical effort to gather the data necessary to answer the priority question within the framework. In a nutshell, the report presents the results from an unprecedented and wide-ranging data collection exercise, which allowed for the worldwide country-level measurement and benchmarking of capital stocks and replacement costs in three sectors: energy, transportation, and digital. The framework can be used to assess whether countries, given their existing infrastructure endowments and their current economic and financial environment, should invest more in certain sectors because the marginal benefit from doing so exceeds the cost.

Moreover, the report advocates for using the model to support a discussion of how the trade-offs might change under different policy interventions, such as lowering the cost of capital through concessional finance or the provision of guarantees, lowering the cost of construction by introducing competition on upstream sectors and better procurement practices, or boosting benefits by providing complementary investments. By allowing for the benchmarking of the different components involved in the computation of social rates of returns, it also provides a way to identify the main bottlenecks hindering countries from maximizing the benefits of infrastructure investments.

THE INFRASTRUCTURE CHALLENGE: DEFINING PRIORITIES

This section illustrates the three realities at the heart of the challenge this report intends to tackle. The following sections expose the fundamental intuition of the framework to address that challenge and outline in more detail the data gaps the report fills.

Infrastructure Access Gaps

Infrastructure needs are well documented, both globally and at the country level. For the three sectors covered in this report, energy, transportation, and digital, the following aggregate numbers provide an idea of the magnitude of the challenge:

- In 2022, 685 million people still lacked electricity access, most of them in Sub-Saharan Africa (IEA et al. 2024).

- One billion people live more than 2 kilometers away from an all-season road (Pirlea et al. 2023, chapter 9).

- Only 51.6 percent of the world's urban population had convenient access to public transportation in 2022 (United Nations 2023).

- In 2023, 2.6 billion people still did not use the internet (ITU 2023).

Although these numbers seem to suggest that the main issue is one of availability, it is useful to think of it in terms of "effective access"—meaning that, for infrastructure services to provide development benefits to households and firms, they must be available, of good quality, and affordable (Straub et al. 2025b). When considering, for example, electricity and digital services, a large fraction of the world's unconnected people lives within reach of the networks, so the fact that they do not use those networks comes down to either poor quality or prices that are too high.

The quality of infrastructure services across the three sectors covers dimensions such as reliability, safety, and convenience. For example, when it comes to energy access, firms are often burdened by frequent outages, which damage equipment, and force investment in suboptimal generator capacity. At the household level, approximately 2.1 billion people worldwide still lack access to clean cooking fuels and technologies, face the burden of collecting biomass fuel, and are exposed to pollution. Similarly, on the roads, 1.19 million people died in 2021 in road crashes because of a lack of safe and well-maintained infrastructure (WHO 2023). Such quality issues lead to low usability and lower the potential benefits of infrastructure, also decreasing the willingness of households to pay for and use the services. In general, we can think of infrastructure investment as addressing all of these dimensions.

Infrastructure's Impact on Development

These access gaps concern the international community, and for good reason: it is well established that essential infrastructure services are key inputs in the development process.

At the microeconomic level, extensive evidence demonstrates that these services can play a crucial role in combatting poverty by improving people's access to jobs, economic opportunities, and basic services such as health and education, and enhancing the affordability and availability of goods and services. In addition, infrastructure generates significant indirect benefits through urban agglomeration economies, including access to ideas and innovation, externalities in the education and health sectors, and resilience against economic and environmental shocks (Berg et al. 2017; Foster et al. 2023, 2025; Straub 2008).

At the macroeconomic level, infrastructure investment is expected to boost productivity and economic growth, although the evidence is mixed. Studies generally support a positive multiplier effect from government public capital spending in the context of developed countries, with estimated multipliers of between 0.6 and 1 (Ramey 2019). By contrast, evidence is more limited and heterogeneous for developing countries, where both null effects and positive ones have been reported (Vagliasindi and Gorgulu 2021). Although data limitations and measurement issues, among other factors, appear partly to explain this lack of consistent results, deeper issues have to do with poorly targeted investments, lack of absorptive capacity, and design and implementation issues, among others (Straub 2011)

The finding that infrastructure investments do not systematically yield high development dividends is also present in the microeconomic literature. A recent meta-analysis of the empirical literature, covering over 1,000 estimates from more than 200 studies conducted in countries all over the world, finds that on average infrastructure has a positive and significant impact on outcomes such as growth, productivity, and jobs, but that a nonnegligible subset of cases displays contrasted results, with null or negative impact (Foster et al. 2025). Figure 1.1, based on over 1,000 estimated output elasticities of infrastructure, illustrates the widespread dispersion in terms of actual impact, with a number of the results falling in the negative and null part of the graph; even among positive results, only a subset appears to be statistically significant. A breakdown by sectors gives a similar picture, with impacts appearing highly heterogenous and context specific.

Large Spending Needs but Constrained Resources

The final piece of the puzzle is the fact that resources available to address the needs are woefully insufficient. It is notoriously difficult to come up with credible figures on infrastructure spending and investment, especially in developing countries. Early studies such as Fay et al. (2019) estimated a total of between US$0.8 billion and US$1.2 trillion in low- and middle-income countries, including both public and private spending. The Global Infrastructure Hub's InfraTracker identified about US$1 trillion of budgeted spending for the Group of Twenty countries only.[1] A recent International Monetary Fund–World Bank Development Committee paper, for example, highlights general agreement that current spending levels are not sufficient to meet the needs and achieve the Sustainable Development Goals (Development Committee 2023).

FIGURE 1.1 Distribution of estimated elasticities from the literature

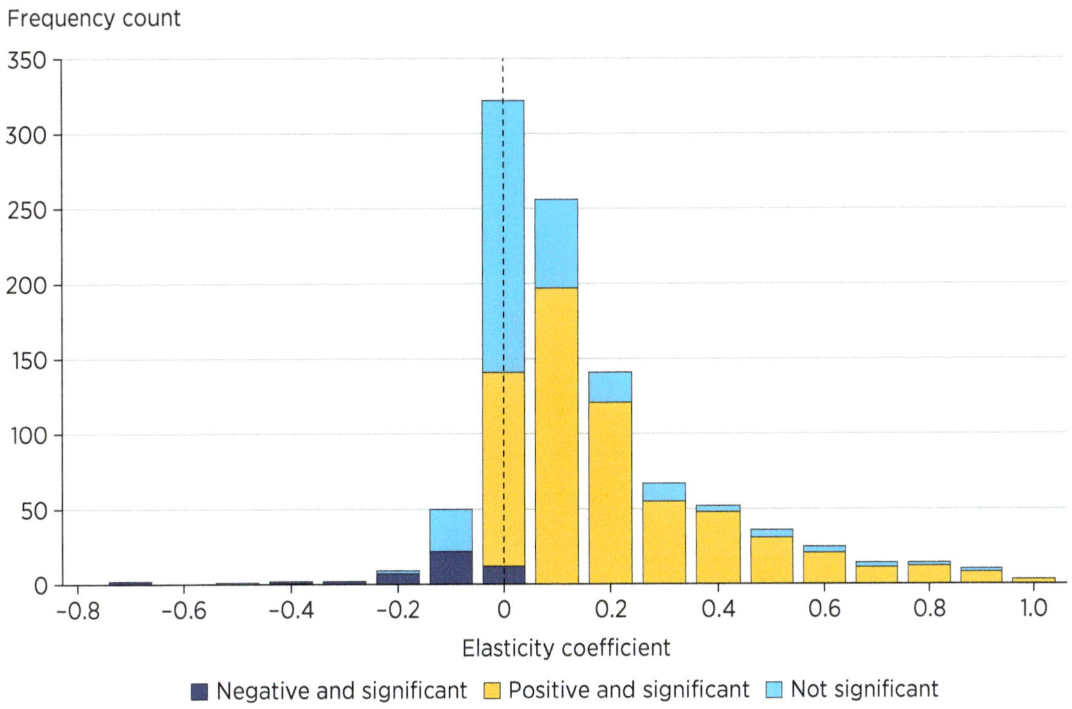

Frequency count

Source: Based on Foster et al. 2025.

Public and concessional funds, in particular, fall short of meeting infrastructure needs despite the fact that the World Bank, for example, invests a large part of its concessional funds in infrastructure projects. In recent years, energy, transportation, urban, and digital investments together represented between a quarter and a third of the institution's investments (table 1.1). As of November 10, 2025, the corresponding portfolio amounted to US$128.3 billion. Although a drop in the bucket of needed investments, which run in the trillions as mentioned before, this amount represents a crucial drop for many low-income countries, which have scarce public resources to invest, can hardly expect to attract large amounts of private money, and thus rely predominantly on these concessional funds to leverage critical infrastructure investments.

To address the shortfalls in those countries, the Independent Experts Group (2023), commissioned by the Group of Twenty, recommended a tripling of financing from all multilateral development banks. This recommendation collides with a political environment in which, for various reasons, development money contributed by major donors is heavily constrained and likely to decrease in coming years. Moreover, uncertainty about the stability of the international economic environment threatens the appetite of private investors for risky long-term investments.

TABLE 1.1 Infrastructure: IBRD + IDA commitments, FY20–FY25 (US$, billions)

Global department	FY20	FY21	FY22	FY23	FY24	FY25
Energy and extractives	4.6	5.5	5.5	8.5	7.7	8.5
Transportation	3.3	3.7	8.2	2.8	5.0	11.2
Urban, resilience, and land	5.0	4.4	5.6	7.4	5.1	6.3
Digital	0.8	0.8	0.9	1.2	2.1	0.6
Total	13.7	14.4	20.2	19.9	19.9	26.6
Share of World Bank lending (%)	23.2	21.6	28.7	27.2	29.1	33.0

Source: Original table for this publication.
Note: FY = fiscal year; IBRD = International Bank for Reconstruction and Development; IDA = International Development Association.

THE FRAMEWORK OF INFRASTRUCTURE CAPITAL INVESTMENT

The growing scarcity described in the previous section allows no room for misdirecting resources to underperforming sectors and projects, which raises the question of how to systematically assess the social returns of infrastructure investments across countries and sectors to establish overarching priorities. Such assessments have generally been addressed through the lens of resource mobilization, trying to estimate the amount of money needed to extend the services and cover the access gaps identified earlier. International organizations and big consulting firms routinely produce such numbers, just to conclude that the amounts are unlikely to be met. However, the methodology for producing such numbers is ill-defined and the underlying data often of bad quality (Fay and Straub 2019; Rozenberg and Fay 2019).

This report wants to shift the infrastructure paradigm from a focus on spending more to one aimed at spending where the social impact is the greatest. In that sense, it starts from the message of the *Beyond the Gap* report, which states, "How much countries need to spend on infrastructure depends on their goals, but also on the efficiency with which they pursue these goals" (Rozenberg and Fay 2019, xiii). It then goes one step further by proposing a transparent methodology to assess, at the country-sector level, the goals that produce the highest social returns, the dimensions that drive these returns, and how policy interventions can boost returns. By helping policy makers facing resource constraints to prioritize across different options, the report provides a clear framework to guide infrastructure choices.

The methodology builds on a simple theoretical framework (Straub et al. 2025a), which expresses the question as a comparison between the marginal benefit of an additional investment in each country-sector and its marginal cost. It can be shown that this comparison is equivalent to comparing the social rate of return of the infrastructure asset base and the cost of raising capital.

To be precise, the social rate of return of infrastructure capital is defined here as the rate of return on capital that includes both the private return to that capital—that is, the part that accrues directly as payment to its services—and additional economic externalities.

As will become clear later in this section, capturing all the externalities associated with infrastructure deployment can be difficult. Although externalities leading to higher growth through different channels, such as agglomeration effects in the urban context, are generally well understood, some longer-term externalities, such as negative environmental externalities, are harder to identify and measure. Thus, the social rate of return as defined in this report must be considered a slightly restrictive one, covering any returns, direct or indirect, that eventually can be appropriated through some mechanism.

Using a simple Cobb-Douglas production function, this social rate of return can be expressed as the combination of three main components: the inverse of the infrastructure capital-output ratio, the output-elasticity of infrastructure (the percentage increase in gross domestic product [GDP] as a result of an increase of 1 percent in infrastructure capital), and the cost of capital (the borrowing cost faced by investors) net of depreciation. In a world in which economic agents—governments and investors—would make optimal decisions unconstrained by any market failures, such as lack of information or credit constraints, it is expected that countries' current capital stocks are such that the marginal benefit of an additional investment in each country-sector is just enough to balance its marginal cost. In practice, extensive evidence shows that investments often fail to flow to where they are likely to have high returns, leading to inefficient allocation of the stock of capital around the world (Caselli and Feyrer 2007; Lowe et al. 2019; Lucas 1990). Considering the large service access gaps that exist today, infrastructure capital in particular appears to be very unevenly distributed across countries at different levels of development and is therefore unlikely to reflect optimal relationships. The present framework can therefore best be viewed as a benchmark to gauge potential misallocation of infrastructure capital distribution in different sectors and places, and to identify areas that warrant more investment.

To formalize these intuitions, consider the following simple model of infrastructure capital investment. For the sake of simplicity and highlighting the main elements of the trade-off, investment is framed as a government decision problem, but this model could be enriched to incorporate the intervention of private investors and the specificities of delegation problems such as public-private partnerships.[2]

Output (GDP) in the economy is produced combining infrastructure capital, K, and other factors of production, which for now are taken as given. This expression can be written as $GDP_t = F(K_t ; .)$, where the subscript t refers to time. Given an initial level of capital, K_0, the government's problem in each period is to decide how much to invest in infrastructure, denoted by I, in order to maximize GDP.

Formally, this is equivalent to solving the following problem:

$$\max_{I_t} \sum_{t=0}^{\infty} \frac{1}{(1+r)^t} \left\{ F\left(K_t; .\right) - P_{K,t} I_t \right\}$$

$$s.t. \, K_{t+1} \le I_t + \left(1 - \delta\right) K_t \tag{1.1}$$

$$K_0 \, given$$

where δ is the rate of depreciation of infrastructure capital, r is the government's discount rate, and P_K is the infrastructure price.

In steady state, the first-order condition of this problem yields the following equality:

$$MPK \equiv \frac{\partial Y}{\partial K} = P_K \left(r + \delta \right). \tag{1.2}$$

Assuming that the function F is a Cobb-Douglas, the previous first-order condition can be written as

$$SRR \equiv \theta_S \frac{P_Y Y}{P_K K} = r + \delta \tag{1.3}$$

with the two terms on the left-hand side representing the social rate of return, often referred to as the marginal product of capital (MPK in the previous expression). As discussed earlier, this equality is expected to hold at equilibrium, absent market failures and other distortions. In practice, this result is very unlikely. A simple way to assess potential misallocations is to compute a ratio R, referred to as the *infrastructure efficiency ratio*:

$$R = \frac{SRR}{r + \delta}. \tag{1.4}$$

Values of R above 1 would imply that additional investments are warranted; ratios below 1 would indicate the contrary. For each specific context, this ratio in turn can be interpreted in terms of the underlying parameters, such as the price of infrastructure P_K, the capital-output ratio $p_K K/p_Y Y$, the cost of capital r, or the impact parameter θ.

The literature includes extensive discussion on how to measure the different elements in this formula—especially the first term, θ, which is sector-specific (thus the subscript s). Generic capital is approximated using the capital share of GDP, as measured from the national account, possibly netting out natural nonreproducible capital (Caselli and Feyrer 2007). When zooming in on infrastructure capital, however, this approach is no longer feasible, because a large part of infrastructure is provided as a public good; the corresponding services are not priced on the market and thus not captured in standard accounts (Lowe et al. 2019). In this case, the common approach has been to use the output-elasticity of infrastructure as estimated from cross-country regressions (Canning and Bennathan 2000; Gardner and Henry 2023). This report acknowledges the limitations of the cross-country literature (Straub 2011) and seeks to generate more robust estimates of θ, using the results from a large-scale meta-analysis, described in more detail in chapter 7 (Foster et al. 2025).

Beyond Y, which is GDP measured at domestic prices and is readily available from reputable sources such as the World Development Indicators, all other elements of equation (1.1) are contributions of this report. The next subsection details the approach for estimating K, the estimated capital stocks; P_K, the unit replacement cost value; r, governments' cost of borrowing; and δ, the infrastructure depreciation rates.

THE DATA

Implementing this framework requires extensive data on several dimensions. The report exploits a variety of data sources, both public and proprietary, as well as internal World Bank documents, to develop a large set of indicators covering issues never systematically documented before in the three main sectors studied here, namely energy, transportation, and digital. The data provided by this report include the following (for a summary, refer to table 1A.1 in the annex):

- A country-specific inventory of physical infrastructure assets necessary to support services (kilometers of roads or railroads, electricity generation plants capacity in MW, kilometers of transmission and distribution grids, number of cell towers, data centers, number of internet exchange points, kilometers of fiber-optic and submarine cables).

- Updated information on country-specific figures for the cost of constructing the underlying infrastructure needed to provide services. The report provides updated information on the cost to produce one megawatt of electricity generating capacity, to build 1 kilometer of road or railroad across countries, or to extend digital network elements such as data centers, fiber-optic cables, and cell towers.

- Leveraging the two previous elements, country-specific estimates of the value of the complete stock of capital that countries possess at the most recent date of collection by sectors and subsectors, and consequently their infrastructure capital-output ratio (defined as the share of capital in GDP). In most cases, the geospatial mapping of the assets allows for the diagnostic to be taken down to second-level administrative divisions (municipalities, districts).

- Estimates of the benefits from infrastructure investments across country groups and geography, based on meta-analysis regressions, and cross-validated by alternative methodologies whenever possible.

- Cost of capital—that is, how much investors must pay to raise resources for infrastructure projects—and depreciation figures across countries and sectors.

- Putting the last two elements together, an infrastructure efficiency ratio grounded in a simple theoretical framework, which compares the social rate of return of infrastructure at the country-sector level to the sum of the cost of capital and depreciation.

The results from the analysis can potentially support several levels of analysis:

- First, the analysis provides a much-needed source of data to precisely identify infrastructure supply gaps or, conversely, overprovision.

- Second, it allows for data-informed benchmarks on the returns across infrastructure sectors in low- and middle-income countries. For the poorest countries and those with weak governance contexts, which generally rely heavily on public and concessional resources because the business climate makes large-scale private investment difficult, it informs the prioritization of these scarce resources to the highest-return investments.

- Third, it provides a basis for estimating optimal allocation of given investment amounts between different infrastructure sectors.

- Fourth, it also provides the basis to analyze different counterfactual scenarios regarding the feasibility of infrastructure investments, as well as identifying the main actionable sources that may tilt the efficiency ratio through policies aimed at lowering the cost of capital through concessional finance or guarantees, lowering the cost of construction, or boosting benefits by providing complementary investments.

- Finally, for more developed countries, such as middle-income countries, the analysis may help identify areas where returns are high enough and could be appropriated to facilitate the attraction of private investors. Attracting private resources raises information and appropriability challenges. Teasing out private (direct) versus social (direct plus indirect) returns can make investments attractive by reducing uncertainty for private players.

ANNEX 1A. BACKGROUND PAPERS AND DATA SUMMARY TABLE

The report builds on a set of accompanying background papers, which will be released in parallel:

- "The Social Rate of Return of Infrastructure," Stéphane Straub, Manuel García-Santana, He He, Yue Li, Xinxin Lyu, Jevgenijs Steinbuks, and Estefanía Vergara Cobos

- "A Global Database of Energy Infrastructure," Ruoyi Li, Xinxin Lyu, Jevgenijs Steinbuks, and Stéphane Straub

- "A Global Database of Transport Infrastructure," He He, Christopher Dann, Yue Li, and Stéphane Straub

- "A Global Database of Digital Infrastructure," Estefanía Vergara Cobos, Julian Hansol, and Stéphane Straub

- "Benchmarking Energy Infrastructure Costs with Machine Learning," Yue Li, Xinxin Lyu, and Jevgenijs Steinbuks

- "Bridging the Infrastructure Investment Data Gap: Leveraging Asset Data to Better Understand Private Investment," Henri Pierre Francis Blas and Stéphane Straub

- "Highway Investments and Local Growth: A Comparative Perspective," Piet Gerrits, Yue Li, Harris Selod, Stéphane Straub, and Yawen Zheng.

All the information (physical assets, unit costs, and stock values) will be provided as a global public good, through World Bank data repositories. Table 1A.1 provides a summary view of the data series provided in this report, for each sector and subsector, listing the specific indicators, the number of countries, and the lowest administrative level included.

TABLE 1A.1 Summary of data provided by the report

Sector	Indicator	Number of countries	Lowest administrative level
Capital stocks			
Energy generation	Capacity	196	local
Energy generation	Stock value	196	local
Energy transmission and distribution	Length	200	local
Energy transmission and distribution	Stock value	200	local
Energy	Total stock value	207	local
Roads	Length	186	local
Roads	Stock value	186	local
Railroads	Length	141	local
Railroads	Stock value	141	local
Transportation	Total stock value	186	local
Digital data centers	Capacity	120	local
	Stock value	120	local
Digital RAN	Number	200	local
	Stock value	202	local
Digital IXPs	Number	173	local
	Stock value	173	local
Digital FOC	Length	186	local
	Stock value	186	local
Digital SMC	Length	164	local
	Stock value	165	local
Digital[a]	Total stock value	216	local
Social rates of return			
Energy SSR		154	country
Transportation SSR		152	country
Digital SSR		158	country
Efficiency ratio			
Energy ratio		150	country
Transportation ratio		149	country
Digital ratio		155	country

Source: Original table for this publication.
Note: FOC = fiber-optic cable; IXP = internet exchange point; RAN = radio access network; SMC = submarine cable; SSR = social rate of return.
a. For the sake of brevity, the table does not include total stock values for each of the five assets listed (although those values are available).

NOTES

1. Global Infrastructure Hub, "InfraTracker," https://infratracker.gihub.org/.
2. Refer, for example, to Fabre and Straub (2023) for an overview of the debate in economics on the role of the government versus the private sector in the provision of goods and services.

REFERENCES

Berg, C. N., U. Deichmann, Y. Liu, and H. Selod. 2017. "Transport Policies and Development." *Journal of Development Studies* 53 (4): 465–80.

Canning, D., and E. Bennathan. 2000. "The Social Rate of Return on Infrastructure Investment." Policy Research Working Paper 2390, World Bank.

Caselli, Francesco, and James Feyrer. 2007. "The Marginal Product of Capital." *Quarterly Journal of Economics* 122 (2): 535–68.

Development Committee (Joint Ministerial Committee of the Boards of Governors of the Bank and the Fund on the Transfer of Real Resources to Developing Countries). 2023. "Ending Poverty on a Livable Planet: Report to Governors on World Bank Evolution." Report DC2023-0004, World Bank.

Fabre, Anaïs, and Stéphane Straub. 2023. "The Impact of Public Private Partnerships (PPPs) in Infrastructure, Health and Education." *Journal of Economic Literature* 61 (2): 655–715.

Fay, M., S. Han, H. I. Lee, M. Mastruzzi, and M. Cho. 2019. "Hitting the Trillion Mark–a Look at How Much Countries Are Spending on Infrastructure." Policy Research Working Paper 8730, World Bank.

Fay, M., and S. Straub. 2019. "Rising Incomes and Inequality of Access to Infrastructure among Latin American Households." *Journal of Infrastructure Policy and Development* 3 (1): 76–100.

Foster, V., N. Gorgulu, S. Straub, and M. Vagliasindi. 2023. "The Impact of Infrastructure on Development Outcomes: A Qualitative Review of Four Decades of Literature." Policy Research Working Paper 10343, World Bank.

Foster, V., N. Gorgulu, S. Straub, and M. Vagliasindi. 2025. "The Impact of Infrastructure on Development Outcomes: A Meta-Analysis." *World Bank Research Observer*, October 7, 2025. https://doi.org/10.1093/wbro/lkaf003.

Gardner, Camille, and Peter Blair Henry. 2023. "Global Infrastructure: Potential, Perils, and a Framework for Distinction." *Journal of Economic Literature* 61 (4): 1318–58.

Independent Experts Group. 2023. *Strengthening Multilateral Development Banks: The Triple Agenda*. Report of the Independent Experts Group to the Indian G20 Presidency.

IEA (International Energy Agency), International Renewable Energy Agency, United Nations Statistics Division, World Bank, and World Health Organization. 2024. "Tracking SDG 7: The Energy Progress Report." World Bank. https://trackingsdg7.esmap.org/.

ITU (International Telecommunication Union). 2023. *Measuring Digital Development Facts and Figures 2023*. Geneva: ITU Publications.

Lowe, Matt, Chris Papageorgiou, and Fidel Perez-Sebastian. 2019. "The Public and Private Marginal Product of Capital." *Economica* 86 (342): 336–61.

Lucas, R. 1990. "Why Doesn't Capital Flow from Rich to Poor Countries?" *American Economic Review* 80 (2): 92–96.

Pirlea, A. F., U. Serajuddin, D. Wadhwa, and M. Welch, eds. 2023. *Atlas of Sustainable Development*. World Bank. https://datatopics.worldbank.org/sdgatlas/goal-9-industry-innovation-and -infrastructure/?lang=en.

Ramey, V. A. 2019. "Ten Years After the Financial Crisis: What Have We Learned from the Renaissance in Fiscal Research?" *Journal of Economic Perspectives* 33 (2): 89–114.

Rozenberg, J., and M. Fay. 2019. *Beyond the Gap: How Countries Can Afford the Infrastructure They Need while Protecting the Planet*. World Bank.

Straub, Stéphane. 2008. "Infrastructure and Growth in Developing Countries: Recent Advances and Research Challenges." Policy Research Working Paper 4460, World Bank.

Straub, Stéphane. 2011. "Infrastructure and Development: A Critical Appraisal of the Macro-Level Literature." *Journal of Development Studies* 47 (5): 683–708.

Straub, Stéphane, Manuel Garcia Santana, He He, Yue Li, Xinxin Lyu, Jevgenijs Steinbuks, and Estefania Vergara Cobos. 2025a. "The Social Rate of Return of Infrastructure." Background paper for this report.

Straub, Stéphane, Tomás Serebrisky, Lisa Bagnoli, and Claudio Rojas. 2025b. "Infrastructure and Poverty Reduction: Innovative Policies for Effective Access." Report for the G20 Brazilian Presidency, Inter-American Development Bank and World Bank.

Vagliasindi, Maria, and Nisan Gorgulu. 2021. "What Have We Learned about the Effectiveness of Infrastructure Investment as a Fiscal Stimulus? A Literature Review." Policy Research Working Paper 9796, World Bank.

United Nations 2023. *The Sustainable Development Goals Report 2023: Special Edition.* New York: United Nations.

WHO (World Health Organization). 2023. *Global Status Report on Road Safety 2023.* WHO.

2

A World of Unequal Endowments

KEY MESSAGES

Global infrastructure endowments are highly unequal and closely correlated with income. Across energy, transportation, and digital infrastructure, physical stocks per capita rise systematically with gross domestic product (GDP) per capita.

When valued in monetary terms, infrastructure capital as a share of GDP exhibits markedly different patterns across sectors. Energy and digital infrastructure capital-output ratios are broadly flat or decline mildly with income, whereas transportation capital-output ratios rise strongly as countries get richer.

Richer countries do not necessarily operate with more infrastructure relative to GDP—except in transportation. For the energy and digital sectors, higher incomes are associated with more efficient systems and partial decoupling between economic growth and physical capacity needs. By contrast, transportation infrastructure expands faster than GDP along the development path, driven by higher construction costs, higher quality standards, and increased investment in lower-density networks.

Consequently, the composition of infrastructure capital shifts systematically with development. As countries move up the income ladder, transportation infrastructure comes to dominate the infrastructure capital stock, increasing from a minority share in the poorest countries to roughly three-quarters in the richest. Energy and digital infrastructure, by contrast, decline as shares of total capital despite rising in absolute terms.

Regional underaccumulation of infrastructure capital is evident even after accounting for income levels. Several regions—most notably Latin America and the Caribbean; the Middle East, North Africa, Afghanistan, and Pakistan; South Asia;

A reproducibility package is available for this book in the Reproducible Research Repository at https://reproducibility.worldbank.org/catalog/536.

and Sub-Saharan Africa—display total infrastructure capital stocks below what their income levels would predict. By contrast, East Asia and Pacific and Europe and Central Asia appear to have accumulated infrastructure more intensively.

INTRODUCTION

The extensive data collection exercise undertaken for the sectors included in this report provides a new picture of the global infrastructure landscape. In the energy domain, the exercise captures 8,851 gigawatts of electricity generation capacity globally and 11.8 million kilometers of power transmission and distribution lines worldwide. For transportation, it maps 19.3 million kilometers of paved roads and 1.1 million kilometers of railway lines. The coverage is likely nearly exhaustive for the assets included, although at this stage the data do not cover off-grid generation and substations for energy, or ports and airports for transportation. For digital, it covers five core subsectors: data centers, internet exchange points (IXPs), radio access networks or mobile cells and sites, terrestrial fiber-optic cables, and submarine cables. The coverage is nearly complete for submarine cables and IXPs (about 100 percent), high for core data centers and mobile cells (about 95 percent), and more limited for terrestrial fiber networks (40–80 percent) because of data constraints. Chapter 4 discusses in detail the sources, collection methodology, assumptions made, and representativity of the data.

PHYSICAL CAPITAL STOCKS AND COUNTRY INCOME

Unsurprisingly, the data show that, across all the sectors and assets covered in this report, endowments of physical stocks behave much in the expected way, with richer countries having larger amounts when expressed in per capita terms. Correlating the physical stock per capita with GDP per capita reveals an upward trend for all categories of assets. More developed countries have, for example, more kilometers of roads, more megawatts of energy generation capacity, and more micro cell towers per person than less developed ones, with also substantial variation both within and across regions (figure 2.1).

Zooming in on each of the sectors provides a more detailed picture of the unequal state of infrastructure assets around the world. Figure 2.2 shows the distribution of power generation technologies—including oil and gas, coal, hydropower, solar, wind, nuclear, bioenergy, and geothermal—across the world's regions. Oil and gas, coal, and hydropower still make up the largest share of installed capacity. The significance of modern renewables—solar and wind plants—in East Asia and Pacific, Europe and Central Asia, and North America highlights regional progress in renewable energy deployment. Last, nuclear, bioenergy, and geothermal power generation represent a relatively small fraction of global capacity. By far the most striking message the figure offers, however, is what is barely visible on it—namely, the very small, limited amount of generation capacity in Sub-Saharan Africa, in red at the bottom.

FIGURE 2.1 **Physical infrastructure stocks per capita versus GDP per capita, by type of infrastructure**

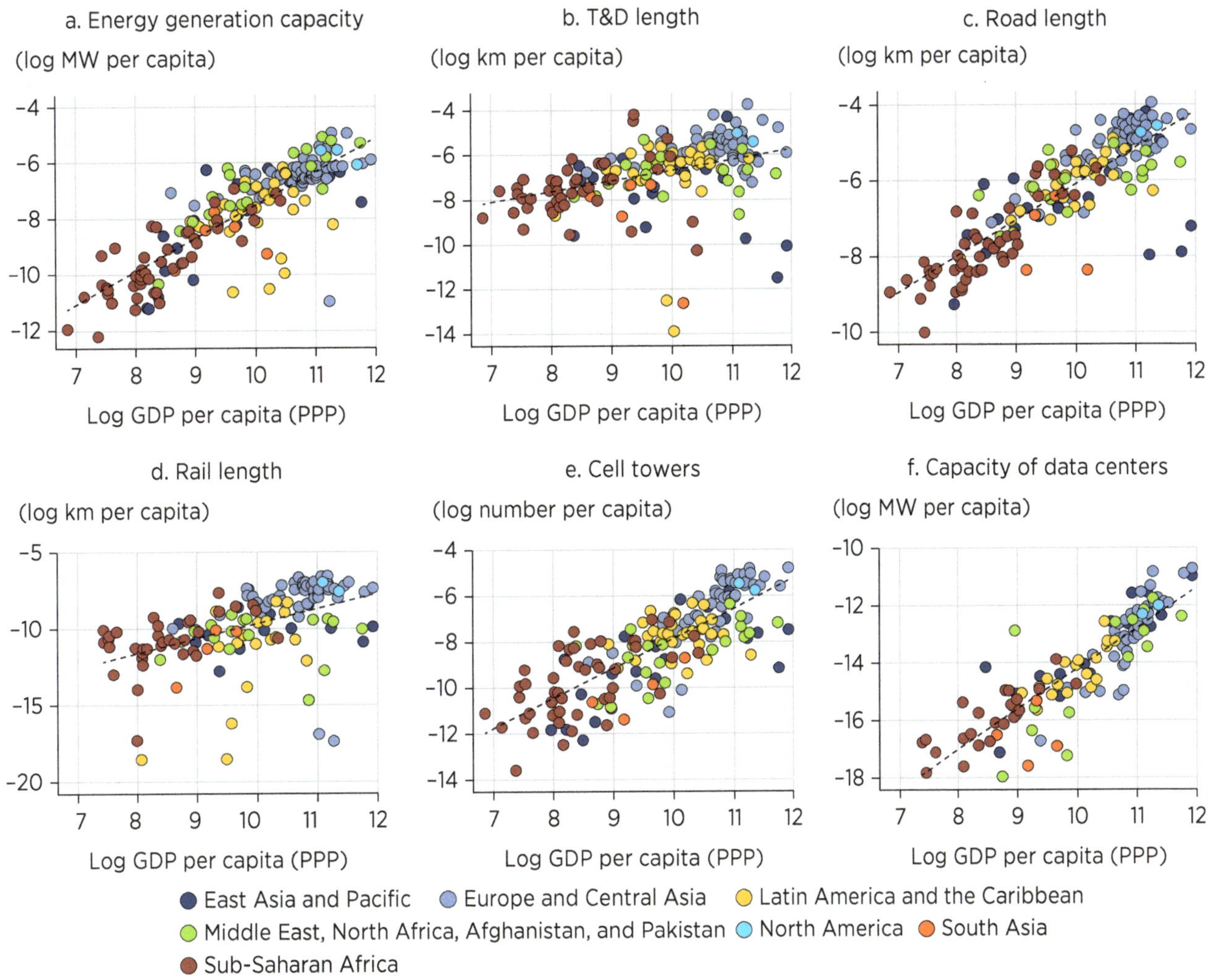

Source: Original figure for this publication.
Note: Although this figure focuses on the six major classes of assets, the pattern is similar for the other three not represented here (terrestrial fiber-optic cables, submarine cables, and internet exchange points). The data are for 2024. km = kilometer; MW = megawatt; PPP = purchasing power parity; T&D = transmission and distribution.

The global pictures of energy and transportation infrastructure convey a similar message. Map 2.1 shows obvious sharp imbalances in energy transmission and distribution lines: high network density in parts of Asia and in Europe and North America contrasts with much lower availability in Africa and Latin America, reflecting different combinations of limited electrification, underdeveloped infrastructure, and large land areas with dispersed populations. In the transportation sector, similarly, the availability of roads and railroads skews greatly toward higher-income countries (map 2.2).

FIGURE 2.2 Distribution of power generation capacity, by region and generation technology

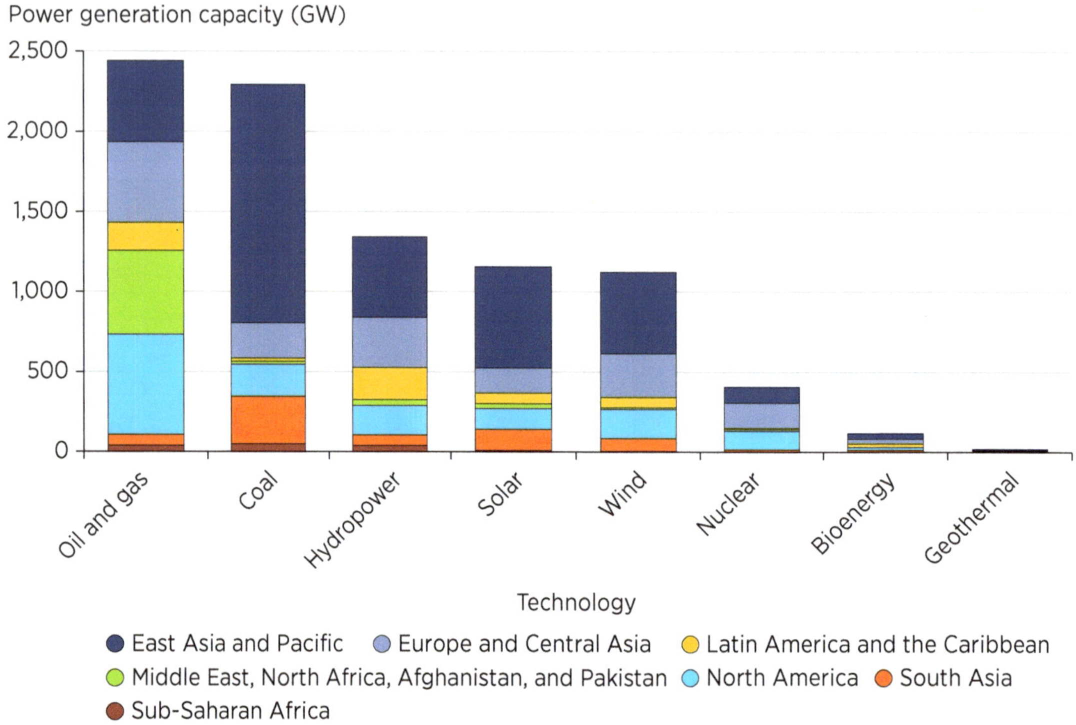

Power generation capacity (GW)

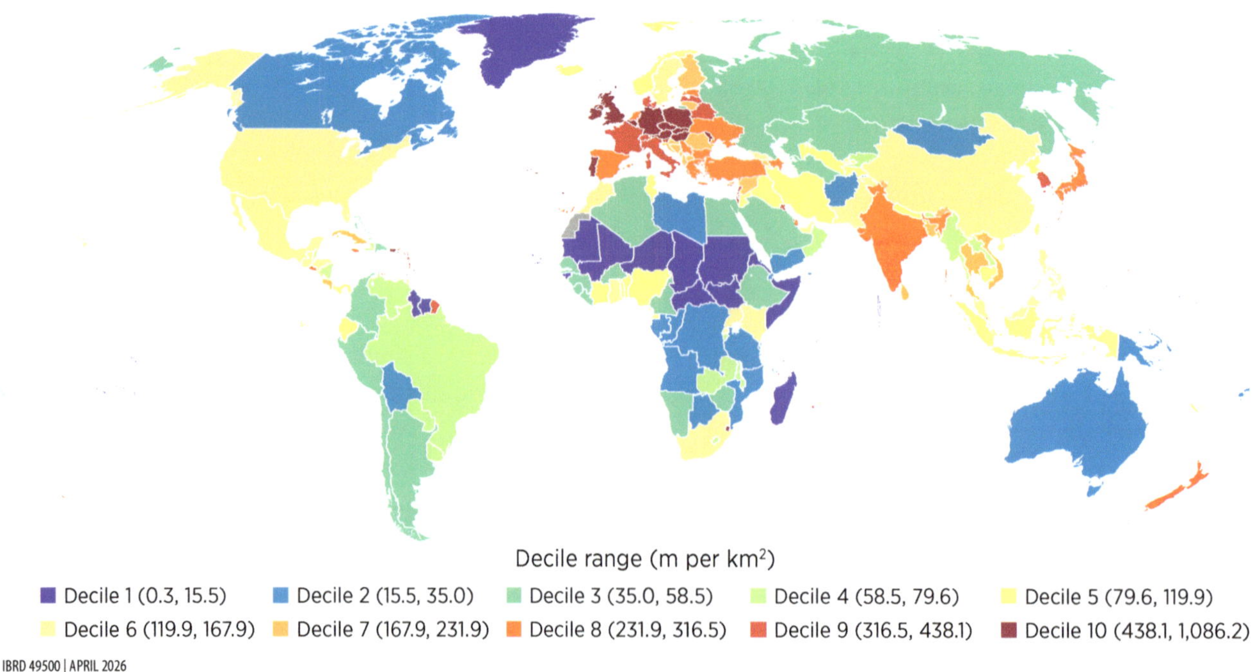

Source: Original figure for this publication.
Note: The data are for 2024. GW = gigawatt.

MAP 2.1 Global distribution of transmission and distribution lines

Source: Original map for this publication.
Note: The map illustrates global distribution in transmission and distribution lines in terms of density, measured as the total length of transmission and distribution lines per unit of land area. Countries are grouped into deciles, with shading indicating their position from lowest (decile 1) to highest (decile 10) in the global distribution. km² = square kilometer; m = meter.

MAP 2.2 Global distribution of transportation infrastructure

a. Roads

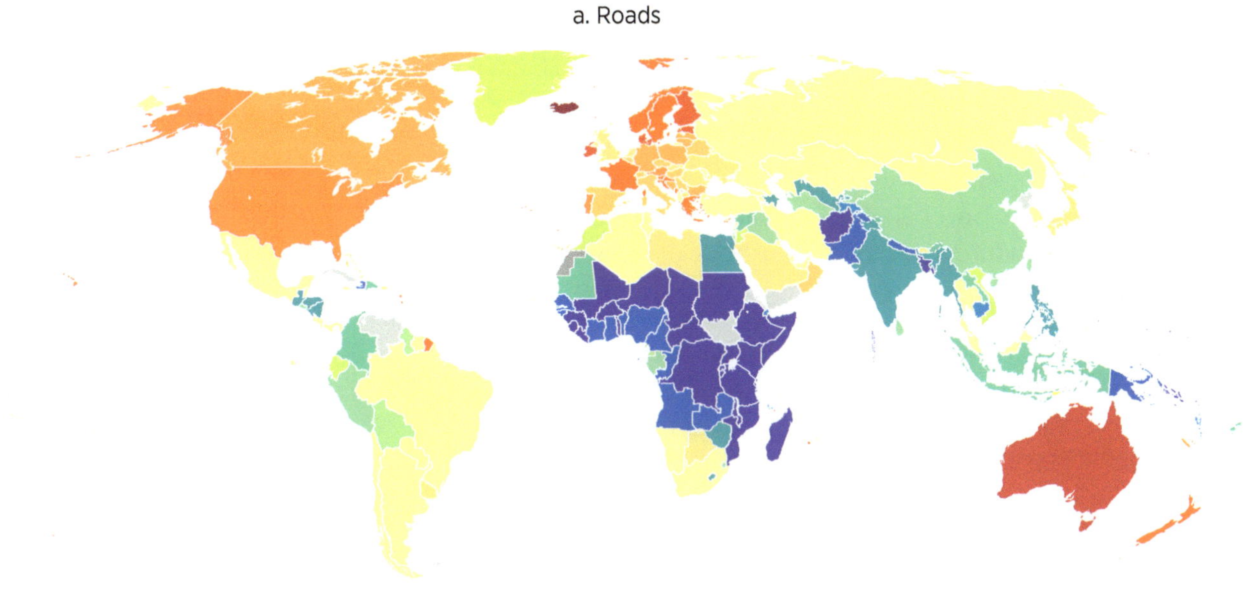

IBRD 49520 | APRIL 2026

b. Railways

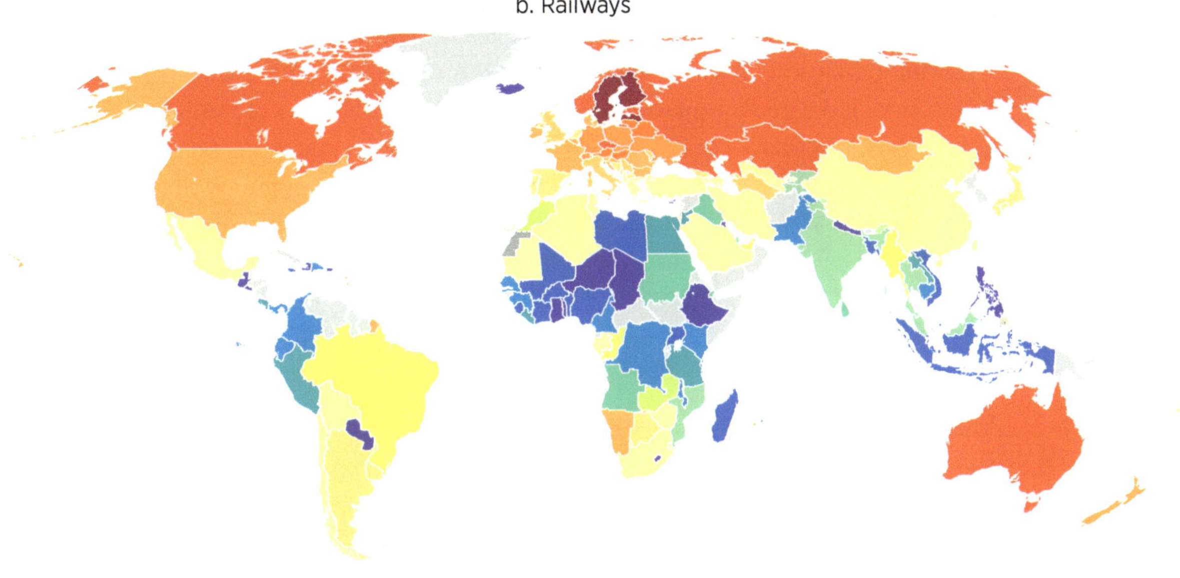

IBRD 49521 | APRIL 2026

Source: Original map for this publication.

In the digital sector, capital-intensive investments in data centers, IXPs, and submarine cables since 2000 have driven increasing evolution toward cloud-driven architectures and cross-border data exchange, with broad effects. Although high-income countries, where assets are still predominantly located, have led much of the expansion, recent submarine cable projects signal increasing global integration, especially in Latin America and the Caribbean and in Sub-Saharan Africa. Similarly, data centers' computational and storage capacities often serve users and firms across borders, meaning that geographical imbalances do not necessarily imply a complete lack of access to digital services, although distance to the primary assets can negatively affect quality.

Growth trajectories have varied, however, by infrastructure type (figure 2.3). Cell tower deployment (micro and macro sites) accelerated rapidly until about 2015 before leveling off; data centers expanded exponentially, reaching peak concentration in 2024 in North America, which accounts for about one-quarter of all data centers and one-third of global capacity; IXPs grew modestly, peaking in 2014 but regaining momentum later in Latin America and the Caribbean, South Asia, and parts of Sub-Saharan Africa; and submarine cables have surged since 2020, extending connectivity across new regional corridors. The evolution between 2015 and 2025 is particularly striking when looking at the spatial coverage of these assets, as shown for example in the case of Asia (map 2.3).

CAPITAL STOCKS AS A SHARE OF GDP

After exploring the data on countries' physical capital stocks, the next step is to determine the value of the stocks relative to countries' GDP. To estimate this value, the report first derives unit replacement cost for each of the assets of interest. It does so using a variety of techniques. For example, using large-scale project databases such as the Global Construction database, which covers over 200,000 large-scale construction projects globally, it runs econometric cost estimations and machine learning techniques to make out-of-sample predictions to recover cost by types of projects and use. In addition, it mines other sources, such as the International Energy Agency and International Renewable Energy Association capital expenditure information by technology in the case of energy, World Bank project information, and engineering tables.

These cost estimates are then multiplied by the physical inventory of each subsector, and the resulting valuations are aggregated to obtain the sector's total replacement cost at current prices. Finally, these replacement costs are adjusted for depreciation over time, in two ways, depending on data availability. When time series data on the quantity of physical assets exist, the exercise assigns a depreciation rate based on the age profile of those assets. Conversely, where historical stock values are unavailable, it applies country-specific ratios to convert replacement cost into a depreciated value. Chapters 4 and 5 provide a full description of the sources and methodologies.

FIGURE 2.3 **Trends in digital infrastructure expansion, by region and type of infrastructure, 2000–25**

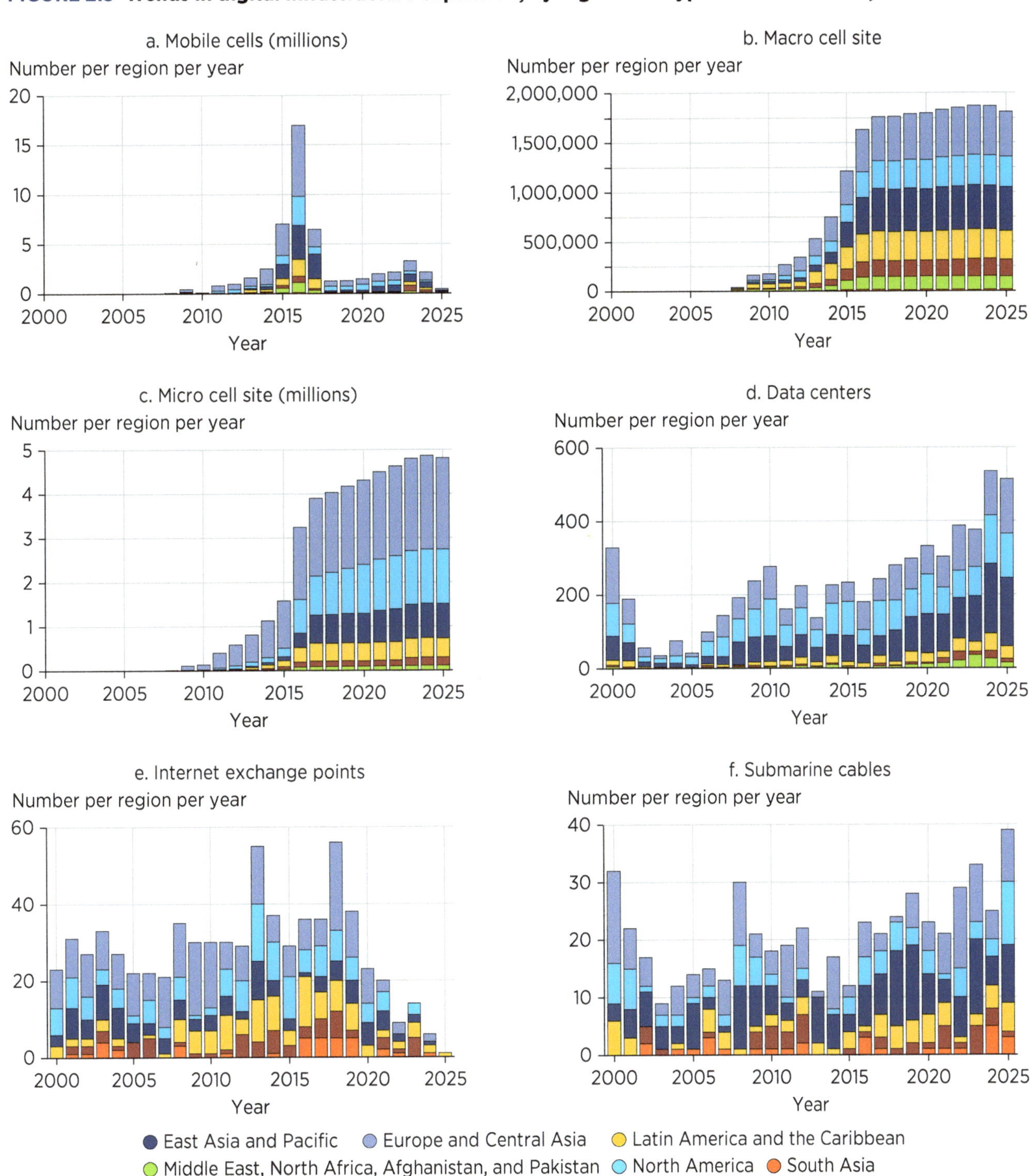

Source: Original figure for this publication.

MAP 2.3 **Digital infrastructure expansion, selected Asian economies, 2015 versus 2025**

a. 2015

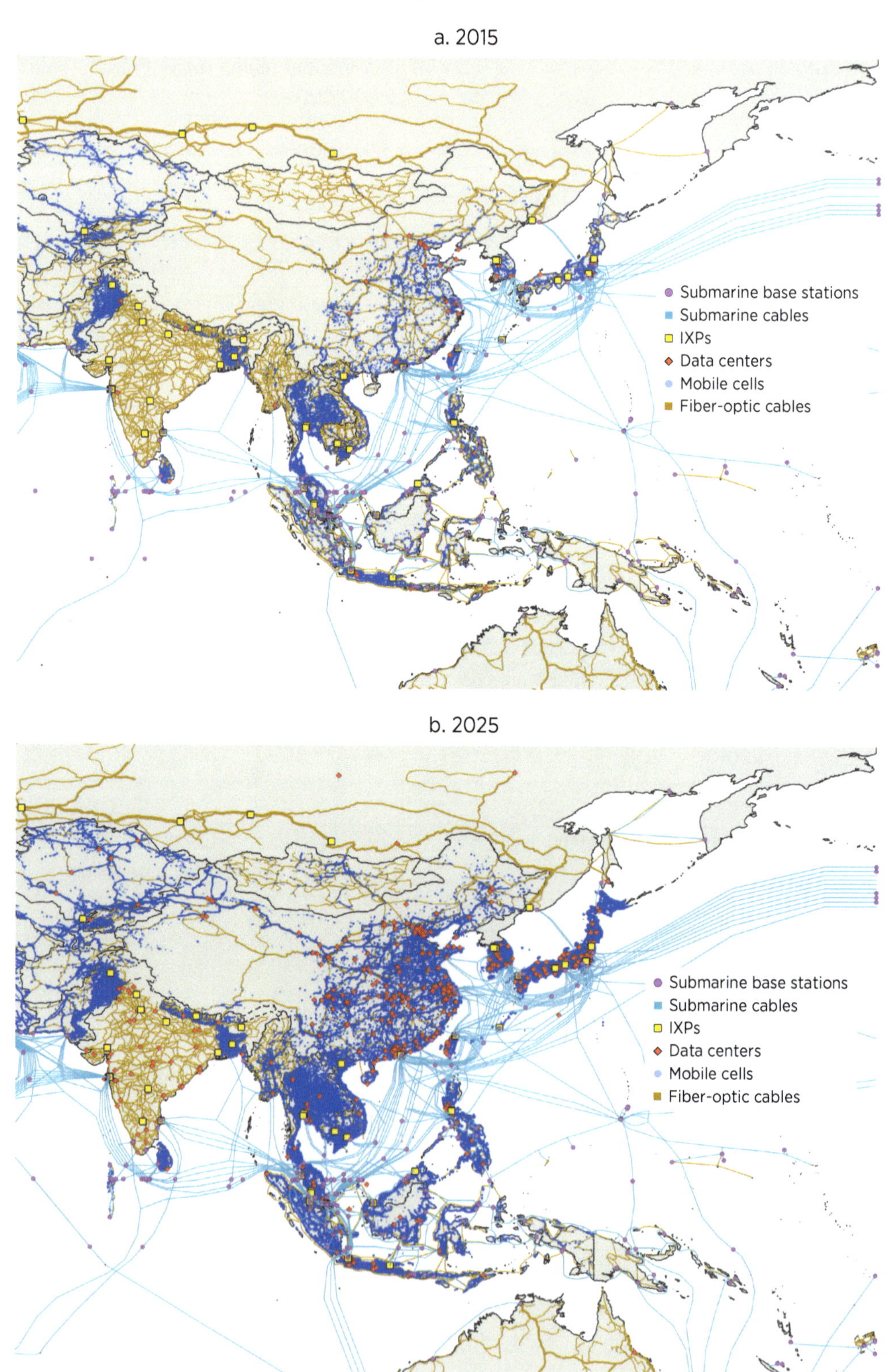

Source: Original map for this publication.
Note: Information on mobile cells is not available for India. IXP = internet exchange point.

The resulting value of the capital stock, when compared to countries' GDP, is the so-called capital-output ratio. Strikingly, the cross-country distribution of infrastructure capital changes quite dramatically when considering its dollar value. Figures 2.4–2.6 plot the capital-output ratio against countries' per capita GDP for the energy, digital, and transportation sectors, respectively.

Ultimately, whether this ratio slopes upward or downward when plotted against per capita GDP depends on whether capital stocks increase faster or more slowly than GDP when moving from low- to high-income countries. For each subsector, this slope depends on the relative amounts of assets that countries hold, the vintage of those assets, and their costs. Energy displays a mostly flat pattern (figure 2.4), as the amount of infrastructure needed to power the economy increases roughly proportionally to the level of income.

Importantly, this pattern persists even though costs increase slightly as countries get richer. The greater dispersion among less developed countries suggests that richer countries may hold slightly smaller capital stocks thanks to a combination of partial decoupling between growth and energy use, greater system efficiency, reduced losses in energy transmission, and better maintenance, among others. However, it appears that, as people get richer and consume more electricity, the quantity of physical assets necessary to supply services does not change much in terms of their share of GDP.

FIGURE 2.4 Energy capital-output ratio versus GDP per capita, by region

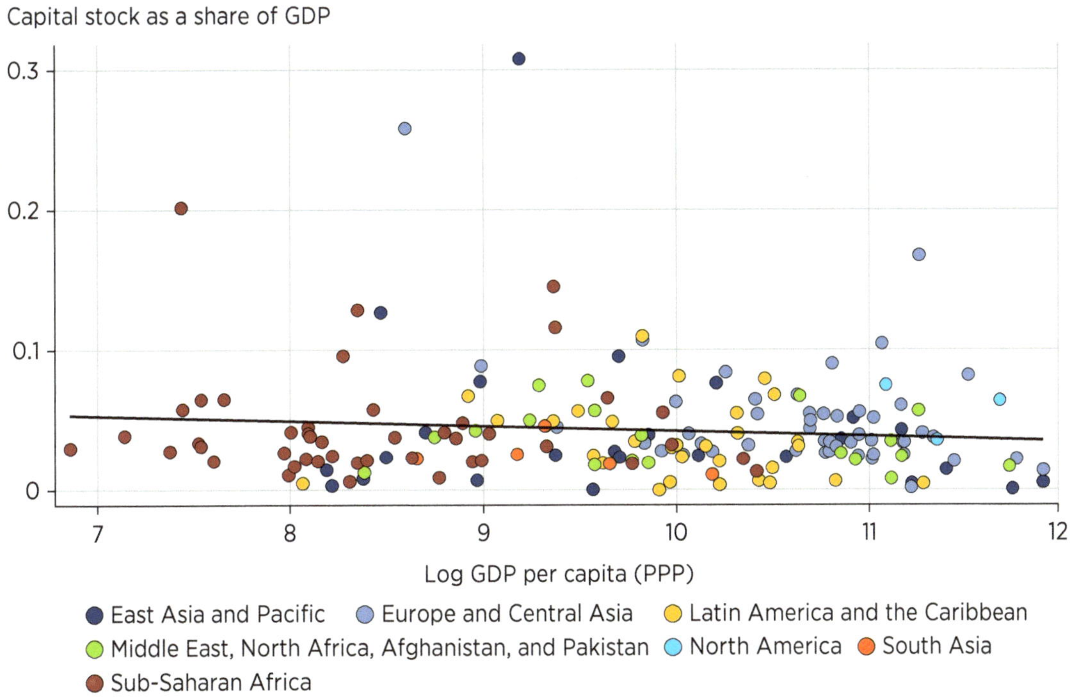

Capital stock as a share of GDP

Source: Original figure for this publication.
Note: The data are for 2024. PPP = purchasing power parity.

The digital capital-output ratio shows a slightly decreasing cross-country correlation (figure 2.5). Note that this trend appears to be driven by the higher dispersion among countries with lower per capita GDP, with a subgroup of countries in East Asia and Pacific and in Sub-Saharan Africa having relatively high stock. Otherwise, the relationship looks relatively flat. Similar conclusions hold when excluding data centers, which constitute about half of the stocks and are less tied to local use.

Transportation presents a very different pattern, with a capital-output ratio that trends strongly upward (figure 2.6). A few factors may explain this pattern. First, transportation capital likely has higher average quality in richer countries, with a larger fraction of the network being paved. Second, in developed countries, most of the new investments tend to cater to secondary roads and rural areas, which have a lower potential efficiency in terms of the number of people they serve. Finally, on the price side, the unit cost of building a new kilometer of road displays a quite steep upward gradient as countries get richer.

One could argue that the amount of infrastructure assets needed varies according to countries' fundamental characteristics. For example, less dense countries may need a larger share of transportation infrastructure relative to GDP to serve a given population, or countries with larger industrial sectors may require relatively more energy generation capacity. Box 2.1 describes how these patterns hold when controlling for such fundamentals.

FIGURE 2.5 Digital capital-output ratio versus GDP per capita, by region

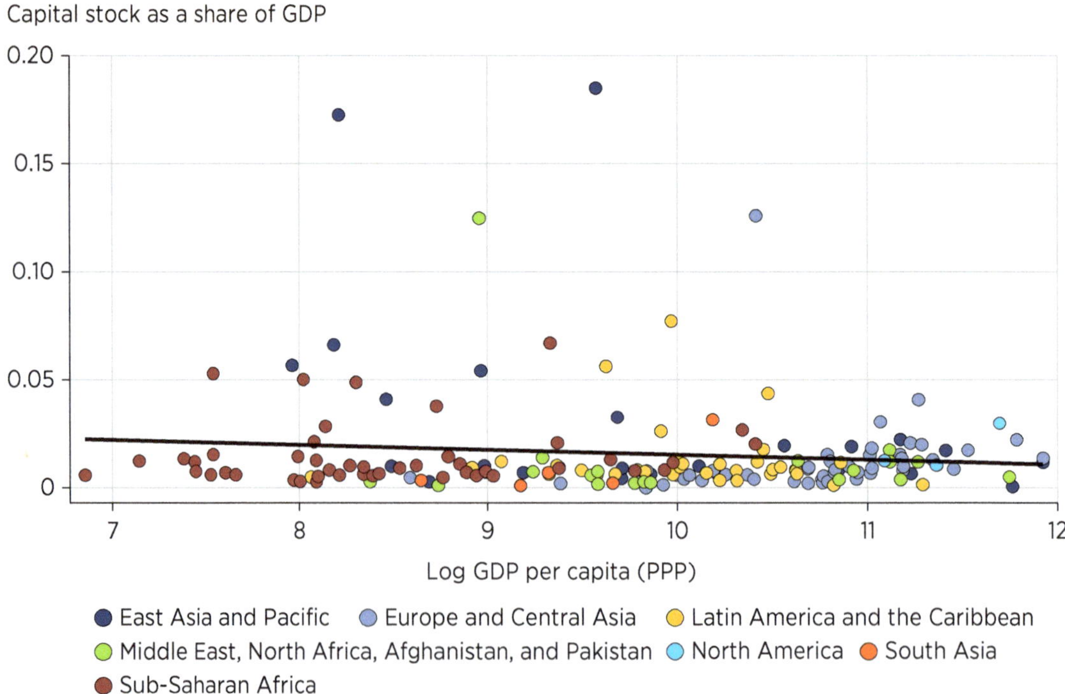

Source: Original figure for this publication.
Note: The data are for 2024. PPP = purchasing power parity.

FIGURE 2.6 **Transportation capital-output ratio versus GDP per capita, by region**

Capital stock as a share of GDP

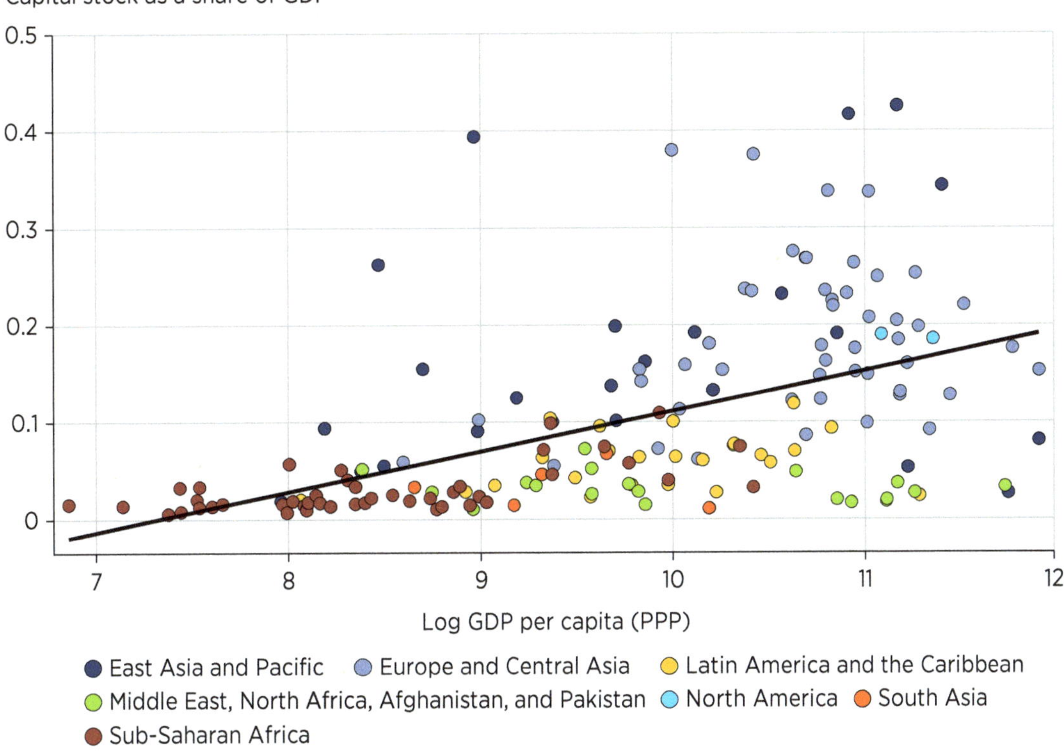

Source: Original figure for this publication.
Note: The data are for 2024. PPP = purchasing power parity.

BOX 2.1

Adjusting for countries' fundamental characteristics: Residualized capital-output ratio

To account for structural differences across countries, this box adjusts capital-output ratios by regressing them on a set of fundamentals including economic size, proxied by gross domestic product, population density, urbanization rates, and the shares of both industry and services in gross domestic product. Figure B2.1.1 shows the resulting residuals— that is, the portion of the capital-output ratio that these fundamentals cannot explain. Importantly, the patterns discussed in the main text hold after doing this adjustment, indicating that they are not simply driven by cross-country differences in scale or economic structure.

(continued)

BOX 2.1   Adjusting for countries' fundamental characteristics: Residualized capital-output ratio *(continued)*

FIGURE B2.1.1 Residualized capital-output ratio versus GDP per capita, by sector

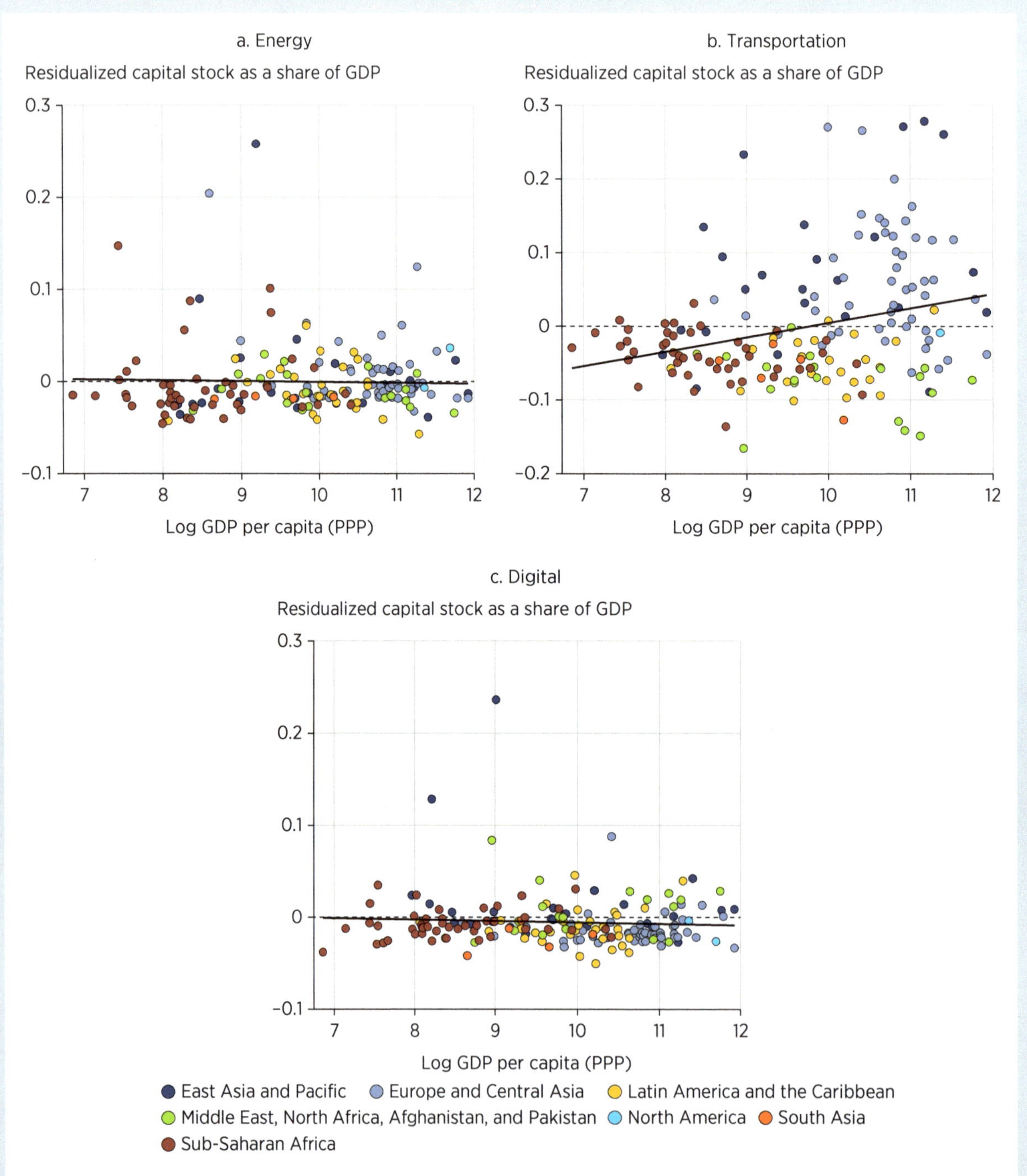

Source: Original figure for this publication.
Note: For readability, panel c excludes residuals greater than 0.4. The data are for 2024. PPP = purchasing power parity.

THE SHIFTING COMPOSITION OF INFRASTRUCTURE CAPITAL ALONG THE DEVELOPMENT PATH

The evolution of the share of each sector's capital in the total infrastructure capital stock across country income deciles illustrates the implication of these patterns (figure 2.7). Whereas energy goes from representing 53 percent of the total stock in the bottom decile (the poorest 10 percent of countries) to only 17 percent in the top decile (the richest 10 percent of countries), and digital decreases from 20 percent to 8 percent, transportation shows the opposite pattern, increasing from 27 percent to 75 percent. Consistently, countries in higher income deciles have significantly more transportation capital, as a share of GDP, but slightly less of both energy and digital.

What overall picture emerges from these patterns? Looking at total infrastructure stocks, summing up the three sectors, the overall infrastructure capital-output ratio clearly trends upward. Richer countries tend to have more infrastructure capital as a share of GDP, although with much variability at given levels of income (figure 2.8). The poorest countries have the equivalent of about 10 percent of GDP or less in infrastructure capital, and the share goes up to between 20 percent and 40 percent for more developed countries. Strikingly, four regions appear to have average capital stocks and total stocks below what their level of income would imply: Latin America and the Caribbean; the Middle East, North Africa, Afghanistan, and Pakistan; South Asia; and Sub-Saharan Africa (figure 2.9). By contrast, the East Asia and Pacific and Europe and Central Asia regions appear to be punching above their weight.[1]

FIGURE 2.7 Shares of total infrastructure capital, by sector and income decile

Average share of total infrastructure capital

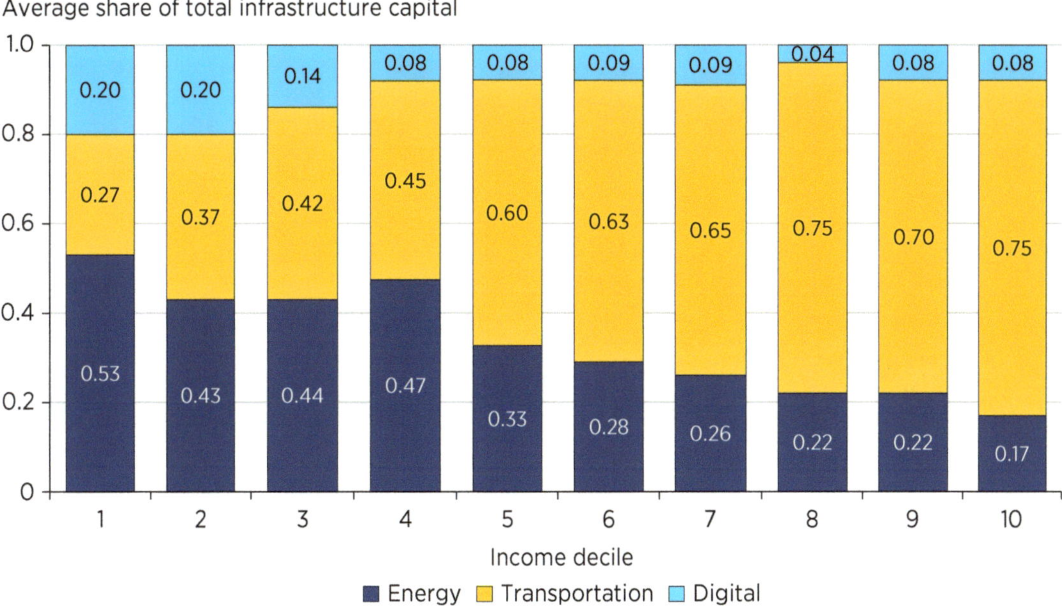

Source: Original figure for this publication.
Note: The data are for 2024.

FIGURE 2.8 Infrastructure capital-output ratio versus GDP per capita, by region

Residualized capital stock as a share of GDP

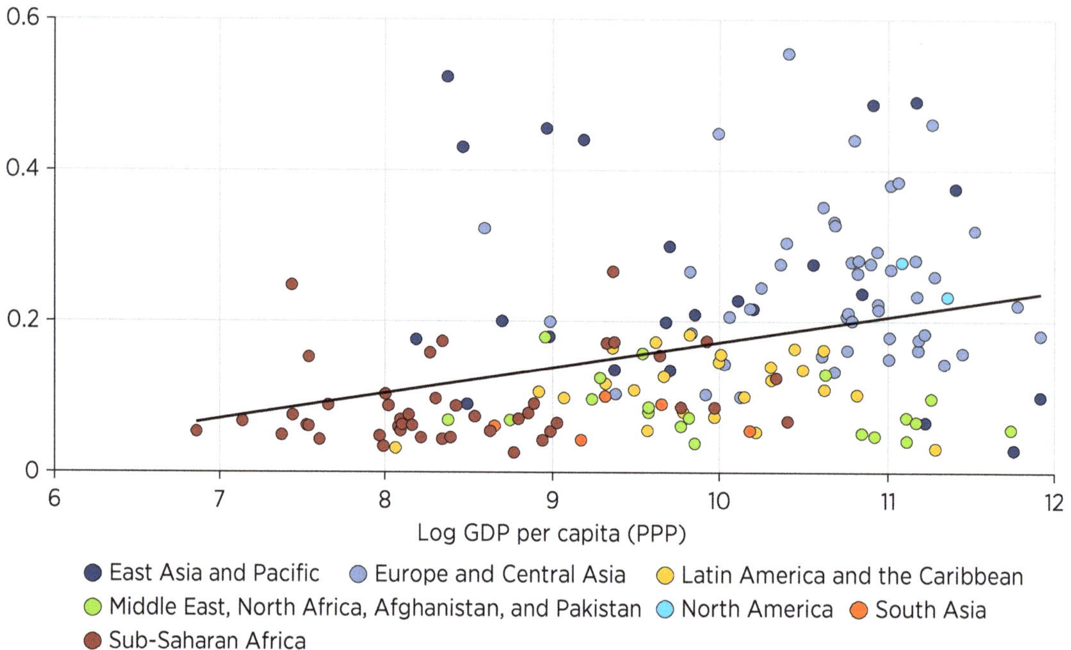

Source: Original figure for this publication.
Note: The data are for 2024. PPP = purchasing power parity.

FIGURE 2.9 Infrastructure capital-output ratio, by sector and region

Average infrastructure capital-output ratio as a share of GDP

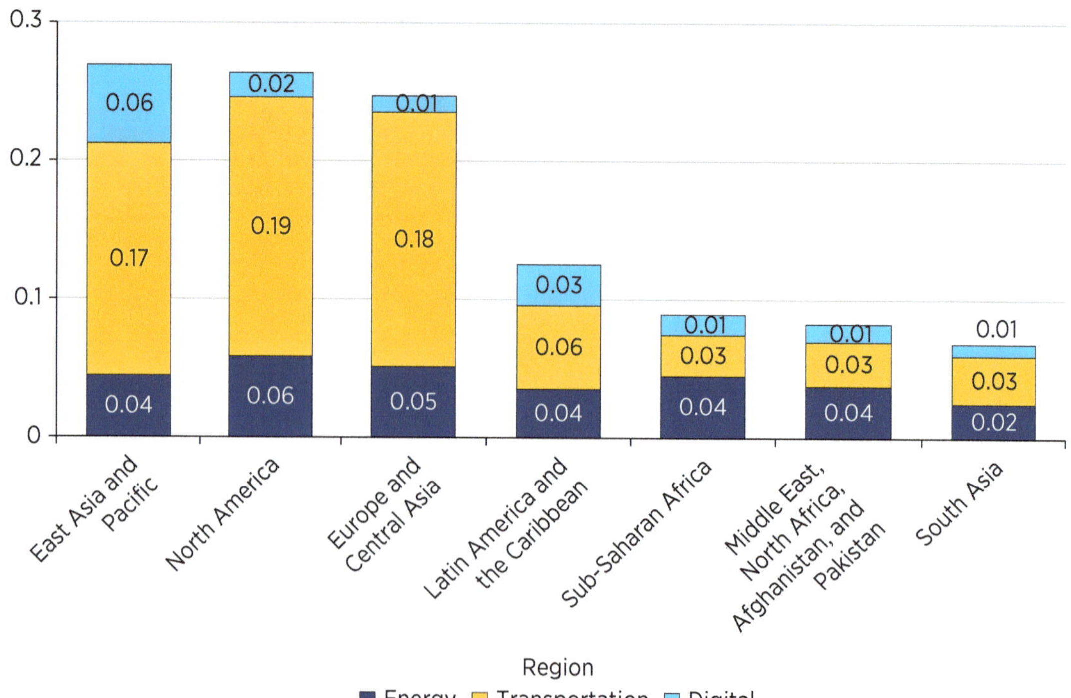

Source: Original figure for this publication.
Note: The data are for 2024.

In any case, an overarching fact becomes apparent: countries and regions that have developed and reached high-income status have done so while accumulating capital in the transportation sector at a faster pace than that of economic growth. Of course, it is worth keeping in mind that more modern transportation services also mean more energy consumption. The energy capital represented here comprises only electricity generation, transmission, and distribution, to the exclusion, for example, of energy consumed in the form of fossil fuels to power transportation services. Consistent with the rising share of transportation, the share of fossil fuel in total energy consumption is approximately 30 percent in low-income countries, 70 percent in lower-middle-income countries, and 80 percent and 85 percent in upper-middle-income and high-income countries, respectively.

This fact points first to a key complementarity between transportation and energy, revealing that the increases in total energy consumption along the development path are in fact possible only if countries accumulate transportation infrastructure capital. In addition, one interesting question going forward is whether emerging countries, as they develop and build more transportation infrastructure, will be able to electrify the related transportation services. If that happens, the pattern in figure 2.7 could well look different a couple of decades from now.

ANNEX 2A. COMPARISON TO OTHER CAPITAL STOCK MEASURES

FIGURE 2A.1 Public capital versus total infrastructure stocks, by region

Public capital as a share of GDP

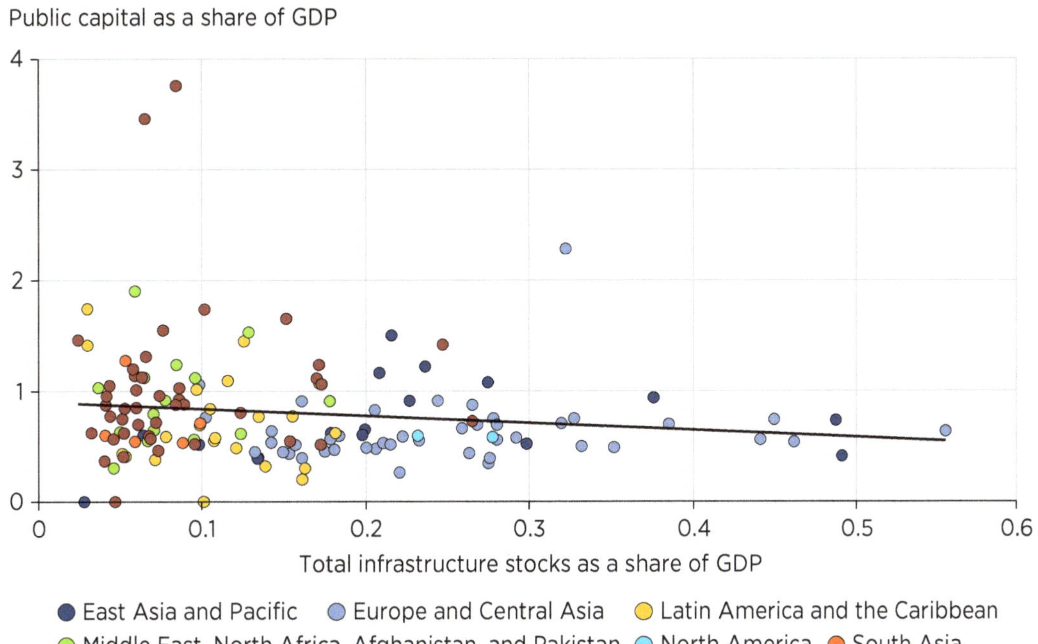

Source: Based on data from International Monetary Fund, "IMF Investment and Capital Stock Dataset, 1960–2019" (accessed November 21, 2025), https://infrastructuregovern.imf.org/content/dam/PIMA/Knowledge-Hub/dataset/IMFInvestmentandCapitalStockDataset2021.xlsx.
Note: The data are for 2024.

FIGURE 2A.2 Capital stocks versus total infrastructure depreciated capital, by region

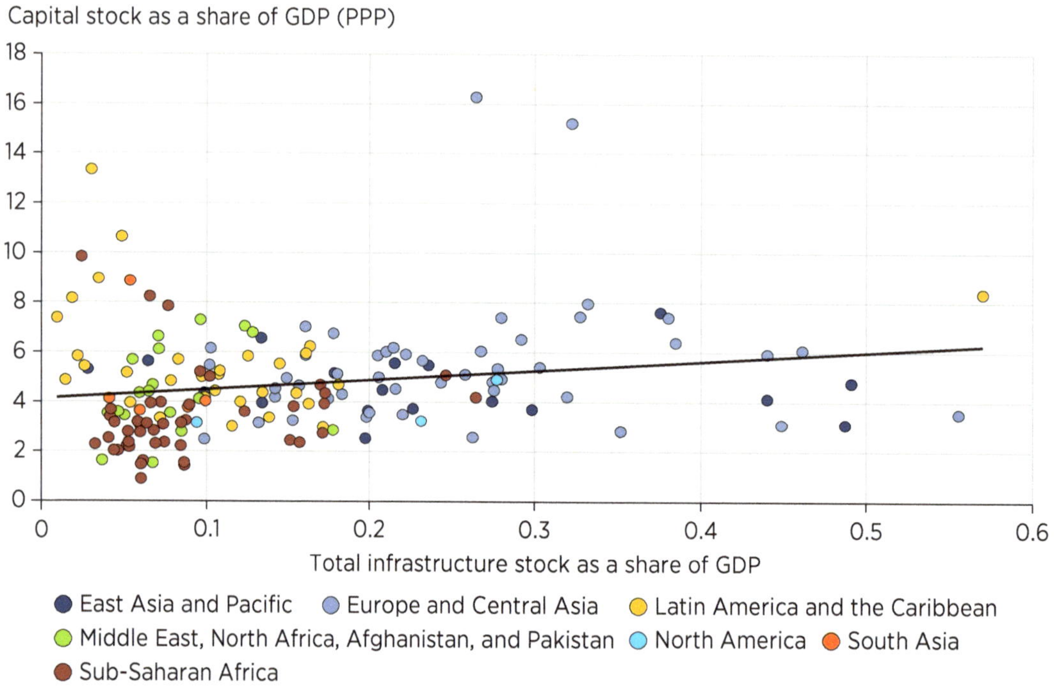

Source: Based on data from Penn World Table (Feenstra et al. 2015).
Note: The data are for 2024.

NOTE

1. Note also that these total stocks correlate negatively (correlation of –0.16) with the stock of public capital from national accounts, according to 2021 data from International Monetary Fund, "IMF Investment and Capital Stock Dataset, 1960–2019" (accessed November 21, 2025), https://infrastructuregovern.imf.org/content/dam/PIMA/Knowledge-Hub/dataset/IMF InvestmentandCapitalStockDataset2021.xlsx. This negative correlation suggests caution on public capital as a proxy for actual infrastructure stocks (illustrated in figure 2A.1 in annex 2A). The correlation with total capital stocks from the Penn World Table data, by contrast, is positive, although it shows that the share of infrastructure in total capital tends to increase with development (figure 2A.2),

REFERENCE

Feenstra, R. C., R. Inklaar, and M. P. Timmer. 2015. "The Next Generation of the Penn World Table." *American Economic Review* 105 (10): 3150–82.

3

Social Rates of Return and Efficiency Ratios

KEY MESSAGES

Social rates of return to infrastructure investments vary systematically across sectors and stages of development. Transportation investments exhibit high social returns in poorer countries, but returns decline sharply with income as networks mature; by contrast, energy investments deliver relatively stable social returns across the income distribution. These patterns reflect both diminishing marginal benefits from accumulated capital and sector-specific differences in benefit elasticities.

Comparing social returns to borrowing costs reveals sizable, unrealized investment opportunities in most countries. For a large majority of countries—92 percent of countries for energy and 98 percent for transportation—social rates of return exceed borrowing costs adjusted for depreciation, yielding efficiency ratios above 1. These efficiency ratios suggest widespread underinvestment in infrastructure from a social perspective, despite heterogeneous financing conditions.

Differences in infrastructure efficiency ratios are driven primarily by existing capital stocks rather than financing costs. More than 90 percent of the cross-country dispersion in efficiency ratios is explained by variation in capital-output ratios, which in turn reflect differences in physical infrastructure quantities. Borrowing costs and construction prices play a secondary—but still policy-relevant—role. High borrowing costs constrain energy investment primarily in poorer economies, whereas low transportation returns are concentrated in richer ones.

Under baseline assumptions, digital infrastructure displays efficiency ratios that far exceed those of energy and transportation in almost all countries. However, these values are sensitive to how benefits are measured—particularly the distinction between adoption and physical capacity—and to strong complementarities

---

A reproducibility package is available for this book in the Reproducible Research Repository at https://reproducibility.worldbank.org/catalog/536.

with energy infrastructure. Adjusting for this sensitivity brings digital returns in line with those of other infrastructure sectors.

Balanced, multisector investment strategies outperform single-sector approaches. Because of diminishing returns within sectors and complementarities across them, allocating infrastructure budgets across energy and transportation typically yields higher aggregate growth effects than concentrating investment in a single sector. Country examples illustrate how the framework can be used to determine optimal sectoral allocations given a fixed investment envelope.

INTRODUCTION

The previous chapter provided a picture of the state of infrastructure around the world. Those important data fill crucial gaps in the existing knowledge on the infrastructure landscape, characterized until now by the scarcity of systematic, relevant, and updated information. Simply knowing how much infrastructure exists, where it is located, and how much its extension would cost can meaningfully inform infrastructure investment plans.

In addition, the data provide the building blocks to derive a summary statistic of how beneficial infrastructure investments would be in each sector and country, and to compare the benefits with the cost of financing such investments. As explained in the framework introduced in chapter 1, the social rate of return, SRR, depends on the product of the impact of marginally increasing the stock of infrastructure assets on economic output and the inverse of the capital-output ratio. Recall the formula, derived in the context of the investment framework of chapter 1:

$$SRR = Cost\ capital + depreciation$$

$$\Leftrightarrow \theta_s . \frac{p_Y Y}{p_K K} = r + \delta_s \tag{3.1}$$

where θ_s is the sector-specific benefit elasticity; $p_Y Y$ is gross domestic product (GDP) at domestic prices; $p_K K$ is the capital stock, computed as the stock of physical assets K evaluated at their domestic price p_K; r is the local borrowing cost; and δ is the sector-specific depreciation rate. As pointed out in chapter 1, this report is specifically interested in the ratio between the social rate of return and borrowing cost adjusted for depreciation rate, because countries are not necessarily at equilibrium:

$$Efficiency\ ratio = \frac{SRR}{r + \delta} . \tag{3.2}$$

In addition to the capital stocks described in chapter 2, the other information needed to compute the social rate of return and the efficiency ratio are the benefit elasticities θ_s and the borrowing costs. Depending on the sector, benefit elasticities can be lower or higher in less developed countries. One interpretation for larger elasticities in richer countries is the existence of network effects. As shown in many contexts, the benefits that households get from accessing infrastructure services may increase as more people in their immediate environment also connect, with reasons that vary across sectors. This is, for example, the case for digital technologies such as cell phone services, mobile money, or internet access, because the benefits depend directly on the number of other individuals who are connected (Katz and Shapiro 1985).[1]

It should therefore come as no surprise that, for digital infrastructure, larger benefit elasticities appear in developed countries than in developing ones. In transportation, the pattern reverses and elasticities are larger in developing countries, indicating that returns are sharply higher at low levels of coverage but diminish thereafter. Finally, for energy, the magnitudes are similar across country groups. Chapter 7 provides details of how these elasticities are derived. Box 3.1 in the next section describes in detail the borrowing cost estimation.

This chapter puts it all together and computes social rate of return values for the three sectors considered in this report. It does so in two parts. First, it details the analysis for energy and transportation, and discusses implications for investment strategies across these two sectors. Second, it separately considers the digital sector, because the nature of the sector and the social rate of return figures that are obtained deserve some qualification. The spotlight after this chapter provides several country examples.

SOCIAL RATES OF RETURN AND EFFICIENCY RATIOS: ENERGY AND TRANSPORTATION

The rates of return in the energy and transportation sectors display very different patterns. The social rate of return of infrastructure investment decreases with per capita GDP for transportation (figure 3.1), both because of lower benefit elasticities in developed countries and a declining $p_Y Y/p_K K$ ratio (the inverse of the capital-output ratio). As discussed in the previous chapter, the amount of transportation infrastructure strongly increases with countries' level of income per capita, which means that any addition to that stock becomes marginally less socially valuable. For energy, by contrast, the social rate of return generally remains stable (figure 3.2).

The next step is to compare these social rates of return figures, which are a proxy for the marginal benefits of additional infrastructure, with the marginal cost of investing— computed as the cost of borrowing adjusted for depreciation, $r + \delta$. The cost of borrowing is the Weighted Average Cost of Capital. Box 3.1 provides a detailed account of how this cost is computed (refer also to box 6.1 in chapter 6 for an explanation of the methodologies used to account for depreciation).

A simple way to get a summary diagnostic is to express the comparison as the ratio of marginal benefit to marginal cost, or the *infrastructure efficiency ratio*, as explained in chapter 1. A ratio above 1 then corresponds to country-sector cases in which investments appear to pass the bar of social profitability—that is, a situation in which the total capital stock of a given sector is below its optimal level.

FIGURE 3.1 **Transportation social rates of return versus GDP per capita, by region**

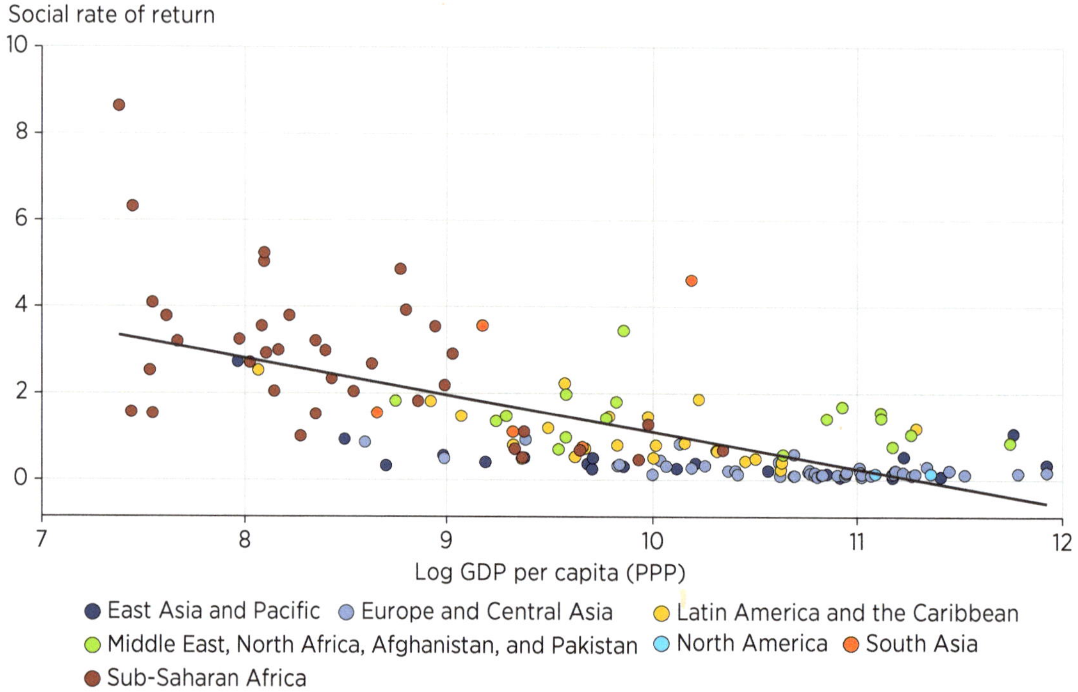

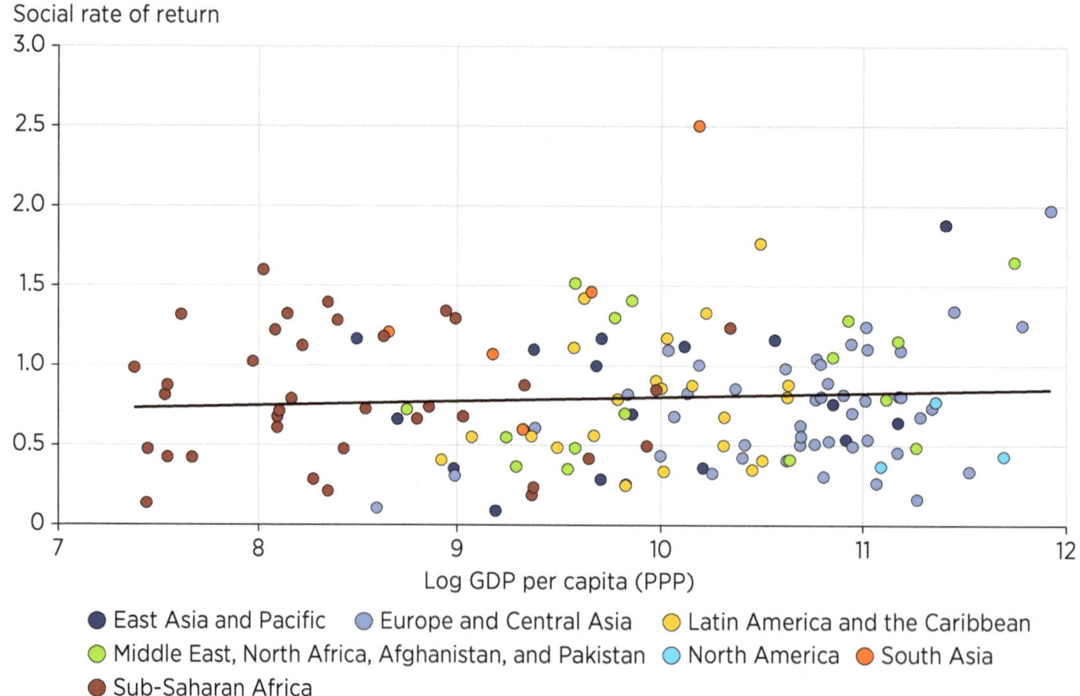

Source: Original figure for this publication.
Note: PPP = purchasing power parity.

FIGURE 3.2 **Energy social rates of return versus GDP per capita, by region**

Source: Original figure for this publication.
Note: PPP = purchasing power parity.

BOX 3.1

Estimating the country-specific cost of borrowing

Infrastructure projects typically span multiple decades and require significant capital expenditures, which largely rely on outside financing. The approach to assess the cost of borrowing builds on the sovereign default spread framework developed by Aswath Damodaran in successive editions of "Country Risk: Determinants, Measures, and Implications" (for example, Damodaran 2025).

The borrowing cost for each country is approximated in a standard way with the Weighted Average Cost of Capital, which combines the cost of debt and the cost of equity. The cost of debt is derived by adding an estimated country risk premium—based on 10-year sovereign credit default swap (CDS) spreads and adjusted country ratings—to a risk-free rate, which this report assumes to be the 30-year US Treasury bond yield, and a lender margin. Tax rate adjustment is ignored in this approximation. This is the standard approach, used for example to estimate the cost of financing for renewable energy (IRENA 2023).

This report used the following key data to estimate the cost of debt:

- *Sovereign CDS spread.* The report used the 10-year sovereign CDS spread as the main indicator of (market based) country risk. The data came from Damodaran (January 2025 update)[a], which covers 10-year CDS spreads for 90 entities, including countries and subnational jurisdictions. These data were used where available to represent each entity's credit risk.

- *Sovereign credit ratings and Political Risk Services (PRS) Group scores.* The report used credit ratings from Fitch, Moody's, and S&P, with values obtained from Damodaran's data set and additional country ratings collected manually from Moody's and rating comparison tables from relevant sources (for example, Moneyland.ch). All ratings were converted into Moody's-equivalent ratings to ensure consistency. For countries with no credit rating data, the report used PRS scores as alternative proxies and converted those scores into Moody's-equivalent ratings using Damodaran's lookup table.[b]

- *US Treasury bond yield.* The 30-year US Treasury bond yield, as of April 2025, was collected from CNBC.

The final data set includes 179 entities, each with at least one source of country risk indicator: CDS spreads, sovereign ratings, or PRS scores.

(continued)

BOX 3.1   Estimating the country-specific cost of borrowing *(continued)*

Estimating country risk premiums using CDS spreads. For countries that had 10-year CDS spread data available, the net CDS spread was used as the country risk premium (CRP). If the resulting value was negative, it was considered zero, following Damodaran's method. The idea was to isolate the risk exclusive to the country, relative to the United States

$$CRP_{Country} = 10Y\ CDS\ spread_{Country} - 10Y\ spread_{United\ States}$$

Estimating CRPs using credit ratings and PRS scores. For countries without CDS data, the CRP was estimated using sovereign credit ratings. Credit ratings from Fitch, Moody's, and S&P were collected and converted into Moody's-equivalent ratings using public conversion tables. Then, for each rating, the average CDS spread was calculated based on countries that had both the CDS spread and rating data. The average CDS spread for AAA-rated countries was subtracted from these values to get the net CDS spread by rating.

Countries with no credit rating but with PRS scores were assigned estimated credit ratings (Moody's-equivalent) using Damodaran's lookup table. The same rating-based risk premium estimation then took place, making it possible to assign a CRP even to countries with limited market data.

Choosing the risk-free rate. Whereas Damodaran uses the 10-year US Treasury bond rate, this report used the 30-year US Treasury bond yield as of April 2025 as the risk-free rate to better align with the investment time span of infrastructure projects.

Calculating the cost of borrowing. The final cost of debt for each country was calculated by adding the estimated CRP to the 30-year US Treasury bond yield and a lender margin of 2 percent. The cost of equity was calculated using the risk-free rate, to which was added the beta (relative volatility of a stock's return against the total market) multiplied by the equity risk premium (additional premium required for investing in equity). This study set beta to 1 as a neutral assumption across sectors/industries. The equity risk premium is the US benchmark (estimated here at 4.33 percent) plus the specific country risk premium. Finally, the study assumed an 80 percent (debt) to 20 percent (equity) leverage ratio to compute the final borrowing cost. Figure B3.1.1 plots the result.

(continued)

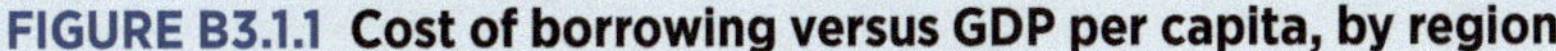

BOX 3.1   Estimating the country-specific cost of borrowing *(continued)*

FIGURE B3.1.1 Cost of borrowing versus GDP per capita, by region

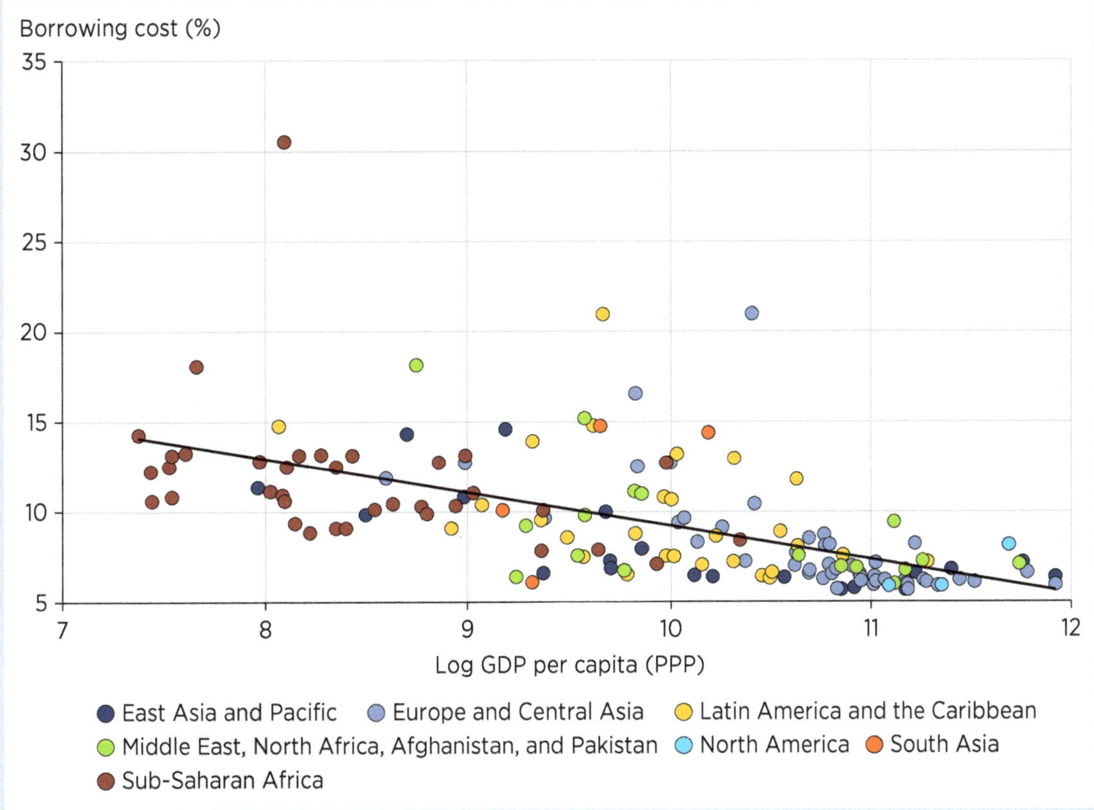

Source: Original figure for this publication.
Note: PPP = purchasing power parity.
a. Data from Damodaran Online, https://pages.stern.nyu.edu/~adamodar/. The raw data file can be located by following the path: Homepage > Data > Current data > Discount Rate Estimation—"Costs of Capital by Industry Sector."
b. Damodaran Online, "Credit Default Spreads and Risk Premiums," https://pages.stern.nyu.edu/~adamodar/New_Home _Page/datafile/ctryprem.html.

Infrastructure efficiency ratios for energy and transportation display different patterns. For energy, the ratio is generally greater than 1 for most countries and displays a slight upward trend (figure 3.3). This result reflects comparable social rates of return across different levels of per capita GDP but higher costs of borrowing in less developed countries, as discussed in box 3.1. For transportation, the ratio is clearly high in less developed countries and declines strongly for richer ones, especially in the Europe and Central Asia region (figure 3.4). This trend appears driven mostly by the large existing physical stocks and high construction costs, which depress the social rate of return.

FIGURE 3.3 Energy infrastructure efficiency ratio versus GDP per capita, by region

Efficiency ratio
10
8
6
4
2
1
0
7
8
9
10
11
12
Log GDP per capita (PPP)
East Asia and Pacific
Europe and Central Asia
Latin America and the Caribbean
Middle East, North Africa, Afghanistan, and Pakistan
North America
South Asia
Sub-Saharan Africa

Source: Original figure for this publication.
Note: PPP = purchasing power parity.

FIGURE 3.4 Transportation infrastructure efficiency ratio versus GDP per capita, by region

Efficiency ratio
20
15
10
5
1
0
7
8
9
10
11
12
Log GDP per capita (PPP)
East Asia and Pacific
Europe and Central Asia
Latin America and the Caribbean
Middle East, North Africa, Afghanistan, and Pakistan
North America
South Asia
Sub-Saharan Africa

Source: Original figure for this publication.
Note: PPP = purchasing power parity.

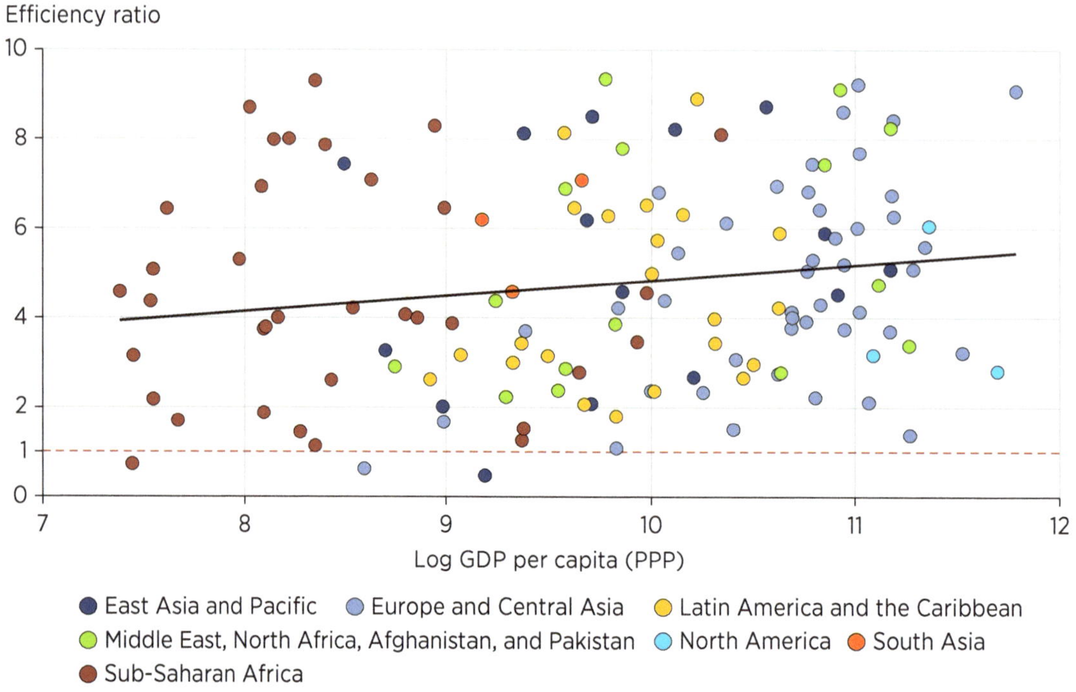

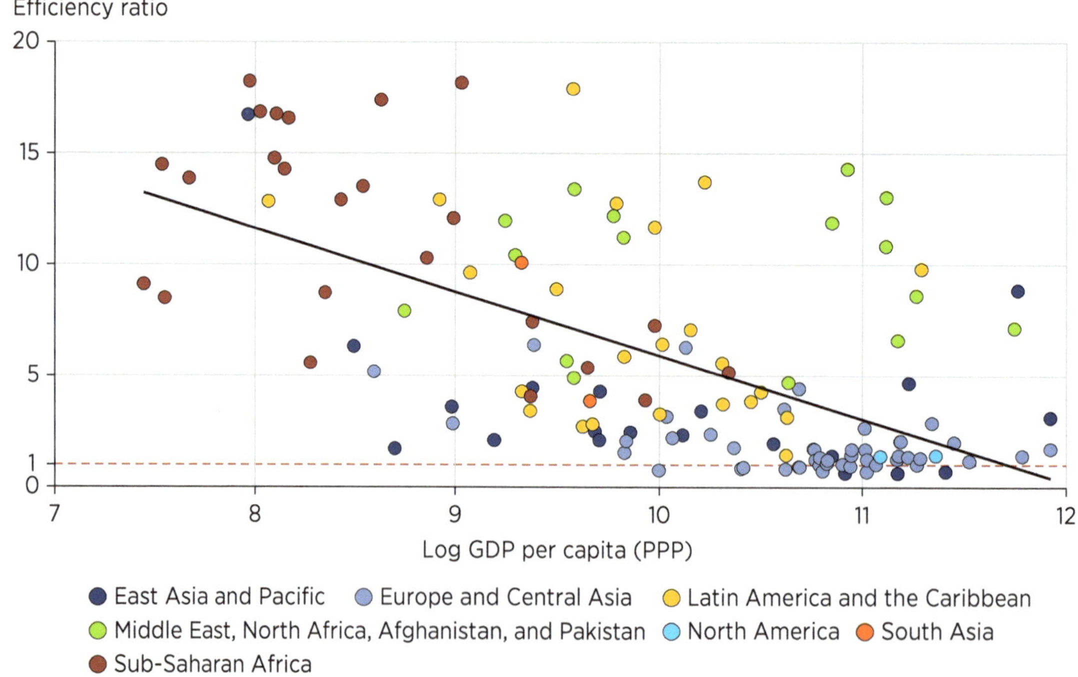

The ratios calculated here come with a few caveats. First, they do not reflect complete coverage of infrastructure subsectors. The report excludes ports and airports in the case of transportation and off-grid assets and some grid elements, such as transformers, in the case of energy. The missing information represents a small part of overall stocks, however—probably no more than 10 percent. Second, the benefit elasticities for this report are based on studies that by their design generally capture wider economic externalities, such as agglomeration effects, but probably miss most of the potential negative environmental elasticities, such as local pollution and greenhouse gas emissions related to the construction and use of physical infrastructure. These externalities are to some extent harder to monetize, and the literature that links infrastructure development to output growth has not systematically addressed them. Both these limitations, if properly included, would lead to lower numbers on the benefit side. For this reason, some of the efficiency ratio near the threshold should be considered carefully; however, the relative patterns across countries and levels of income are likely to hold. A simple way to visualize the inclusion of the missing information is to think of it as pushing the dashed red line up.

Summaries of efficiency ratios and social rates of return, by region, highlight a few facts (table 3.1; refer to table 3A.1 in the annex for individual economy numbers). First, with a few exceptions, the ratios reported are generally greater than 1 (92 percent of countries for transportation and 98 percent for energy). This finding can be seen as good news in the sense that more infrastructure investment might be warranted, because it passes a basic benefit-cost threshold. It could also mean that most economies fail to act on investment opportunities that have large potential social benefits, possibly because of different market failures.

Second, the ratios in table 3A.1 show high dispersion across economies, even at similar levels of development. Box 3.2 analyzes in more detail the determinants of this high variability, noting in particular the amount of capital economies already have and, to a lesser extent, the level of replacement costs. The situation is, however, very different when one compares energy and transportation. Although economies with low energy

TABLE 3.1 Social rates of returns and infrastructure efficiency ratios, by region

Region	Energy		Transportation	
	SRR	Efficiency ratio	SRR	Efficiency ratio
East Asia and Pacific	0.61	4.46	0.39	3.30
Europe and Central Asia	0.73	5.18	0.30	2.29
Latin America and the Caribbean	0.73	4.35	1.00	7.65
Middle East, North Africa, Afghanistan, and Pakistan	0.89	4.88	1.94	11.55
North America	0.73	5.75	0.16	1.42
South Asia	0.67	4.79	1.38	11.44
Sub-Saharan Africa	1.19	6.72	3.89	22.54

Source: Original table for this publication.
Note: The regional averages are population-weighted. SRR = social rate of return.

BOX 3.2

Determinants of the dispersion of efficiency ratios

Infrastructure efficiency ratios show dispersion across countries. Two exercises help understanding the drivers of these different patterns across sectors. The first exercise, a simple variance decomposition using order-neutral Shapley decomposition, provides a first indication of which components have a larger impact on the final ratio of social rates of return to borrowing cost. That decomposition is conducted in two stages. First, it independently assesses whether the cross-country variations in the value of the capital stock are mostly due to differences in prices (the unit costs) or volumes of physical assets, which helps disentangle two alternative mechanisms: countries could already have large physical stocks, so additional investments will likely have low returns because of the large amount of assets supporting services to the population, or they could have relatively low stocks but be facing inefficiently high costs of investments. Second, it gauges the respective weights of the capital-output ratio (the result of combining these price and volume effects) and of the borrowing cost in driving the dispersion of net returns. These weights provide an additional indication of the constraints related to the premium that specific countries face on the capital market. Table B3.2.1 shows the results from these decompositions, pulling together the three sectors.

Table B3.2.1 shows that, most of the variance in the efficiency ratio, 91–93 percent, is explained by that of the capital-output ratio, with only a small remaining share corresponding to the borrowing cost. By component of the capital-output ratio, most of the variation is explained by differences in physical stocks (from 71 percent

TABLE B3.2.1 Variance decomposition of the efficiency ratio, by sector

Component	Energy	Transportation	Digital
Y/K block	93	93	91
(r + delta)	7	7	9
Price 1 (energy generation/road/DC)	2	19	9
Quantity 1 (energy generation capacity/road quantity/DC quantity)	55	52	46
Price 2 (energy T&D/rail/CT)	7	10	2
Quantity 2 (energy T&D quantity/rail quantity/CT quantity)	36	20	43
Total prices	8	29	11
Total quantities	92	71	89

Source: Original table for this publication.
Note: CT = cell tower; DC = data center; K = capital; r = borrowing cost; T&D = transmission and distribution; Y = total output.

(continued)

 Determinants of the dispersion of efficiency ratios *(continued)*

for transportation to 92 percent for energy and 89 percent for digital) and only the residual part by differences in prices, although they feature a bit more prominently in the case of roads and railroads.

To extract more specific policy relevant conclusions, the second exercise focuses specifically on energy and transportation, and on the group of countries with a relatively lower efficiency ratio. This exercise adds valuable information on the specific bottlenecks these countries face. Considering the previous results, choosing a threshold to separate high- from low-performing countries must be sector specific. Regarding energy, 4 countries appear to have a ratio lower than 1, and 14 lower than 2. In the case of transportation, 12 countries have a ratio lower than 1, and 32 lower than 1.5. Although this choice is arbitrary, the relative findings are not strongly dependent on the exact threshold used. The exercise therefore uses 1.5 as a threshold for energy and 2 for transportation.

Figure B3.2.1 presents simple box plots situating countries' ratios according to three characteristics: unit cost, capital-output ratio, and domestic borrowing cost. Countries below the threshold are represented in yellow if their borrowing cost is below the full sample median, and in red otherwise. Countries with higher ratios are represented in light blue for the sake of comparison.

In panels a and b, countries with low efficiency ratios are almost all in the upper right quadrant, meaning that they have above-median capital-output ratios, as well as above-median generation replacement costs, although a number of countries have high ratios despite high costs. Most of these countries appear also to have a high borrowing cost (red dots). Overall, these results fit the previous conclusions, indicating that unfavorable conditions for energy investment are mostly found in countries with relatively high borrowing costs (thus, mostly low- and middle-income countries), high stocks given their level of development, and to some extent high replacement costs.

Panels c and d show some notable differences for transportation. First, the countries with low ratios are all in the upper right quadrant, indicating a combination of high costs and high capital-output ratios; most other countries appear in the lower left quadrant, indicating low costs and low capital-output ratios. Second, almost all low performers have low borrowing costs, meaning they are richer countries. This result is consistent with the downward sloping trend in figure 3.4 in the main text characterizing the ratio in terms of per capita gross domestic product and indicates that the countries facing low potential net returns from transportation investments are more developed countries that have large stocks and face high construction costs.

(continued)

BOX 3.2   Determinants of the dispersion of efficiency ratios _(continued)_

FIGURE B3.2.1 Efficiency ratios: Generation costs, capital stocks, and borrowing costs

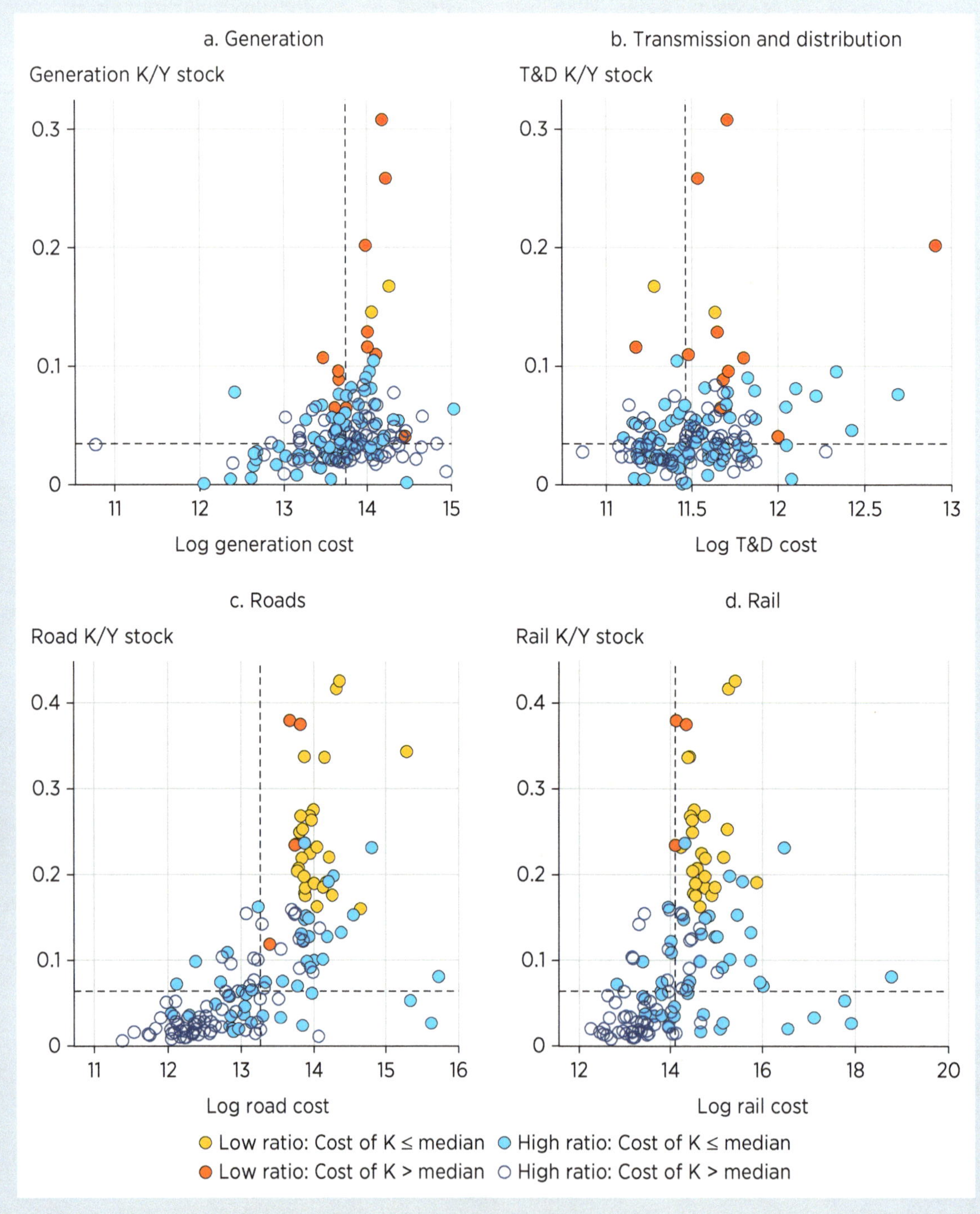

Source: Original figure for this publication.
Note: K = capital; T&D = transmission and distribution; Y = total output.

efficiency ratios overwhelmingly have high borrowing costs, which compound high replacement costs and thus seem amenable to policy interventions, the reverse is true for transportation. Almost all economies with low transportation efficiency ratios are in the low borrowing cost group, meaning that they have likely overaccumulated basic transportation infrastructure.

The results shown in tables 3.1 and 3A.1 suggest different implications for energy and transportation. For energy, regional averages are high across the board, and highest in Sub-Saharan Africa despite low ratios in a handful of countries there. Transportation shows much higher variability, with again the highest ratio for Sub-Saharan Africa, where social returns on investment appear to exceed costs by a factor of more than 22. More developed countries, including all of North America and most of Europe and Central Asia, have low ratios. For the countries with close to negative net returns under prevailing conditions, the question is to assess how credible policy interventions may help maximize the impact of specific operations, lower construction costs, and improve borrowing conditions, as discussed in the following subsection.

Focusing on the comparison between the ratios in energy and transportation, table 3.2 shows that efficiency ratios are higher for the latter in Sub-Saharan Africa (97 percent of countries in the region), South Asia (75 percent), and the Middle East, North Africa, Afghanistan, and Pakistan (74 percent), and to a lesser extent Latin America and the Caribbean (73 percent). This result is again consistent with the evidence from figure 3.4, showing that these four regions have relatively lower amounts of transportation infrastructure capital than their level of development would predict.

TABLE 3.2 Comparing energy and transportation efficiency ratios, by region

Region	Number of countries with energy > transportation	Number of countries with energy < transportation	Share of countries with transportation > energy (%)
East Asia and Pacific	15	4	21.05
Europe and Central Asia	40	7	14.89
Latin America and the Caribbean	6	16	72.73
Middle East, North Africa, Afghanistan, and Pakistan	4	13	76.47
North America	2	0	0
South Asia	1	3	75.00
Sub-Saharan Africa	1	35	97.22
World	69	78	53.06

Source: Original table for this publication.

PRIORITIZATION AND COMPLEMENTARITY

One question raised by these estimates is what they imply in terms of prioritization of investments. A key insight is that there is a case for most countries not to put all their eggs in the same basket. Instead, with some exceptions, a balanced strategy is generally optimal. Importantly, the terms of the social rate of return and the efficiency ratio can be used to determine the optimal budget allocation across sectors.

Before proceeding, it is important to note the limitations of the analysis. This analysis provides a methodology to decide how to optimally allocate a given budget dedicated to infrastructure. It abstracts, however, from the broader question of how much should be allocated overall across both infrastructure and noninfrastructure sectors such as health, education, and a host of other public goods, and what the shares each should receive. Figure 3.5 shows the optimal country-level allocations between the energy and transportation sectors for an investment of 10 percent of GDP. The vertical axis shows the share of the investment allocated to energy: points at the top correspond to the whole budget being allocated to energy, and points at the bottom indicate 100 percent investment allocated to transportation. For each country, the figure provides a range, represented by the vertical bar, using the elasticities in table 7.2, panels a and b. Box 3.3 provides the detailed methodology used to translate the efficiency ratios into these allocations.

Figure 3.5 has several important implications. First, as mentioned, the optimal strategy for most countries involves investing in both energy and transportation. The exact mix depends on the relative capital stocks and the relative output elasticities, with important variations both within and across regions. In panel a, economies are ordered within regions by increasing shares of energy investment. For the East Asia and Pacific and Europe and Central Asia regions, the results cover the whole range of possibilities, whereas developing regions generally display a mix slightly more biased toward transportation. For almost half of the countries in Europe and Central Asia, an exclusive focus on energy appears optimal, whereas the reverse is true for a significant number of Sub-Saharan African countries, with about half of them having optimal shares of transportation investment over 75 percent. Panel b, which orders economies within regions by their level of GDP per capita, shows a positive correlation between the optimal share of energy investment and the level of development, but also shows variation that depends on current capital stocks levels.

FIGURE 3.5 **Optimal allocation of 10 percent of GDP investment between energy and transportation**

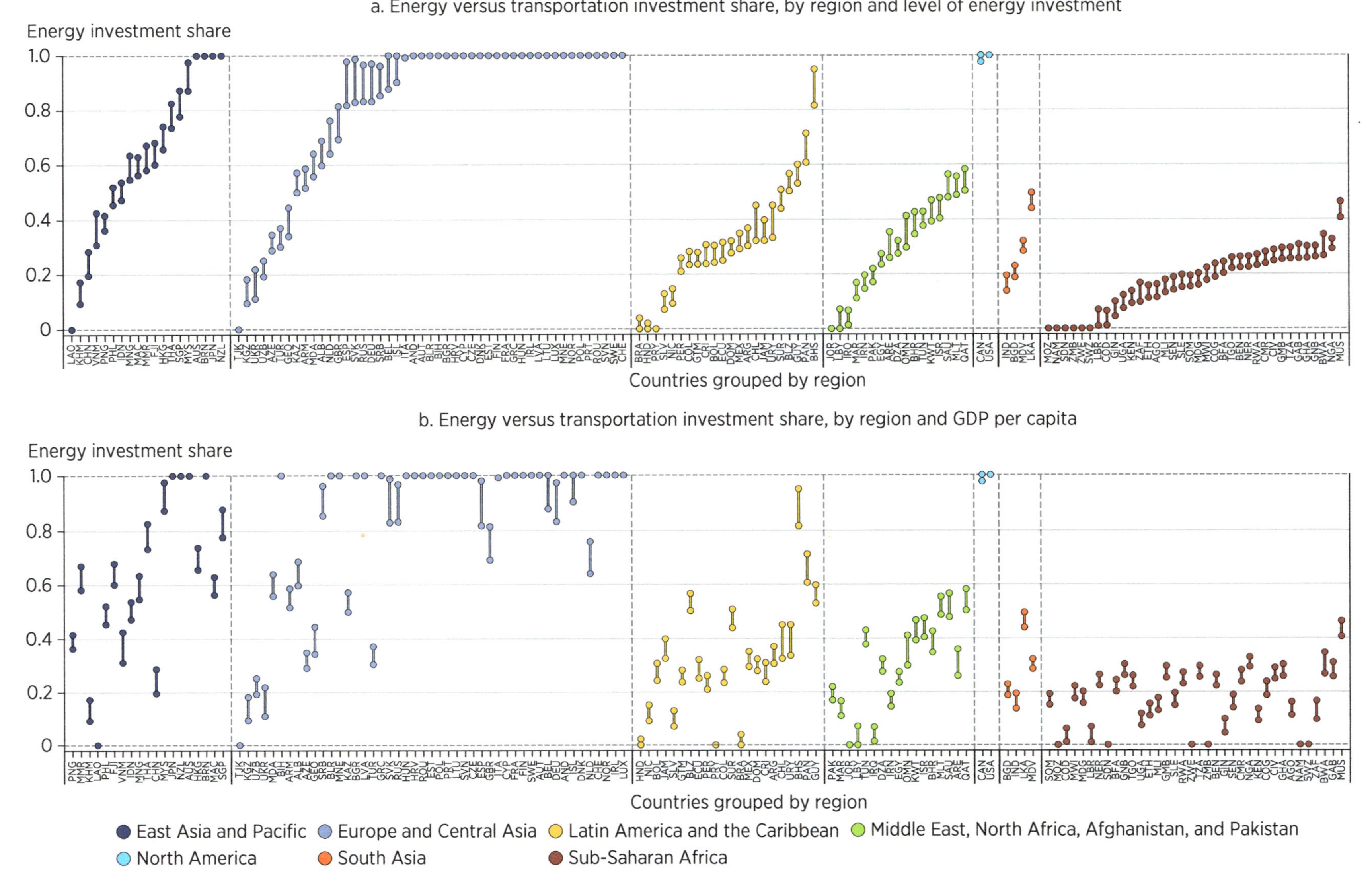

Source: Original figure for this publication.

Note: In panel a, economies are ordered within their regions by increasing shares of energy investment. In panel b, economies are ordered within their regions by increasing GDP per capita. Refer to https://www.iso.org/obp/ui/#search for country codes.

Determining optimal investment allocation

Efficiency ratios guide this report's prioritization of investment across infrastructure sectors. Specifically, putting the next dollar in the sector with the greatest efficiency ratio yields the greatest "bang for the buck." Continued investment in one sector yields diminishing returns; however, investment in other sectors becomes more efficient because of complementarities. In other words, as investments flow to a sector, the efficiency ratio for that sector will decrease and the efficiency ratios of the other sectors will increase. When the efficiency ratios of two or more sectors equalize, the optimal investment involves simultaneous investment in those sectors with investment shares split according to their benefits and costs.

Put differently, the optimal investment path can be described as the following stepwise approach:

1. Invest in the sector(s) with the highest efficiency ratio. For sector s with capital K_s, elasticity θ_s, and depreciation rate δ_s, given a cost of borrowing r and total output Y, the efficiency ratio is given by

$$\text{Efficiency ratio} = \frac{\theta_s}{r+\delta_s}\frac{p_Y Y}{p_K K_s}.$$

Investment should continue until the efficiency ratio of this sector equals the next highest efficiency ratio.

2. Once multiple sectors have the same efficiency ratio, allocate I_s of the remaining budget B to sector s, which ensures that the efficiency ratios remain equal to I_s:

$$I_s = \frac{\phi_s}{\sum_i^N \phi_i} B$$

$$\text{where } \phi_s = \frac{\theta_s}{\gamma+\delta_s}$$

3. Finally, if some of the budget remains available and all the efficiency ratios equal 1, stop new investments. At this point, maintain the current assets to counteract depreciation

In conceptual terms, the complementarity arises from two mechanisms—diminishing returns on the one hand, and amplification effects on the other. First, because of diminishing returns, allocating part of the total investment to both sectors will often dominate a single-sector focus. The relative shares will be defined by the different components of the social rate of return and borrowing cost formula.

The potential second—amplification—component of complementarity implies that the "total" return exceeds the sum of the individual returns from investments in transportation and energy, making the whole greater than the sum of its parts. Intuitively, this complementarity captures the fact that it is more effective to build roads between economically active places. Conversely, powering factories connected to logistics networks makes it easier to sell the goods produced.[2] Putting these two channels together illustrates why a balanced infrastructure investment strategy can yield greater returns than one that focuses on a single sector, and how the results in this report can help identify the optimal complementarities between the sectors that seem to characterize successful countries.

The overall message is that access to the right data is key in defining countries' overarching priorities given their budget and financing constraints. Of course, implementing such a strategy requires more analysis. A few aspects need to be addressed, leaving aside, as mentioned earlier, the broader question of how the returns unveiled here compare with alternative opportunities in the noninfrastructure sectors at an aggregate level. First, although setting the right targets is important, achieving the right mix of public and private investment runs into well-known issues of implementation capacity, predictability of the economic and institutional environment, access to finance, and other aspects of the enabling environment.

Second, these are *social* rates of returns. Whether they can be privately appropriated to support the funding part of investments—that is, the repayment of initial financing outlays (Fay et al. 2019)—will be key to attracting private investors in a context of generally scarce public and concessional funds, as highlighted in chapter 1. Although this report does not address these important questions, instead focusing on providing a framework to define high-level priorities, the data presented here provide a crucial building block for answering the two questions. Follow-up work, discussed later in the chapter, will focus on how the data unveiled here can be used to address some of these issues.

SOCIAL RATES OF RETURN AND EFFICIENCY RATIOS: DIGITAL

Using the simple functional form used so far, this section turns to the digital sector, which displays very high social rates of return and, consequently, very high efficiency ratios (figures 3.6 and 3.7). Countries consistently have efficiency ratios above 2, with higher ratios in developed countries (figure 3.7); the figure excludes a few extreme outliers (countries with a ratio above 30). Almost all countries (99 percent) appear to have digital efficiency ratios above 1, exceeding the ratios of other sectors by roughly an order of magnitude.

FIGURE 3.6 Digital social rate of return versus GDP per capita, by region

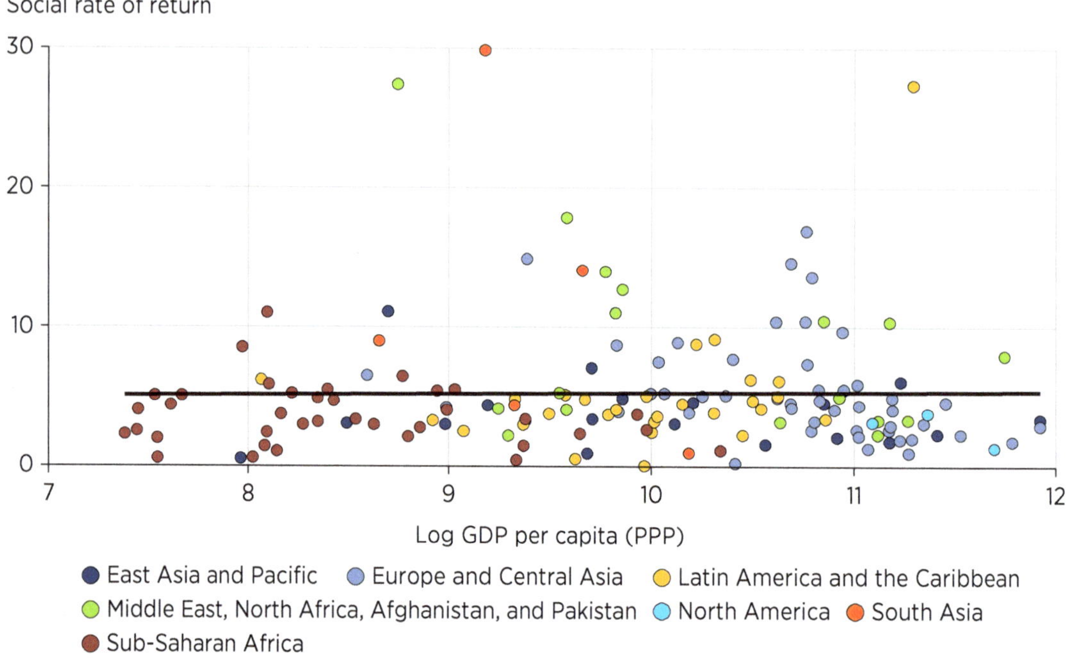

Source: Original figure for this publication.
Note: PPP = purchasing power parity.

FIGURE 3.7 Digital efficiency ratio versus GDP per capita, by region

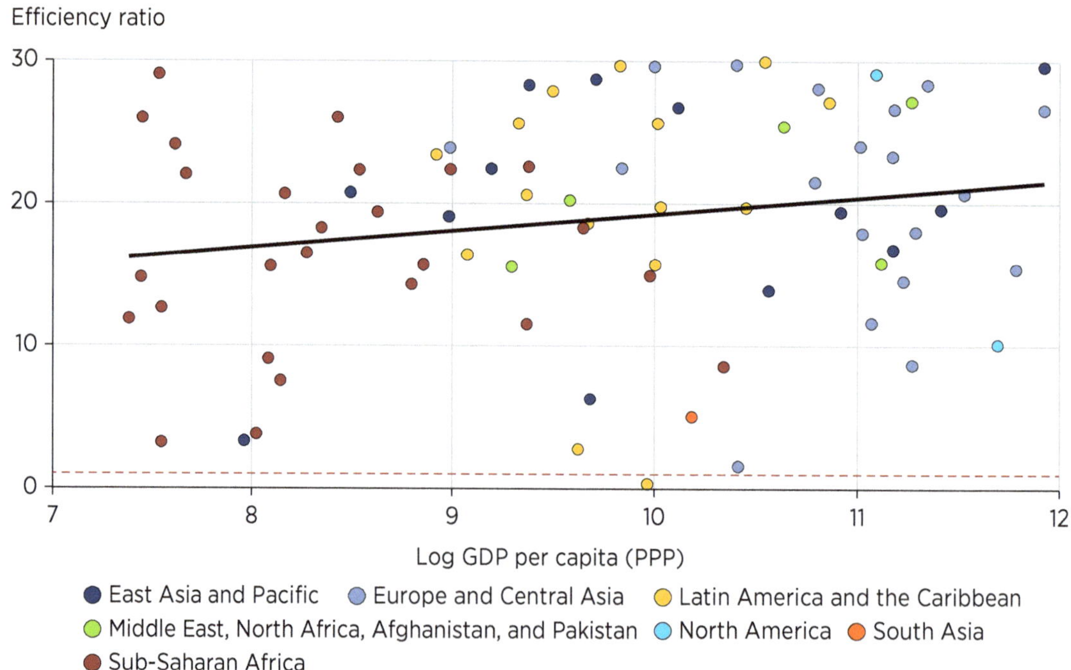

Source: Original figure for this publication.
Note: PPP = purchasing power parity.

At face value, these figures provide a powerful argument to support investment in the digital sector across the board. However, they also display important dispersion, particularly within regions, indicating that appropriate policy interventions to lower the cost of construction and the financing costs could help some countries reap even larger benefits. It is important to interpret these high values cautiously, for at least two reasons.

First, although the energy and transportation sectors have well-established underlying assets and technologies, and a relatively abundant impact literature to rely on, the digital sector is a fast evolving one, with new services and delivery modes emerging at high frequency. Consequently, the elasticities considered in Foster et al. (2025) and in chapter 7 may not fully align with the nature of the digital capital assets covered in this report. Many studies included in the meta-analysis look at the impact of adoption of mobile phone or internet penetration rates, but almost none at physical capacity expansion of cables or data centers. A recent paper provides separate estimates for adoption versus capacity for 32 Organisation for Economic Co-operation and Development countries between 2002 and 2020 (Briglauer et al. 2023). Interestingly, it finds an elasticity of GDP per capita with respect to fixed broadband adoption of between 0.026 and 0.034, similar in magnitude to the values used here, but finds coefficients for fiber-based capacity that are an order of magnitude smaller, between 0.002 and 0.003. Taking a midrange value of 0.0025, this is about 1/12th of the elasticity for developing countries used earlier.

A second caveat has to do with the fact that digital infrastructure displays a very high degree of complementarity with other types of infrastructure—especially with energy. The functioning of most digital devices, and underlying physical infrastructure such as data centers and cell towers, depends on the existence of a reliable energy supply. Taking this aspect into account would to some extent compensate for the fact that the digital capital stock alone is small. To address this issue, an alternative estimation was performed with a different production function specification, including some complementarity between energy and digital. Under specific calibration of the parameters, the resulting digital elasticity is eight times smaller than the one from chapter 5.[3]

Table 3.3 shows the social rates of returns and efficiency ratios by region under the initial assumption, and adjusted as mentioned in the preceding paragraphs. The values in the columns on the right, reflecting adjustments with a lower elasticity and factoring in complementarities, are broadly in a similar range to those for energy and transportation.

TABLE 3.3 Digital social rates of returns and efficiency ratios, by region

Region	Basic scenario		Lower elasticity		Production complementarities	
	SRR	Efficiency ratio	SRR	Efficiency ratio	SRR	Efficiency ratio
East Asia and Pacific	4.51	38.26	0.38	3.19	0.56	4.78
Europe and Central Asia	8.36	63.77	0.70	5.31	1.05	7.97
Latin America and the Caribbean	4.46	32.98	0.37	2.75	0.56	4.12
Middle East, North Africa, Afghanistan, and Pakistan	16.86	91.20	1.40	7.60	2.11	11.40
North America	3.75	34.36	0.31	2.86	0.47	4.30
South Asia	7.24	56.74	0.60	4.73	0.90	7.09
Sub-Saharan Africa	5.12	28.05	0.43	2.34	0.64	3.51

Source: Original table for this publication.
Note: The regional averages are population-weighted. SRR = social rate of return.

FUTURE WORK

Beyond the results covered in this report, the methodology and data open the way for several strands of future research. All nonproprietary data will be made available to researchers interested in exploiting them, and this section highlights a few immediate areas of interest. The social rate of return computations reported here are only a first step in what should be a complete prioritization exercise. A more precise prioritization framework for World Bank Group projects would benefit from progress in several directions.

- One critical factor is the existence of relevant complementarities between different infrastructure investments and other additional policy interventions. Future work will extend and generalize the analysis.

- Looking also at more spatially disaggregated data, joint follow-up work will assess how complementarities between digital and energy may shape firms' productivity gains.

- Large-scale infrastructure investments do not happen in a vacuum; instead, they likely have macro-fiscal implications and affect financing conditions through feedback loop effects. Better understanding of how macroeconomic conditions and social rate of return implications interact is important in a world in which numerous developing countries face fiscal constraints and high debt services.

- Relatedly, the social rates of return figures presented here can be integrated in a broader framework considering the returns of alternative investment opportunities, to assess both the best investment strategies for policy makers and the attractiveness of specific contexts to private investors. Doing so also implies analyzing how these returns could be appropriated, because they partially include externalities.

- Environmental externalities, such as greenhouse gas emissions and pollution, need to be assessed and incorporated in the return estimates to provide a fuller picture of the social dimension of infrastructure returns.

- Assets not currently covered in this report will be integrated next. In transportation, ports and airports are a natural extension. Work is also under way to determine unit costs and capital stocks in water and sanitation sectors across countries for different levels of services. Although a companion piece reporting on this work will be published later, the water sector raises specific issues in terms of a more comprehensive integration of environmental externalities in the estimation of social benefits. That later work will provide the opportunity to reflect on how to better account for such externalities when estimating the returns from infrastructure investments in general.

ANNEX 3A. ADDITIONAL SOCIAL RATES OF RETURN AND EFFICIENCY RATIOS RESULTS

Table 3A.1 presents the social rates of return and infrastructure efficiency ratios for the energy and transportation sectors in individual economies, broken down by region.

TABLE 3A.1 Social rates of return and efficiency ratios, by economy

		Energy		Transportation	
Region	**Economy**	**SRR**	**Efficiency ratio**	**SRR**	**Efficiency ratio**
EAP	Australia	0.64	5.09	0.07	0.64
EAP	Brunei Darussalam	1.88	13.43	0.08	0.71
EAP	Cambodia	0.35	2.02	0.57	3.60
EAP	China	0.36	2.68	0.39	3.42
EAP	Fiji	1.00	6.20	0.38	2.51
EAP	Hong Kong SAR, China	5.84	42.19	0.54	4.67
EAP	Indonesia	1.17	8.52	0.51	4.30
EAP	Japan	0.76	5.90	0.15	1.41
EAP	Lao People's Democratic Republic	0.09	0.47	0.41	2.11
EAP	Macau	34.85	241.74	1.08	8.86
EAP	Malaysia	1.16	8.74	0.22	1.96
EAP	Mongolia	0.70	4.59	0.32	2.46
EAP	Myanmar	0.66	3.27	0.33	1.73
EAP	New Zealand	0.54	4.53	0.07	0.64
EAP	Papua New Guinea	1.17	7.44	0.94	6.33
EAP	Philippines	1.10	8.14	0.52	4.46
EAP	Singapore	5.17	38.02	0.36	3.13
EAP	Solomon Islands	—	—	2.73	16.73
EAP	Thailand	1.12	8.23	0.27	2.35
EAP	Viet Nam	0.29	2.08	0.26	2.12

(continued)

TABLE 3A.1 Social rates of return and efficiency ratios, by economy *(continued)*

Region	Economy	Energy		Transportation	
		SRR	Efficiency ratio	SRR	Efficiency ratio
ECA	Albania	0.68	4.39	0.33	2.22
ECA	Andorra	16.27	105.31	0.18	1.36
ECA	Armenia	1.10	6.81	0.46	3.18
ECA	Austria	0.81	6.75	0.16	1.42
ECA	Azerbaijan	0.83	5.47	0.84	6.29
ECA	Belarus	0.42	1.51	0.22	0.85
ECA	Belgium	1.09	8.43	0.23	2.07
ECA	Bosnia and Herzegovina	0.44	2.37	0.14	0.77
ECA	Bulgaria	0.41	2.76	0.10	0.82
ECA	Croatia	1.01	7.45	0.12	1.02
ECA	Cyprus	1.11	7.70	0.09	0.71
ECA	Czechia	0.70	5.21	0.16	1.45
ECA	Denmark	0.68	5.10	0.15	1.31
ECA	Estonia	0.31	2.23	0.09	0.74
ECA	Finland	0.26	2.12	0.12	1.03
ECA	France	0.54	4.14	0.14	1.25
ECA	Georgia	0.33	2.34	0.34	2.38
ECA	Germany	0.81	6.27	0.22	2.07
ECA	Greece	0.56	4.02	0.11	0.92
ECA	Hungary	1.05	6.83	0.16	1.23
ECA	Iceland	0.17	1.38	0.11	1.02
ECA	Ireland	1.25	9.09	0.16	1.41
ECA	Italy	1.25	9.23	0.19	1.70
ECA	Kazakhstan	0.98	6.96	0.42	3.52
ECA	Kyrgyz Republic	0.31	1.68	0.51	2.85
ECA	Latvia	0.51	3.78	0.11	0.93
ECA	Lithuania	0.82	5.80	0.12	1.04
ECA	Luxembourg	1.98	15.12	0.19	1.73
ECA	Moldova	0.82	4.23	0.36	2.08
ECA	Montenegro	0.51	3.08	0.14	0.89
ECA	Netherlands	0.73	5.60	0.31	2.89
ECA	North Macedonia	1.01	—	0.29	—
ECA	Norway	0.34	3.23	0.13	1.18
ECA	Poland	0.89	6.43	0.13	1.09
ECA	Portugal	0.53	4.30	0.13	1.23
ECA	Romania	0.81	5.31	0.18	1.35

(continued)

TABLE 3A.1 **Social rates of return and efficiency ratios, by economy** *(continued)*

Region	Economy	Energy		Transportation	
		SRR	Efficiency ratio	SRR	Efficiency ratio
ECA	Russian Federation	0.79	5.06	0.23	1.71
ECA	Serbia	0.86	6.13	0.22	1.78
ECA	Slovak Republic	0.51	3.92	0.20	1.73
ECA	Slovenia	1.14	8.62	0.11	0.95
ECA	Spain	0.50	3.75	0.19	1.71
ECA	Sweden	0.46	3.70	0.14	1.26
ECA	Switzerland	1.34	12.47	0.23	2.01
ECA	Tajikistan	0.11	0.63	0.87	5.18
ECA	Türkiye	0.63	4.14	0.60	4.43
ECA	Ukraine	0.26	1.09	0.33	1.55
ECA	United Kingdom	0.78	6.02	0.29	2.67
ECA	Uzbekistan	0.61	3.71	0.94	6.40
LAC	Argentina	0.68	3.44	0.67	3.74
LAC	Bahamas, The	0.80	4.23	0.24	1.45
LAC	Barbados	1.17	5.75	—	—
LAC	Belize	1.42	6.47	0.54	2.73
LAC	Bolivia	0.60	3.00	0.81	4.30
LAC	Brazil	0.34	2.37	0.80	6.43
LAC	Chile	0.35	2.67	0.44	3.85
LAC	Colombia	0.91	6.53	1.47	11.69
LAC	Costa Rica	0.50	3.98	0.68	5.58
LAC	Dominican Republic	1.33	8.91	1.87	13.73
LAC	Ecuador	0.56	2.07	0.73	2.83
LAC	El Salvador	0.49	3.15	1.21	8.90
LAC	Guatemala	1.11	8.15	2.24	17.92
LAC	Guyana	6.08	42.11	1.20	9.81
LAC	Haiti	5.57	—	2.54	12.84
LAC	Honduras	0.41	2.62	1.82	12.93
LAC	Jamaica	0.56	3.43	0.50	3.43
LAC	Mexico	0.88	6.32	0.85	7.08
LAC	Nicaragua	0.55	3.17	1.48	9.63
LAC	Panama	0.88	5.91	0.41	3.15
LAC	Paraguay	0.25	1.80	0.81	5.88
LAC	Peru	0.79	6.29	1.47	12.77
LAC	Suriname	0.86	5.00	0.51	3.28
LAC	Trinidad and Tobago	1.77	13.05	—	—

(continued)

TABLE 3A.1 Social rates of return and efficiency ratios, by economy *(continued)*

Region	Economy	Energy		Transportation	
		SRR	Efficiency ratio	SRR	Efficiency ratio
LAC	Uruguay	0.41	2.97	0.50	4.27
MENAAP	Algeria	1.30	9.35	1.43	12.21
MENAAP	Bahrain	0.79	4.75	1.56	10.84
MENAAP	Egypt, Arab Rep.	1.41	7.80	3.46	21.64
MENAAP	Iran, Islamic Rep.	0.70	3.87	1.81	11.23
MENAAP	Iraq	0.48	2.87	1.98	13.41
MENAAP	Israel	1.29	9.12	1.71	14.32
MENAAP	Jordan	0.37	2.24	1.48	10.42
MENAAP	Kuwait	1.06	7.44	1.42	11.90
MENAAP	Libya	0.35	2.38	0.71	5.68
MENAAP	Malta	3.43	25.94	1.44	13.05
MENAAP	Morocco	0.55	4.38	1.36	11.98
MENAAP	Oman	0.41	2.79	0.59	4.70
MENAAP	Pakistan	0.72	2.91	1.83	7.91
MENAAP	Qatar	1.65	11.53	0.87	7.16
MENAAP	Saudi Arabia	1.15	8.26	0.78	6.61
MENAAP	Tunisia	1.52	6.90	0.99	4.91
MENAAP	United Arab Emirates	0.49	3.39	1.06	8.61
NA	Bermuda	0.43	2.82	—	—
NA	Canada	0.37	3.17	0.15	1.40
NA	United States	0.77	6.06	0.16	1.43
SA	Bangladesh	1.07	6.20	3.57	23.66
SA	India	0.60	4.59	1.12	10.09
SA	Maldives	2.50	11.60	4.63	23.87
SA	Nepal	1.21	—	1.55	—
SA	Sri Lanka	1.46	7.09	0.77	3.88
SSA	Angola	0.68	3.88	2.92	18.18
SSA	Benin	1.28	7.88	2.99	21.22
SSA	Botswana	0.50	3.47	0.47	3.91
SSA	Burkina Faso	1.02	5.31	3.25	18.25
SSA	Cabo Verde	0.88	—	0.72	—
SSA	Cameroon	1.18	7.09	2.69	17.40
SSA	Congo, Dem. Rep.	0.48	3.15	6.32	40.55
SSA	Congo, Rep.	0.74	4.00	1.83	10.29
SSA	Côte d'Ivoire	1.34	8.30	3.55	23.15
SSA	Eswatini	0.24	1.53	1.12	7.44

(continued)

TABLE 3A.1 Social rates of return and efficiency ratios, by economy *(continued)*

Region	Economy	Energy		Transportation	
		SRR	Efficiency ratio	SRR	Efficiency ratio
SSA	Ethiopia	0.68	1.88	5.25	14.78
SSA	Gabon	0.85	4.57	1.29	7.27
SSA	Gambia, The	1.32	7.99	2.05	14.29
SSA	Ghana	1.30	6.46	2.19	12.09
SSA	Guinea	0.48	2.61	2.34	12.91
SSA	Guinea-Bissau	1.60	8.72	2.72	16.86
SSA	Kenya	0.67	4.08	3.92	26.37
SSA	Liberia	0.42	2.18	1.54	8.49
SSA	Madagascar	0.87	5.09	4.09	25.88
SSA	Malawi	0.81	4.37	2.53	14.49
SSA	Mali	0.71	3.80	2.93	16.76
SSA	Mauritius	1.24	8.12	0.69	5.16
SSA	Mozambique	0.14	0.73	1.57	9.12
SSA	Namibia	0.19	1.26	0.52	4.08
SSA	Niger	1.32	6.44	3.79	20.76
SSA	Nigeria	3.06	17.66	4.88	31.91
SSA	Rwanda	1.13	8.01	3.80	27.46
SSA	Senegal	0.73	4.22	2.04	13.52
SSA	Sierra Leone	0.79	4.01	3.00	16.58
SSA	Somalia, Fed. Rep.	0.98	4.58	8.64	44.90
SSA	South Africa	0.42	2.79	0.69	5.37
SSA	Sudan	0.42	1.70	3.20	13.88
SSA	Tanzania	1.40	9.31	3.22	22.83
SSA	Togo	1.22	6.94	3.56	22.36
SSA	Uganda	0.61	3.75	5.05	32.39
SSA	Zambia	0.21	1.14	1.53	8.74
SSA	Zimbabwe	0.29	1.45	1.01	5.58

Source: Original table for this publication.
Note: EAP = East Asia and Pacific; ECA = Europe and Central Asia; LAC = Latin America and the Caribbean; MENAAP = Middle East, North Africa, Afghanistan, and Pakistan; NA = North America; SA = South Asia; SRR = social rate of return; SSA = Sub-Saharan Africa; — = not available.

Finally, the main messages and the case for complementary investments are reinforced when using the specific regional elasticities (from table 7.3 in chapter 7). Figure 3.A1 presents the four regions for which such elasticities are available. Panel a shows almost all positive energy ratios, whereas panel b shows the high potential returns from transportation investment in Sub-Saharan Africa, highlighting the argument made earlier for a big push strategy.

FIGURE 3A.1 **Efficiency ratios for energy and transportation, with regional elasticities, selected regions**

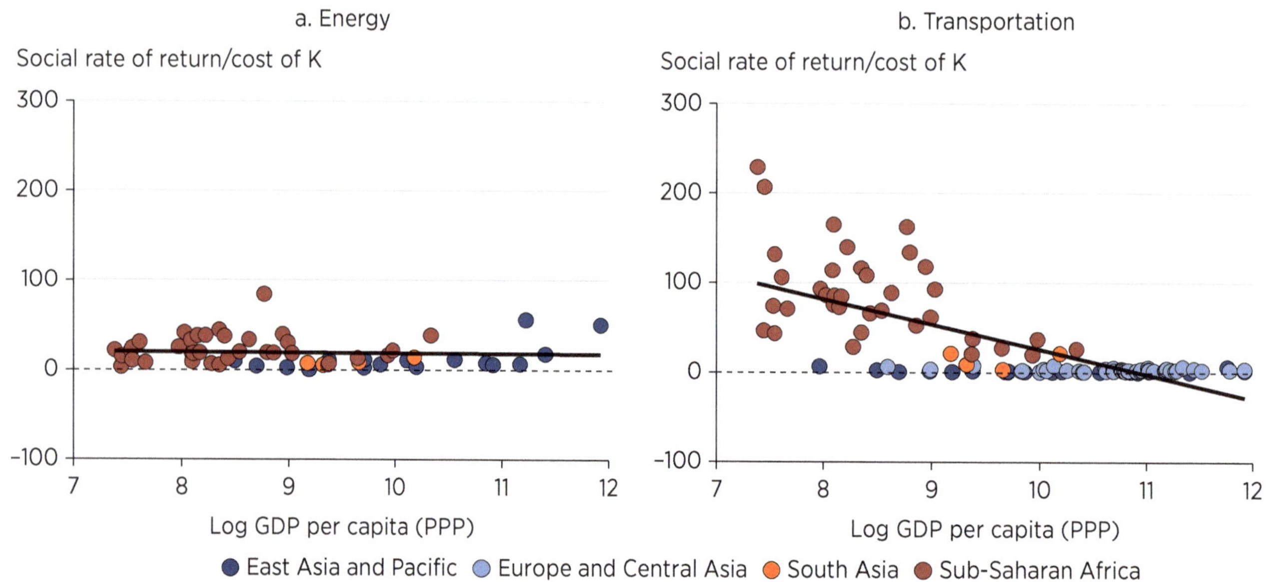

Source: Original figure for this publication.
Note: K = capital; PPP = purchasing power parity.

NOTES

1. Similarly, in water and sanitation, the benefits from safely managed access are felt only if enough households in the neighborhood also enjoy it, thus avoiding cross-contamination effects (Gautam et al. 2025).
2. The colocation effect shifts the optimal allocation—albeit only slightly in this case. This result is an artifact of the Cobb-Douglas production function, which does not allow for strong complementarities between production factors. Using a functional form explicitly incorporating complementarities between transportation and energy, like a constant elasticity of substitution production function, would reinforce the share of this second colocation effect. Note also that the complementarities due to diminishing returns will imply more balanced outcomes when considering bigger, longer-term investments.
3. Specifically, the basic Cobb-Douglas production function is augmented with a constant elasticity of substitution aggregator term for energy and digital. The calibration uses the observed average ratio of digital to energy capital of 0.17 and an elasticity of substitution of 2 (a value above 1 corresponds to factors being gross complements). Of course, the results are for illustration purposes only, because the choice of value for the elasticity of substitution is to some extent arbitrary.

REFERENCES

Briglauer, Wolfgang, Carlo Cambini, and Klaus Gugler. 2023. "Economic Benefits of High-Speed Broadband Network Coverage and Service Adoption: Evidence from OECD Member States." Research Paper No. 23, EcoAustria—Institute for Economic Research.

Damodaran, Aswath. 2025. "Country Risk: Determinants, Measures and Implications—The 2025 Edition." New York University Stern School of Business. http://dx.doi.org/10.2139/ssrn.5354459.

Fay, Marianne, David Martimort, and Stéphane Straub. 2019. "Funding and Financing Infrastructure: The Joint-Use of Public and Private Finance." *Journal of Development Economics* 150 (May): 102629.

Foster, V., N. Gorgulu, S. Straub, and M. Vagliasindi. 2025. "The Impact of Infrastructure on Development Outcomes: A Meta-Analysis." *World Bank Research Observer*, October 7, 2025. https://doi.org/10.1093/wbro/lkaf003.

Gautam, S., M. Gechter, R. Guiteras, and A. M. Mobarak, 2025. "To Use Financial Incentives or Not? Insights from Experiments in Encouraging Sanitation Investments in Four Countries." *World Development* 187 (March): 106791.

IRENA (International Renewable Energy Agency). 2023. *The Cost of Financing for Renewable Power.* IRENA.

Katz, M. L., and C. Shapiro. 1985. "Network Externalities, Competition and Compatibility." *American Economic Review* 75 (3): 424–40.

Spotlight 3.1. Zooming in on Specific Country Cases

CASE 1: INVESTMENT PRIORITIES IN BRAZIL AND NIGERIA

Consider Brazil and Nigeria, two countries that, despite having similar population sizes, differ greatly in land area and income. Brazil's mature and widely distributed energy infrastructure supports resilience and long-distance transmission. By contrast, Nigeria's capacity is concentrated in a few southern states, leaving large northern areas underserved. Transmission and distribution networks also reflect these disparities: Brazil has a much larger and more extensive network, whereas Nigeria's is denser in urban and southern regions but sparse elsewhere, highlighting the country's greater vulnerability and reliance on transmission.

The aggregate results are consistent with these elements. The total capital stock of energy assets to gross domestic product (GDP) is about nine times higher in Brazil than in Nigeria (8.1 percent versus 0.9 percent of GDP), reflecting not only larger physical stocks but also higher replacement costs (two times higher for transmission and distribution investments, and three times higher for generation investments). Consequently, whereas Brazil has achieved universal access, only 60.5 percent of Nigeria's population has access to electricity.[1]

How do these results translate into investment returns? Unsurprisingly given the large service gap, the social rate of return of energy is an order of magnitude higher in Nigeria. Even facing a borrowing rate about 3 percentage points higher than that of Brazil (10.3 percent versus 7.5 percent), Nigeria has a largely favorable infrastructure efficiency ratio, at over 18.0 compared to only 2.4 for Brazil. This simple comparison offers a few lessons.

The gaps in Nigeria clearly call for more investment. For energy, however, the high efficiency ratio signals a failure of markets to deliver on socially beneficial investments at scale, in a context of limited fiscal space, and even though Nigeria is one of the main recipients of International Development Association funds (World Bank 2025). This failure is consistent with an electrification rate that has not increased significantly in recent years and that remains especially low in rural areas, at less than 30 percent. Broadening the lens to transportation reveals an even larger efficiency ratio, at almost 32, consistent with the fact that only 25 percent of the rural population lives within 2 kilometers of an all-season road. The strong spatial gaps in both sectors point to the opportunity of a multisector strategy. As noted earlier, for a given infrastructure budget, the data indicate that the optimal allocation should consider spending approximately two-thirds on transportation and the rest on energy.

Brazil, by contrast, appears to be at a different stage in terms of infrastructure access, with much higher coverage rates and both energy and road networks that have gradually extended to the whole territory. Nevertheless, efficiency ratios—2.4 for energy and

6.4 for transportation—indicate that the benefits of additional investments still exceed the costs. Electrification has yet to reach close to 700,000 unconnected people in rural areas, and transmission and distribution losses are higher than in Nigeria. In the transportation sector, both roads and railroads display unequal quality and spatial coverage, with over one-third of the capital stock concentrated in only 2 states (Minas Gerais and São Paulo) out of 27. Clearly, in Brazil the returns to addressing these shortcomings translate into positive efficiency ratios, with a needed focus on improving quality and a potential priority to the transportation sector; however, the debt level, currently one of the highest among emerging countries, constrains the country's ability to invest more. Brazil will need a lower overall amount of investment than will Nigeria, and, given the imbalances in efficiency ratios, the data support a clear prioritization of the transportation sector.

CASE 2: THE ROADS OF HISPANIOLA

The island of Hispaniola, home to both the Dominican Republic and Haiti, presents a stark dichotomy in development—illustrated here by the road subsector—driven by divergent socioeconomic trajectories and institutional capacities. The Dominican Republic, leveraging its status as an upper-middle-income economy, has successfully integrated road network expansion with key economic drivers like tourism and agriculture, using public-private partnerships and a relatively stable Ministry of Public Works and Communications to maintain decent connectivity and pavement quality despite shared climate risks such as hurricanes and flooding. Conversely, Haiti remains stifled by chronic political instability, weak institutional governance, and a low-income economy, resulting in a critically underfunded and deteriorating road network with investment that remains largely reactive and donor-dependent rather than systemic. Although both nations grapple with the engineering challenges posed by rugged, mountainous topography and high seismic activity, they present asymmetrical investment landscapes: the Dominican Republic focuses on modernization and corridor efficiency, whereas Haiti faces an existential struggle to provide basic all-weather access.

Using results of the data collection effort in chapter 4, map S3.1.1 shows the road network of Hispaniola, with 3,748 kilometers of road in Haiti compared to 14,713 kilometers in the Dominican Republic. Panel a shows the network by hierarchy status, with each road segment geocoded and, when data are available, described by detailed attributes, for example number of lanes and surface type. The granularity of these data makes them useful for detailed spatial analyses, such as evaluating flood proneness for disaster risk management—vitally important for Hispaniola, given its frequent exposure to major hurricanes. Panel b shows the paved road density in each municipality in the Dominican Republic and each commune in Haiti, highlighting the more densely built-up urban areas of both countries. However, this presentation paints only a partial picture of the scale and quality of the road infrastructure. Applying the valuation methodology developed in chapters 5 and 6 allows for producing a map of the road asset value per capita (panel c). Here, the border between the two countries stands out as a sharp discontinuity: the population of the Dominican Republic is much better endowed with road transportation infrastructure than that of Haiti.

MAP S3.1.1 The roads of Hispaniola

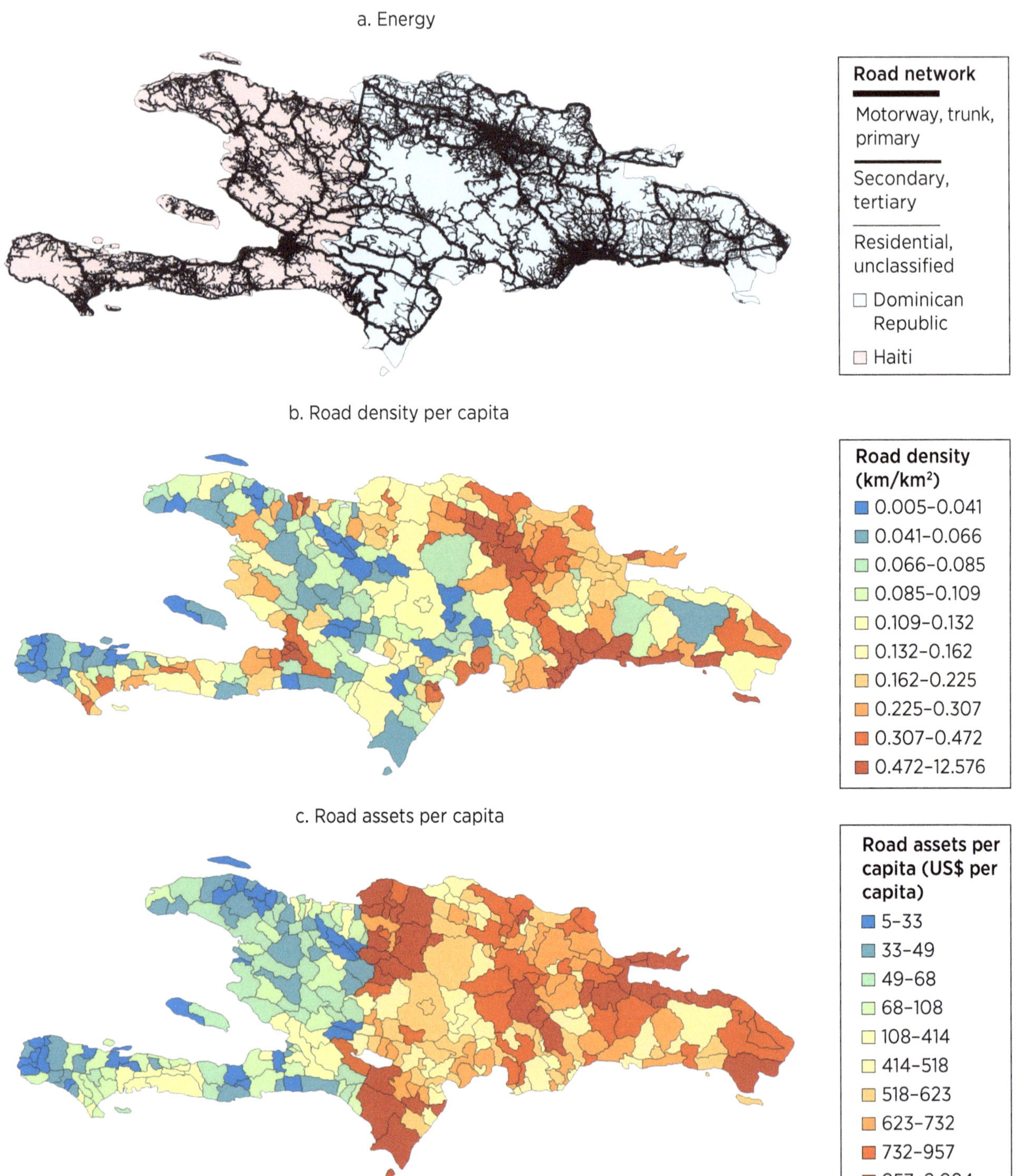

Source: Original map for this publication.
Note: km = kilometer; km² = kilometer squared.

Does the larger transportation infrastructure gap in Haiti necessarily imply that it is the better place to target investments? Even after accounting for productivity differences, the social rate of return of transportation infrastructure investment is indeed greater in Haiti (2.54) than in the Dominican Republic (1.87). In other words, the marginal dollar invested in Haiti will yield a larger development impact than in the Dominican Republic. However, the less stable environment of Haiti also has impacts for borrowing costs and depreciation rates, effectively making that marginal dollar more expensive in Haiti. Consequently, the infrastructure efficiency ratio for roads is slightly more efficient in the Dominican Republic (13.73) than in Haiti (12.84).

CASE 3: LANDLOCKED VERSUS COASTAL—THE DIGITAL ECONOMY IN ETHIOPIA AND KENYA

Cut off from the sea and burdened with higher deployment costs, landlocked countries have usually watched their digital networks grow more slowly, accumulating less digital capital than their coastal peers. This very disadvantage, however, could make each new investment more powerful. Across Sub-Saharan Africa, the returns tell the story clearly: landlocked economies have a median digital efficiency ratio about 50 percent higher than that of coastal countries.

Two countries examined for this report, Ethiopia and Kenya, highlight this dichotomy. They share the same estimated elasticity of digital infrastructure to GDP and have roughly similar GDP levels, although Ethiopia faces a higher borrowing cost (30.5 versus 9.8 percent in Kenya). Despite the similarities between the two countries, Ethiopia—a large, landlocked economy with a long history of underdeployment in digital infrastructure—stands out with a digital efficiency ratio more than twice that of Kenya.

With no submarine cables and historically limited deployment of cell sites and data centers, Ethiopia's higher efficiency ratio emerges from its modest starting point: a digital capital stock of only US$1.21 billion (4.5 times smaller than Kenya's) and a low baseline of internet usage at 19 percent of the population of 25 million, compared with 35 percent of Kenya's 20 million people.[2] These conditions make each additional investment far more transformative, consistent with the classical diminishing marginal returns to capital theory.

However, infrastructure alone does not tell the full story. Adoption barriers, especially affordability of telecommunications services, may also shape how infrastructure investment turns into adoption. Kenya's mobile data and voice baskets (US$2.50 for low consumption and US$5.00 for high consumption) are considerably more expensive than Ethiopia's (US$1.10 and US$2.00, respectively), according to the International Telecommunication Union.[3] Although higher prices in Kenya may reflect adequate pricing and thus affect the sustainability of providing infrastructure, lower affordability barriers may amplify the economic impact of each additional unit of digital capital in Ethiopia by enabling broader diffusion and use, reinforcing the high marginal returns suggested by the digital infrastructure efficiency ratio estimates.

CASE 4: ENERGIZING HONDURAS

Honduras's high generation capital cost raises the marginal cost of new investment and depresses the social rate of return relative to peer countries, resulting in a low efficiency ratio of energy capital (2.62). The country's current generation unit cost stands at US$2.2 million per megawatt, placing Honduras in the 82nd percentile globally and far above regional comparators. This elevated cost structure reflects Honduras's reliance on fossil fuels, which still account for 41 percent of generation, as well as its exposure to volatile global oil prices, hydropower-related drought risks, and delays in new generation investments. Scenario analysis makes clear how costly generation depresses investment attractiveness: if Honduras converged to neighboring Panama's unit generation cost (US$1.7 million per megawatt), the efficiency ratio would rise to 3.45. Aligning with the average for Latin America and the Caribbean (US$1.58 million per megawatt) would raise Honduras's ratio further to 3.58, and even a modest 10 percent cost reduction would lift the ratio to 2.92. Achieving such reductions would significantly strengthen the economic case for new generation and enhance Honduras's appeal to energy investors by shifting the system toward a more resilient and lower-cost trajectory.

NOTES

1. Based on values for 2022 from the World Bank, World Development Indicators.
2. Based on World Bank Data 360, https://data360.worldbank.org/.
3. International Telecommunication Union, "ICT Price Baskets (IPB)," https://www.itu.int/en /ITU-D/Statistics/Dashboards/Pages/IPB.aspx.

REFERENCE

World Bank. 2025. *International Debt Report 2025*. World Bank. doi:10.1596/978-1-4648-2262-9.

PART 2

Mapping Infrastructure Physical Stocks

KEY MESSAGES

The chapter documents a systematic undertaking to assemble comprehensive data on the physical stocks of the principal subsectors within energy, transportation, and digital infrastructure. It covers close to 200 countries and provides location down to second-level administrative divisions (municipalities, districts). The compilation draws upon a broad spectrum of leading public and proprietary data sources.

Global infrastructure physical stocks are extremely uneven across countries and closely track income and geography. Across the energy, transportation, and digital sectors, richer countries systematically hold larger quantities of physical infrastructure per capita, whereas low-income regions—most notably South Asia and Sub-Saharan Africa—remain severely underendowed in almost all asset classes.

Physical infrastructure inequality persists not only between countries but also within them. Geolocated data reveal pronounced subnational disparities: infrastructure assets cluster around urban cores, coastal corridors, and economic hubs, leaving large inland or rural areas thinly served. These internal gaps are especially large in lower-income countries and amplify regional inequality.

INTRODUCTION

This chapter documents a systematic undertaking to assemble comprehensive data on the physical stocks of the principal subsectors of energy, transportation, and digital infrastructure across nations. The compilation draws upon a broad spectrum of leading public and private data sources (refer to annex 4A). For power generation, for instance, four major repositories—including the Global Energy Monitor Integrated Power Tracker and the Global Power Plant Database—were consulted. In addition, information on data centers comes from TeleGeography Inc., Global Data Plc, and Datacenters Map.

A reproducibility package is available for this book in the Reproducible Research Repository at https://reproducibility.worldbank.org/catalog/536.

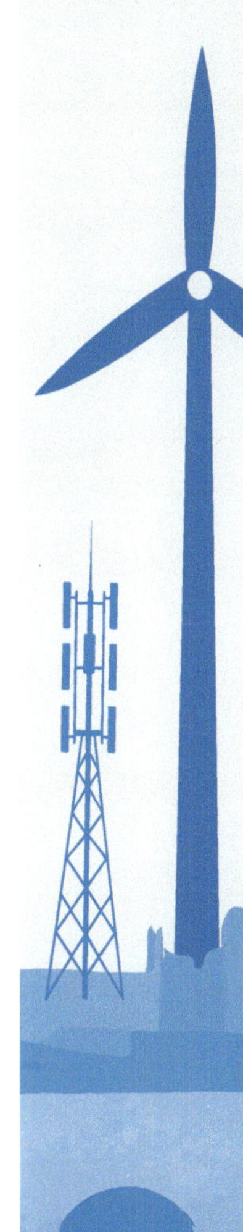

The exercise is unprecedented both in the rigor of its quality assurance procedures and in the breadth and consistency of its coverage. In the energy domain, meticulous cross-checking and alignment of disparate databases yield a unified, coherent foundation that captures 8,851 gigawatts of electricity generation capacity globally and 11.8 million kilometers (km) of power transmission and distribution lines worldwide. For transportation, road and railway networks are extracted from OpenStreetMap and subsequently harmonized to enhance cross-country comparability, resulting in a data set encompassing 19.3 million km of paved roads and 1.1 million km of railway lines. In the digital sphere, extensive integration and triangulation produce a consolidated view of five core subsectors of digital infrastructure, attaining an average coverage of 80 percent across components and representing the essential systems that underpin global data transmission, processing, and interconnection.

ENERGY

This section provides a full inventory of energy physical assets, including on-grid generation, transmission, and distribution, as well as stylized facts regarding their distribution worldwide and in selected countries.

Data and methodology

Figure 4.1 illustrates the overall structure of the electric power system, encompassing both on-grid and off-grid configurations. Electricity generation begins with conventional sources such as coal, gas, and nuclear, and renewable sources including solar, wind, and hydropower. Power generated at these plants passes through a step-up transformer, which raises voltage for long-distance transmission through high-voltage overhead or underground lines connected to transmission substations and switchyards. From there, the voltage is stepped down for distribution substations, where medium-voltage electricity is carried through distribution networks and electric poles to end users. A pole-mounted transformer further reduces the voltage to supply residential, commercial, and industrial customers. In parallel, off-grid systems often operate independently through a charge controller, battery storage, and DC/AC inverter, delivering electricity directly to households, businesses, or small industries not connected to the main grid. Together, these components form an integrated view of how energy is generated, transmitted, distributed, and consumed across different infrastructure contexts.

To assess physical stocks in the energy sector, this chapter focuses on two key assets: (1) power generation and (2) grid transmission and distribution lines. Because of the difficulty in obtaining reliable, globally consistent data, the chapter does not cover off-grid generation, transmission, distribution, and storage as well as grid substations. The omission of off-grid technologies is not expected to have a material effect on estimates of physical energy assets (IRENA 2025).[1] Effects of the omission of grid transmission and distribution substations are more difficult to assess, given the high uncertainty about their share in total investment cost.[2]

FIGURE 4.1 On-grid and off-grid electric power system architecture

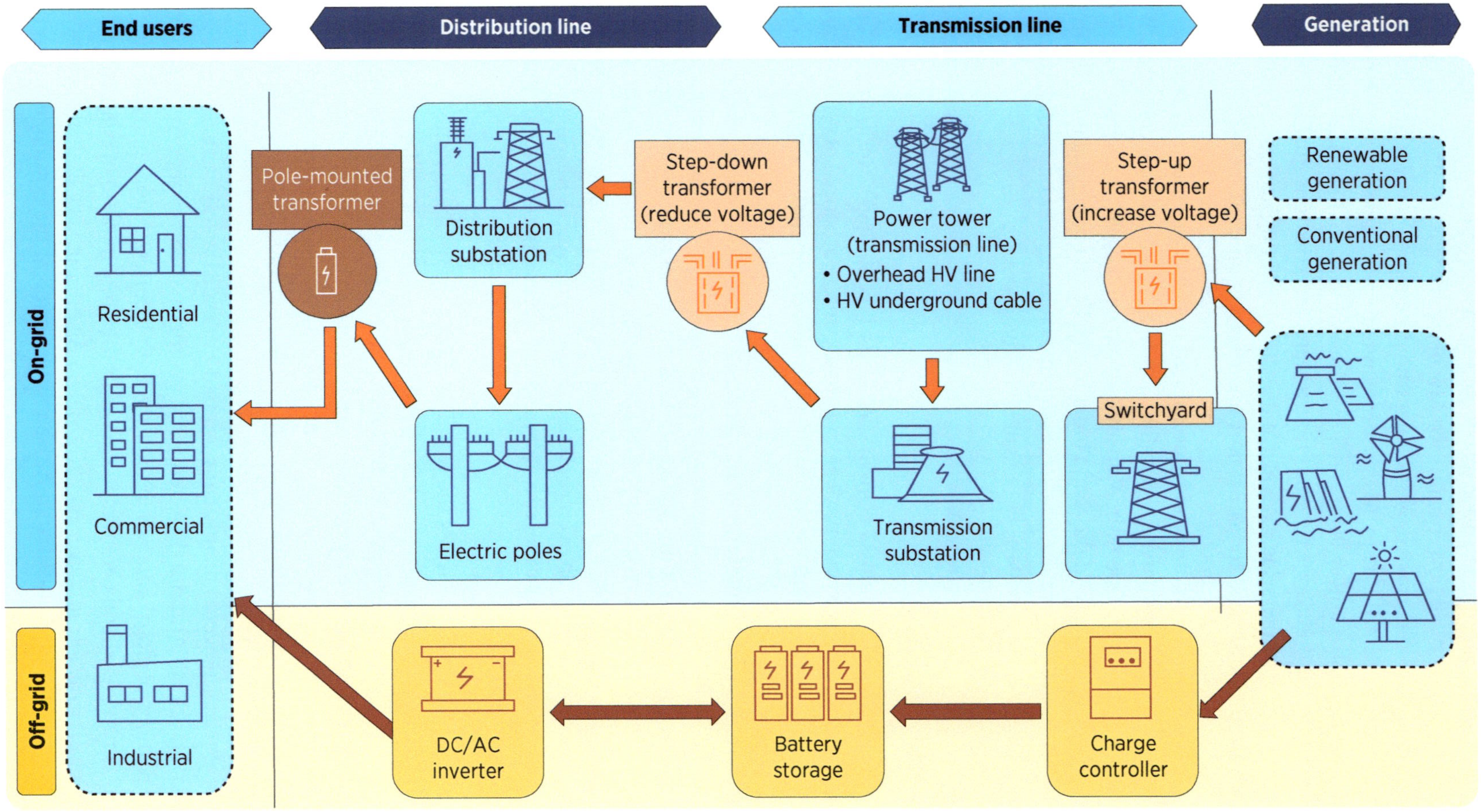

Source: Original figure for this publication.
Note: HV = high voltage

For power generation, a comprehensive global data set has been developed that maps the locations and capacities of all power plants worldwide, totaling 8,851 gigawatts of installed capacity. The data set is constructed by systematically integrating records from multiple authoritative sources: Global Energy Monitor Integrated Power Tracker, the World Resources Institute Global Power Plant Database, the World Bank Electricity Planning Model, and the Global Data Construction Projects Database. Rigorous quality checks and careful matching ensure wide coverage and avoidance of duplications, resulting in a unified and reliable foundation for global power generation analysis.

For transmission and distribution, worldwide data on transmission and distribution lines—amounting to approximately 11.8 million km in total length—are compiled. This information is sourced from OpenInfraMap and supplemented with data from the World Bank's EnergyData platform and the Grid Finder tool. Official country geometries from the World Bank are used to accurately allocate power lines to countries or sovereign entities, with each line assigned on the basis of its geographic location.

Power generation

Power generation assets encompass a broad spectrum of technologies, including oil and gas, coal, hydropower, solar, wind, nuclear, bioenergy, and geothermal. As shown in figure 4.2, stark regional disparities exist in installed power-generation capacity per capita, with the lowest capacity in Sub-Saharan Africa—under 0.2 kilowatt per person, which corresponds to roughly 1/10th of the world average and reflects severe power supply constraints. The South Asia region also remains well below the average, whereas Latin America and the Caribbean and the Middle East, North Africa, Afghanistan, and Pakistan approach but still trail it. East Asia and Pacific and Europe and Central Asia are modestly above the global mean, and North America stands out at about 4 kilowatts per person, more than three times the world average. The gradient underscores how limited capacity in low-income regions constrains electricity access and reliability relative to higher-income regions.

Technology distribution varies across the world's regions. Thermal generation—including oil and gas, and coal power plants—makes up the largest share of installed capacity, primarily driven by the energy-intensive East Asia and Pacific and North America regions (figure 4.3). Hydropower is widely distributed, with notable concentrations in East Asia and Pacific and in Latin America and the Caribbean. Modern renewables, including solar and wind plants, are especially significant in East Asia and Pacific, Europe and Central Asia, and North America, highlighting regional progress in renewable energy deployment. Nuclear power is mainly concentrated in East Asia and Pacific, Europe and Central Asia, and North America. Bioenergy and geothermal power generation account for smaller portions of global generation capacity, with bioenergy more prevalent in Europe and Central Asia, and geothermal energy limited to a handful of countries where this technology is available and economically viable. Again, the very limited amount of generation capacity in the Sub-Saharan Africa region, in red at the bottom, is apparent from the figure.

FIGURE 4.2 Per capita power generation capacity, by region

Average generation capacity (kW per capita)

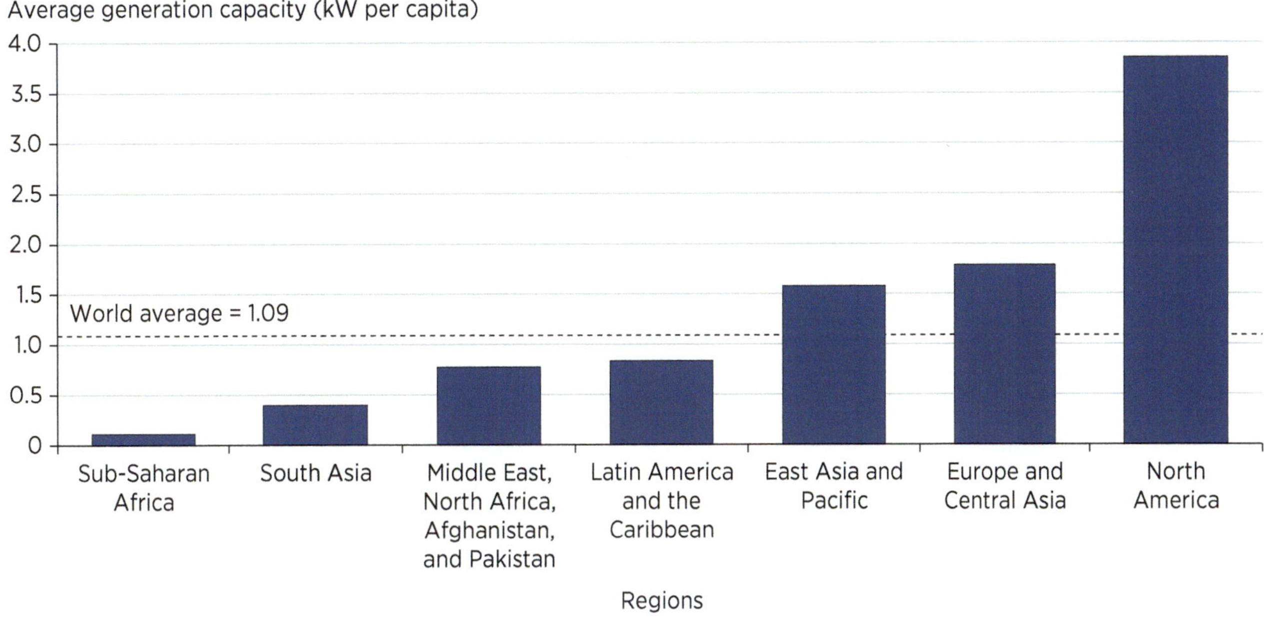

Source: Original figure for this publication.
Note: The data are for 2024. kW = kilowatt.

FIGURE 4.3 Distribution of power generation capacity, by region and generation technology

Power generation capacity (GW)

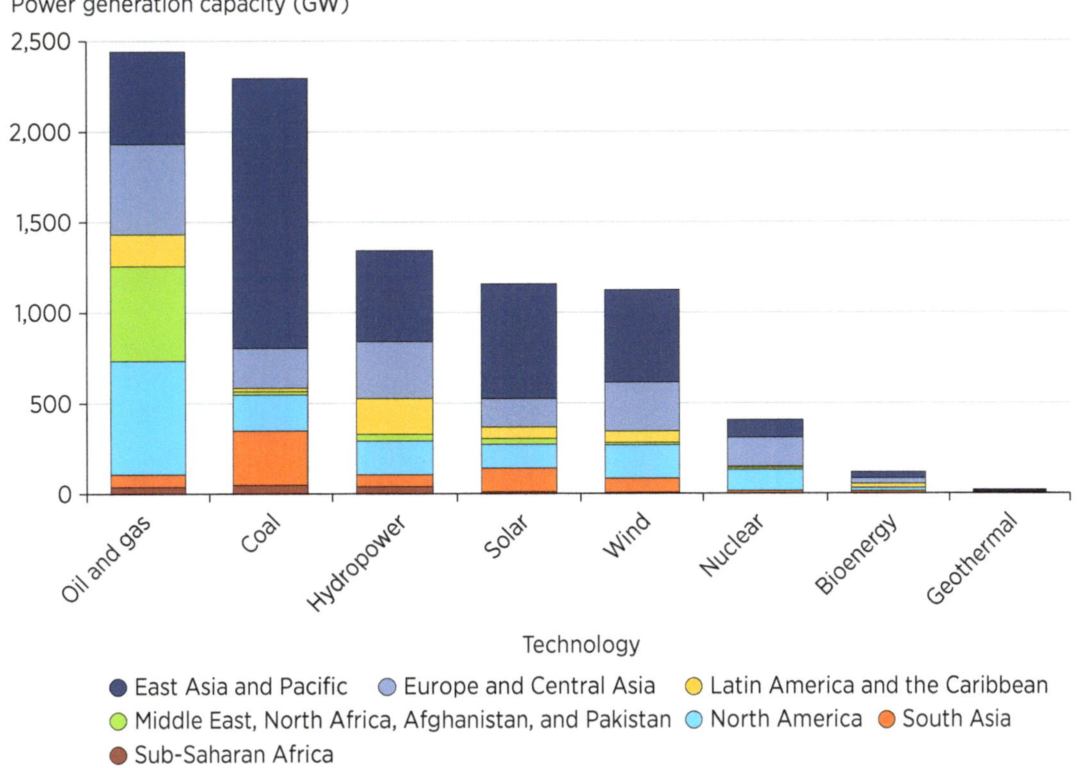

Source: Original figure for this publication.
Note: The data are for 2024. GW = gigawatt.

Transmission and distribution networks

The combined transmission and distribution line data reveal significant regional differences in total network density. Map 4.1 shows the global distribution of transmission and distribution line density by decile. Europe stands out as the most densely networked region, with many of its countries falling into the top deciles (particularly decile 10), reflecting both high levels of electrification and compact geographies. In contrast, many countries in Sub-Saharan Africa fall into the lowest deciles, indicating sparse power line networks relative to their territorial extent. These low densities often reflect a combination of limited electrification, underdeveloped infrastructure, and large land areas with dispersed populations.

Subnational distribution

Importantly, all the assets covered here are geolocated, allowing for a precise mapping down to the second-level administrative division—that is, the municipality/district/county level. Maps 4.2 and 4.3 show the examples of Brazil and Nigeria, mapping both generation and transmission and distribution assets at the regional and district levels. These countries offer a useful comparison because they have broadly similar population sizes but markedly different land area and income levels: Brazil has a far larger territory and greater wealth per capita, whereas Nigeria is far more spatially compact. The maps show that, across the first-level administrative division (the regional or state level) within each country, Brazil's median installed capacity (approximately 6.7 gigawatts) is an order of magnitude larger than Nigeria's (about 0.48 gigawatt), yielding far higher capacity per person and per square kilometer.

MAP 4.1 Global distribution of transmission and distribution lines

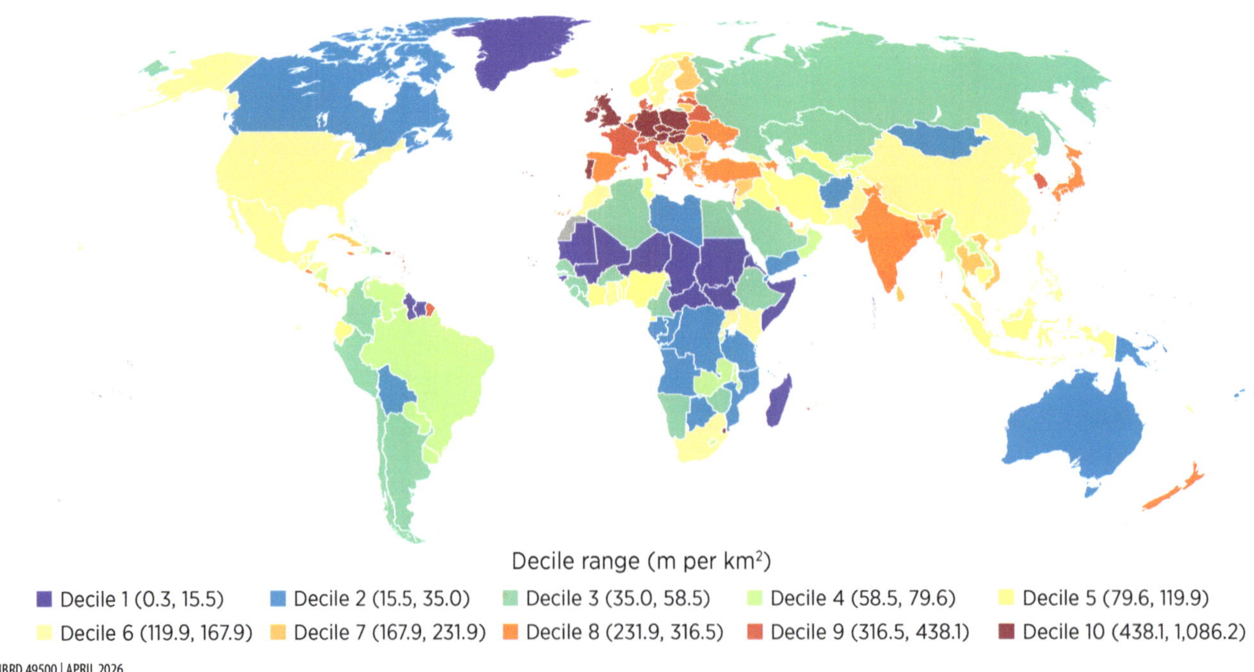

Source: Original map for this publication.
Note: This map illustrates global distribution in transmission and distribution lines in terms of density, measured as the total length of transmission and distribution lines per unit of land area. Countries are grouped into deciles, with shading indicating their position from lowest (decile 1) to highest (decile 10) in the global distribution. km² = square kilometer; m = meter.

MAP 4.2 Subnational generation capacity (MW), Brazil and Nigeria

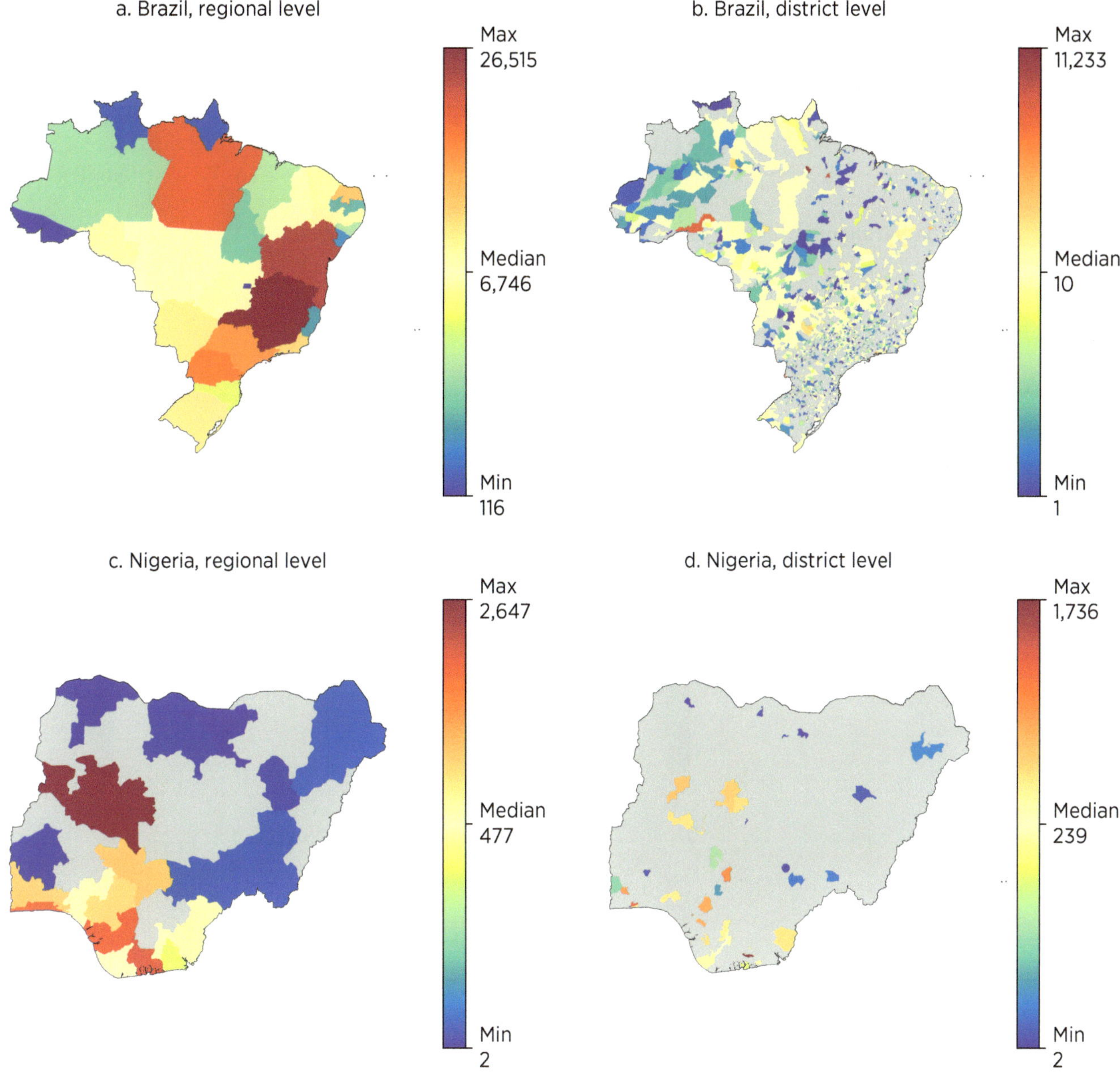

Source: Original map for this publication.
Note: The map shows total generation capacity, excluding some power plants without spatial information. The data are for 2024. MW = megawatt.

In Brazil, most states host substantial generation, and the municipal-level mosaic reveals a dense, granular spread of plants—consistent with a mature, diversified system that distributes supply across territory and fuels, supporting resilience and long-distance transmission. By contrast, in Nigeria, capacity is concentrated in a handful of southern states, with municipal-level generation sites clustered around the coastal gas corridor and a few urban hubs; large areas—especially in the north—remain thinly served.

This spatial concentration, combined with a much smaller national resource base, implies tighter supply margins, greater vulnerability to regional shocks, and a heavier reliance on transmission to move power to demand centers.

Looking at transmission and distribution reveals a far larger network in Brazil (median length of about 13,000 km) than in Nigeria (about 1,600 km), yielding substantially more line-kilometers per capita even though Brazil's vast territory lowers its network density per square kilometer (map 4.3). At the state level, Brazil shows extensive south/southeast

MAP 4.3 Subnational transmission and distribution lines (km), Brazil and Nigeria

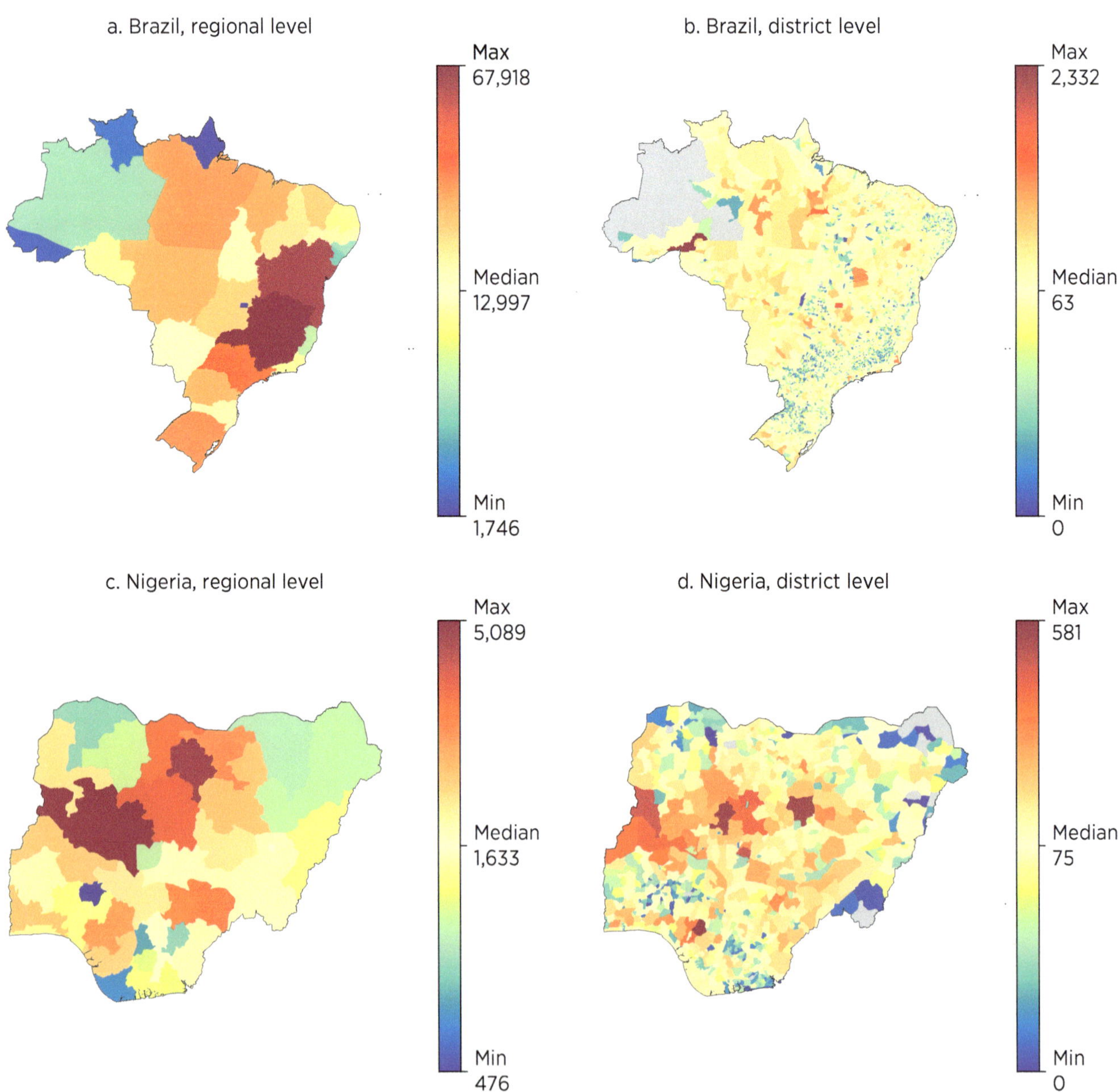

Source: Original map for this publication.
Notes: The data are for 2024. km = kilometers.

coverage with long interregional trunks reaching the interior; the municipal level reveals broad line penetration with thinner reach across the Amazon. Nigeria has a more concentrated state-level pattern, with higher intensities around the southwest/central corridor and gas-rich south; municipal level disaggregation shows dense urban webs (Abuja, Lagos–Ibadan, Port Harcourt) and sparser coverage in the northeast and northern border areas.

TRANSPORTATION

For the transportation sector, the scope of the report spans road and rail networks. These linear infrastructures make up the vast majority of transportation infrastructure capital.[3] Whereas ports, airports, and other nodal infrastructure represent large concentrations of infrastructure, the vastness of road and rail networks dominates the overall capital value.

Data and methodology

Data availability and formats are more uniform for road and rail, compared to the more complex and heterogeneous nature of air and maritime infrastructure. Consequently, the focus on roads and rail enables a more consistent methodological approach. For the road subsector, the scope is further narrowed to paved roads. Similarly, this focus enforces a level of homogeneity in the captured infrastructure and implicitly restricts the focus to links of adequate economic significance.

The study uses OpenStreetMap (OSM) as its primary data source to create a globally consistent and spatially explicit inventory of road and rail assets.[4] A global, open-source, and crowdsourced geospatial database, OSM is built and continuously maintained by a global community of volunteers, resulting in a data set of unparalleled scale and detail; it was previously used for a similar stocktaking exercise (Meijer et al. 2018). The global coverage and consistency of OSM data are its principal advantages. Although local data sources are often more definitive, idiosyncratic measurement approaches and data formats make aggregation and comparisons across local data sets challenging. Furthermore, its "live" crowdsourcing makes OSM extremely cost-effective and one of few feasible ways of keeping current with the rapid infrastructure expansion in many developing economies.

Despite its benefits, the crowdsourced nature also presents challenges. Although data structures are globally consistent, the reliance on volunteers to contribute data inevitably introduces variations in data completeness and variable interpretation. In particular, data completeness tends to be higher in denser and more developed areas. This variability could create a bias that exacerbates apparent spatial inequality, however the validation and robustness checks for this report indicate that the OSM data are at least as comprehensive as alternative data sources.[5]

For a detailed description of the processing of the OSM data, please refer to annex 4B.

Roads and railways

In total, the estimated lengths of the world's linear transportation infrastructure add up to 19.3 million km of paved roads and 1.1 million km of railroads (map 4.4). Much like in other infrastructure sectors, the distribution is highly uneven across the world. Large economies, such as the United States, China, and India top the list of countries with most kilometers of paved roads. The United States, China, and the Russian Federation top the list of countries with most kilometers of railroads.

Subnational distribution

To illustrate the granularity of the data, map 4.5 shows the examples of the Dominican Republic and Uzbekistan, countries with comparable nominal gross domestic product but differing land area. The maps of the main roads (excluding residential and unclassified roads) of the two countries are displayed with the same spatial scale. The vastness of Uzbekistan (roughly nine times larger than the Dominican Republic) and the spread of its population across numerous distant cities necessitates a far more extensive road network (36,579 km) compared to the Dominican Republic (14,713 km).

MAP 4.4 Global distribution of line transportation infrastructure, roads and railways

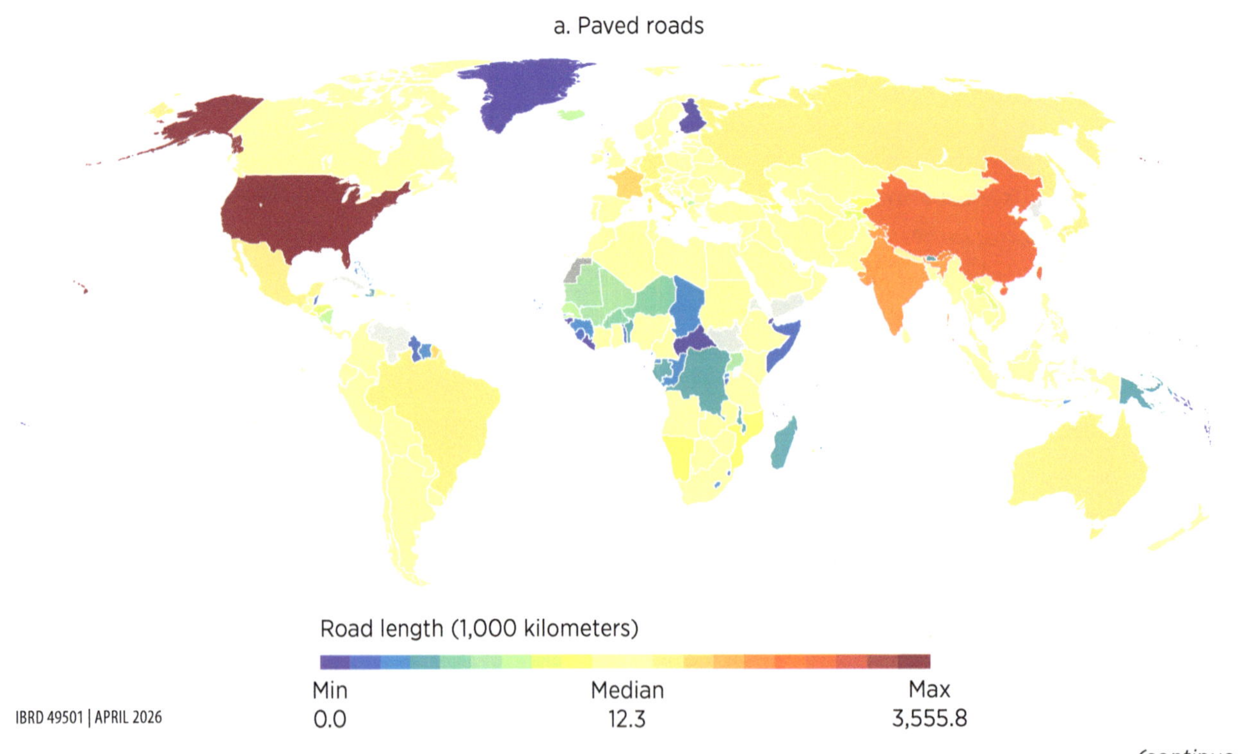

(continued)

MAP 4.4 **Global distribution of line transportation infrastructure, roads and railways** *(continued)*

b. Railways

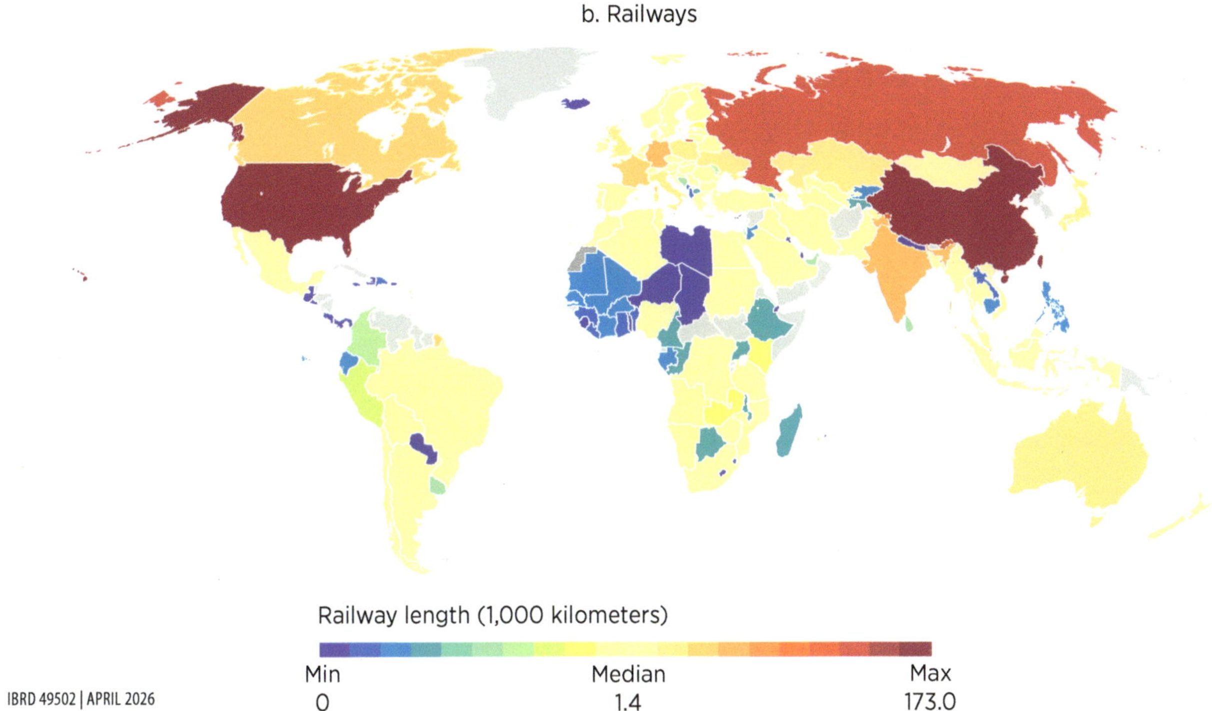

IBRD 49502 | APRIL 2026

Source: Original map for this publication.
Note: The data are for 2025.

DIGITAL

From the broad landscape of digital infrastructure (figure 4.4), the following core
components stand out for their indispensable roles in global connectivity and resilience:

- *Data centers*—facilities that house computer servers, storage systems, and networking
  equipment used to store, process, and deliver digital data and applications

- *Internet exchange points (IXPs)*—physical locations where different networks connect to
  exchange internet traffic directly, improving speed, reducing costs, and enhancing reliability

- *Radio access networks*—the part of a mobile network that connects user devices, such as
  phones, to the core network through wireless communication using antennas and base
  stations

- *Terrestrial fiber-optic cables*—land based networks that transmit data as light signals at very
  high speeds, forming the backbone of broadband, 5G, and the interconnection of digital
  systems

- *Submarine cables*—underwater fiber optic cables laid on the ocean floor that transmit
  data between countries and continents, forming the backbone of international internet
  connectivity[6]

MAP 4.5 **Subnational distribution of line transportation infrastructure, Dominican Republic and Uzbekistan**

a. Dominican Republic

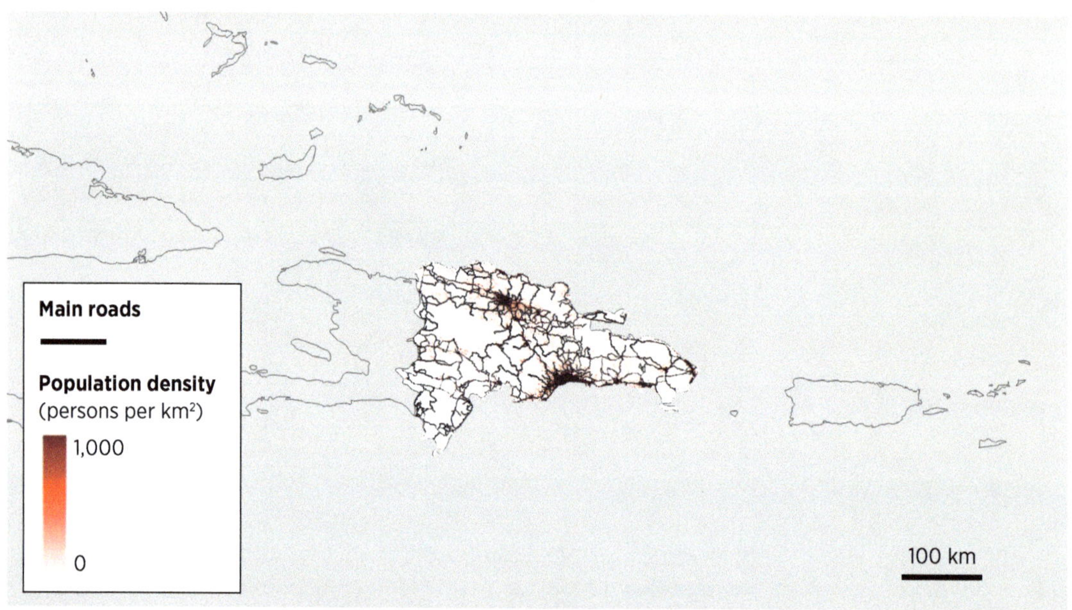

b. Uzbekistan

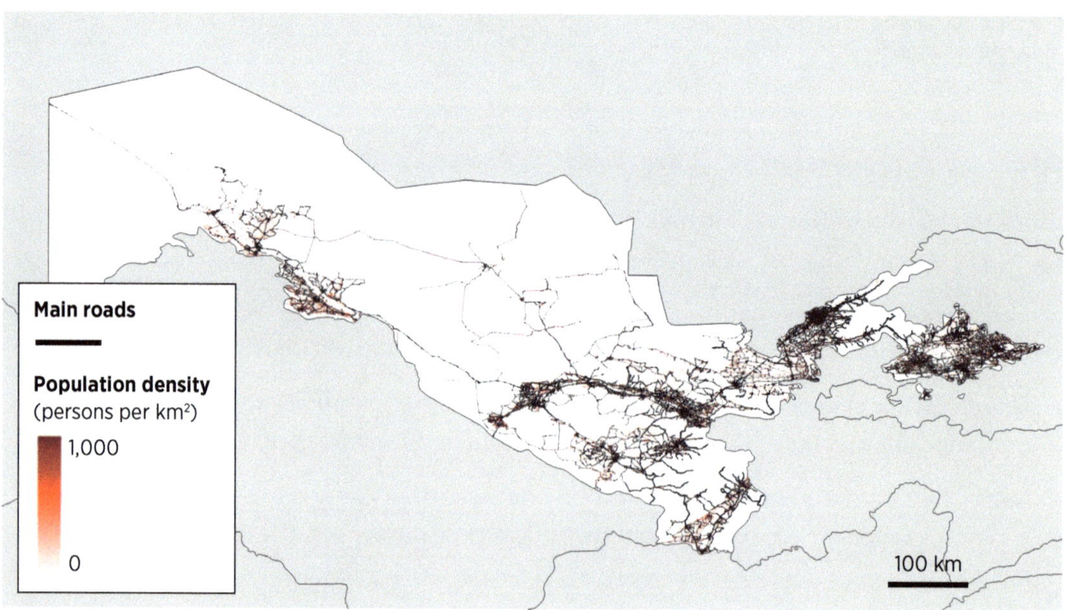

Source: Original map for this publication.
Note: The data are for 2025. km = kilometer; km² = kilometer squared.

FIGURE 4.4 Architecture of the digital ecosystem

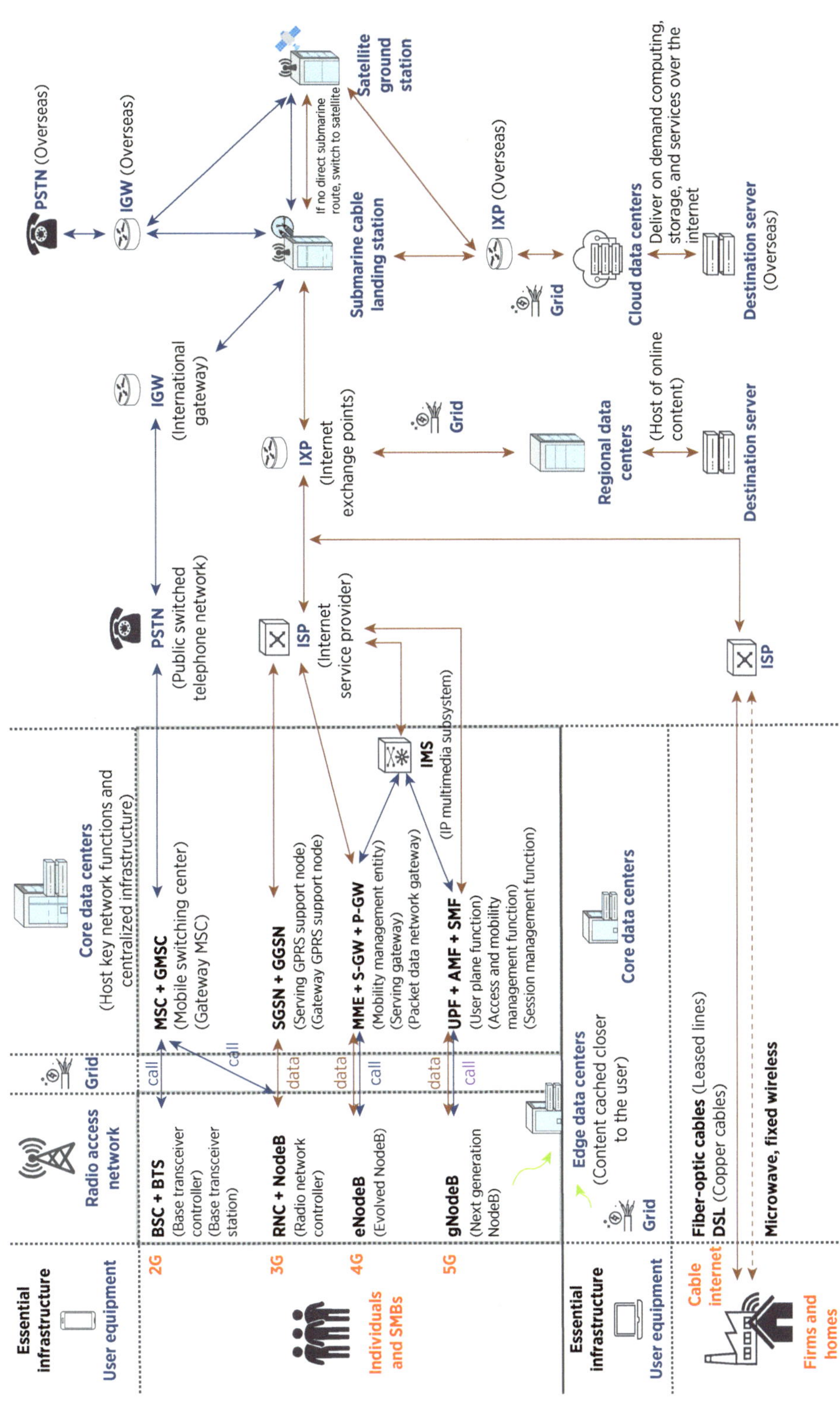

Source: Original figure for this publication.

Note: Brown lines indicate infrastructure mapped for this figure. 2G, 3G, 4G, 5G = second, third, fourth, fifth generation; DSL = digital subscriber line; GPRS = general packet radio service; IP = internet protocol; SMBs = small and medium businesses.

Data and methodology

This report uses the five core components because together they form the complete chain of digital connectivity, from user access (cell towers) to global data transportation (fiber and submarine cables) and core data processing (data centers and IXPs). Data on the five pillars of digital infrastructure were developed by integrating leading public and private sources (annex 4A), representing the first comprehensive global consolidation of digital infrastructure information. This collection of digital assets achieves about 80 percent average coverage across components, capturing the core systems that enable connectivity.[7]

The shifts in digital infrastructure reflected in the last two decades show a global pivot toward cloud-driven architectures and cross-border data exchange as the defining forces of digital integration, transitioning from broad-based tower rollouts to more strategic, capital-intensive investments in data centers, IXPs, and submarine cables (figure 4.5). Although high-income countries led the initial expansion, recent submarine cable projects signal increasing global integration, especially in Latin America and the Caribbean and in Sub-Saharan Africa. Growth trajectories now differ by infrastructure type: cell tower deployment accelerated rapidly until about 2015 before leveling off; data centers expanded exponentially, reaching peak concentration by 2024 in North America; IXPs grew modestly, peaking in 2014 but regaining momentum later in Latin America and the Caribbean, South Asia, and parts of Sub-Saharan Africa; and submarine cables have surged since 2020, extending connectivity across new regional corridors.

Radio access networks

Countries have made uneven progress toward next-generation mobile connectivity, as seen through high concentration of high-capacity Long-Term Evolution (LTE) (4G) and New Radio networks (5G) in high-income countries (HICs), compared to dependence in non-HICs largely on Global System for Mobile Communications (GSM) (2G) and Universal Mobile Telecommunications System (3G).[8] As of 2025, developing countries hosted only 30 percent of global mobile cells yet served 77 percent of the world's mobile subscribers, revealing severe infrastructure strains. Network efficiency and coverage disparities are also evident. HICs operate with roughly 500 cells per 1,000 km² and median latency of 26 milliseconds, whereas low-income countries average fewer than 20 cells and latency above 30 milliseconds, leaving countries such as Burundi, the Republic of Congo, Eritrea, and the Republic of Yemen among the most underserved.[9]

With respect to physical sites, developed countries are densifying through quick micro site expansion, and developing countries remain focused on extensive coverage via macro sites (refer to annex 4C for estimation of physical sites from mobile cells data).[10] This densification, adding more sites within already connected areas, serves to boost network capacity, speed, and reliability, allowing users to enjoy faster data transfer and lower latency. In contrast, reliance on macro site expansion in less developed regions often results in broader but thinner coverage, meaning that more people gain access to mobile service but with continuing limited connection quality and data throughput.

FIGURE 4.5 Trends in digital infrastructure expansion, by region and type of infrastructure, 2000–25

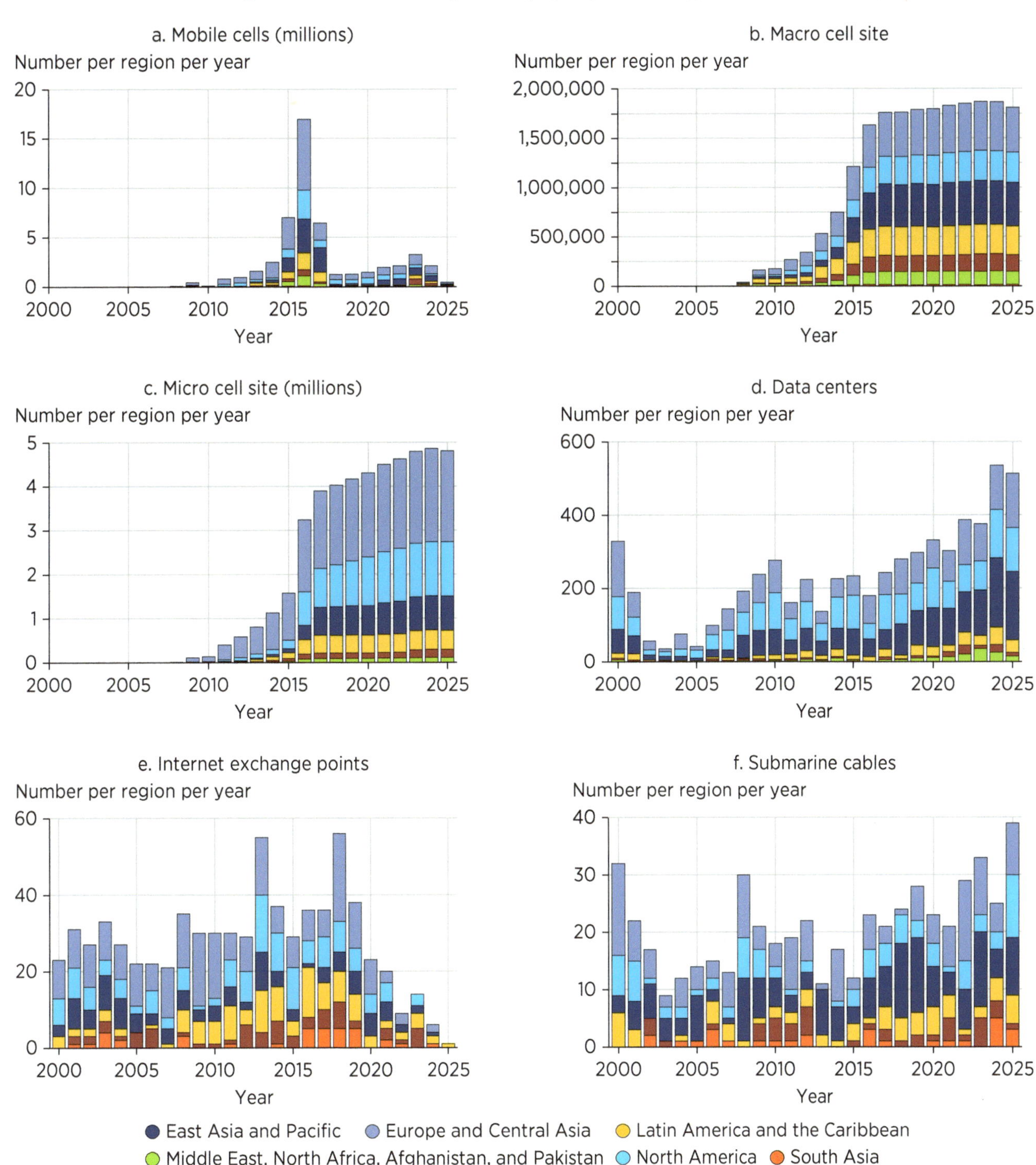

Source: Original figure for this publication.

As of 2025, Europe and Central Asia led with over 2.5 million total sites, 82 percent of which are micro sites, reflecting sustained network densification in mature markets and the deployment of advanced mobile technologies, particularly 5G. In contrast, South Asia and Sub-Saharan Africa continue to rely predominantly on macro deployments with over 50 percent and 80 percent, respectively.[11]

Data centers

Although data centers are physically concentrated in certain locations, their computational and storage capacities often serve users and firms across borders, meaning that geographical imbalances do not necessarily imply a complete lack of access to digital services. Still, the data show a stark global divide in data center development. The United States alone accounts for roughly one-quarter of all data centers and one-third of global capacity, nearly double that of the combined total of the 110 countries of Latin America and the Caribbean, the Middle East and North Africa, Southeast Asia, and Sub-Saharan Africa. Across income groups, HICs host 72 percent of global facilities, compared to only 7 percent and 0.2 percent in lower-middle-income and low-income countries, respectively. On a per capita basis, HICs average about 4 data centers per million people and about 94 megawatts in capacity, whereas low-income countries have just 0.04 data centers and about 0.4 megawatts.

Internet exchange points

The Europe and Central Asia region leads on IXPs, hosting nearly 380 mostly medium- or high-capacity facilities, equivalent to 0.41 IXPs per 1 million citizens and about 15 times the number in South Asia (figure 4.6). However, IXP presence alone does not guarantee performance. Resilience and speed depend on the number of active peers, such as internet service providers, content delivery networks, and cloud providers. Many low- and lower-middle-income countries host IXPs with minimal participation, causing local traffic to be routed internationally and increasing costs and latency. On average, HICs have about four participants per IXP compared to just two and a half in non-HICs, underscoring the need to deepen local peering ecosystems to unlock full connectivity.[12] Traffic capacity, measured by peak megabits per second (Mbps), also varies widely, reaching a median of over 470,000 Mbps in North America and over 340,000 Mbps in East Asia and Pacific, compared to just 556 Mbps in Sub-Saharan Africa.

Terrestrial fiber-optic cable

The compilation of terrestrial fiber-optic cable covers about 3.94 million km of long-haul, national, regional, and metro routes. The findings point to a widening "fiber divide," with nearly half of the global population living in 60 countries that fall below the median in fiber coverage both per capita and by land area. They include much of Sub-Saharan Africa and several rapidly growing economies such as Kenya and Nigeria. Countries like the Democratic Republic of Congo, Sierra Leone, and the Republic of Yemen have severe gaps, and even small high-income economies such as Kuwait and Qatar lag relative to their potential. The data also show that countries with denser terrestrial fiber enjoy significantly faster fixed broadband speeds, reinforcing the critical role of national fiber infrastructure in digital performance (figure 4.7).

FIGURE 4.6 Number of IXPs, by region and capacity

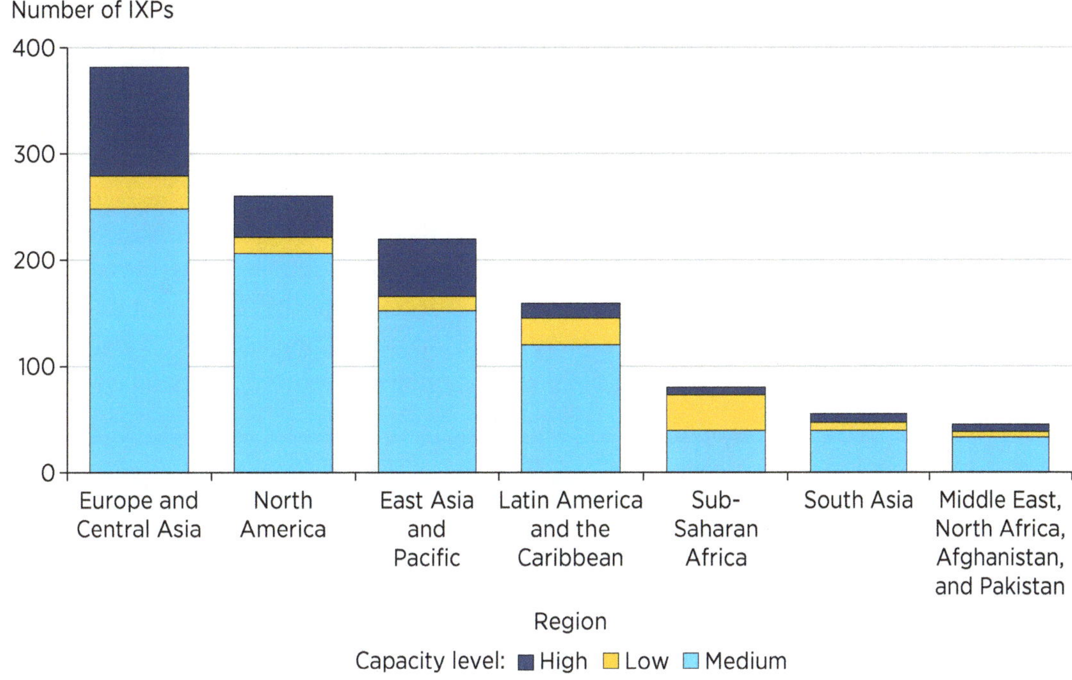

Source: Original figure for this publication.
Note: Capacity level is a composite of participants and peak traffic. The data are for 2025. IXP = internet exchange point.

FIGURE 4.7 Terrestrial fiber density and fixed download speed, by region

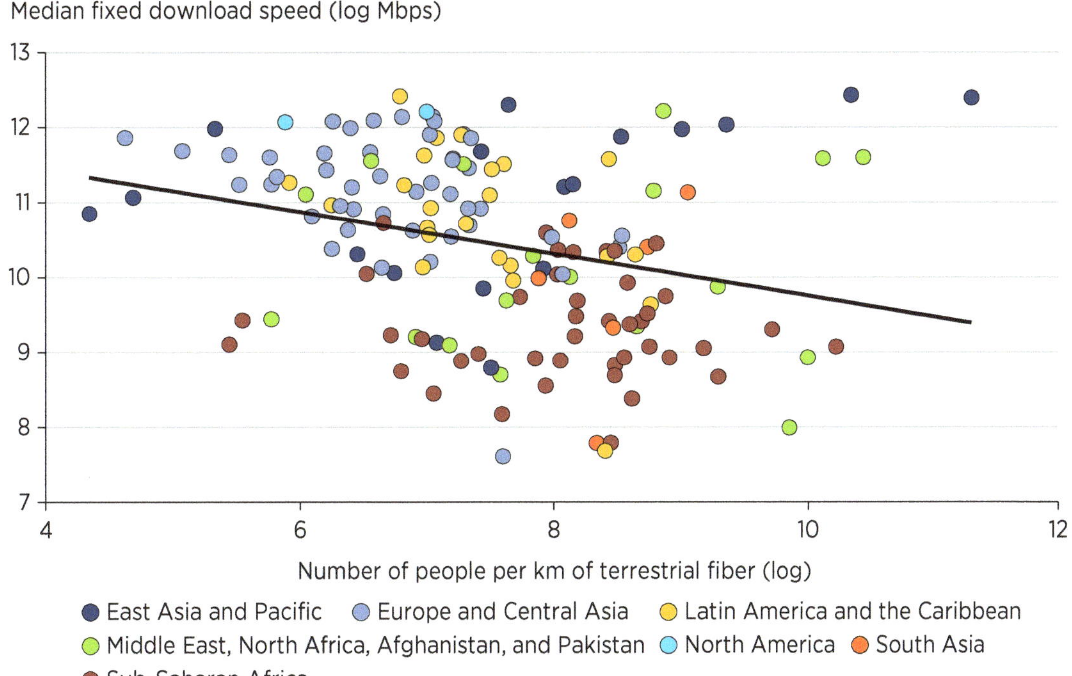

Sources: Original calculations based on data from Ookla, International Telecommunication Union, and Africa Bandwidth.
Note: The data are for 2025. km = kilometer; Mbps = megabits per second.

Submarine cables

Out of nearly 630 submarine cables, HICs dominate both total installed length and capacity, averaging about 85 terabits per second per million people, compared to the under 10 terabits per second seen in other income groups. Connectivity disparities remain sharp with 42 percent of low-income countries relying on just one or two landing points, and over a quarter of landlocked developing countries depending on neighbors with similarly limited access (figure 4.8). Regional differences are also striking, Europe and Central Asia and North America each averages over 0.6 cable per million people, about 4 times the levels in East Asia and Pacific and Sub-Saharan Africa, and 20 times the level in South Asia. In terms of capacity, the Europe and Central Asia region has a per capita capacity (192 terabits per second per million) roughly 74 times higher than South Asia's, underscoring the global asymmetry in international data connectivity.[13]

Subnational distribution

Africa's digital infrastructure remains highly concentrated along coastal corridors and major urban centers, where submarine cable landings, terrestrial backbones, data centers, and IXPs cluster around economic hubs. Large inland areas, particularly in the Sahel and Central Africa, show thinner coverage despite significant population presence (map 4.6).

FIGURE 4.8 Countries with submarine cable landing points, by income level

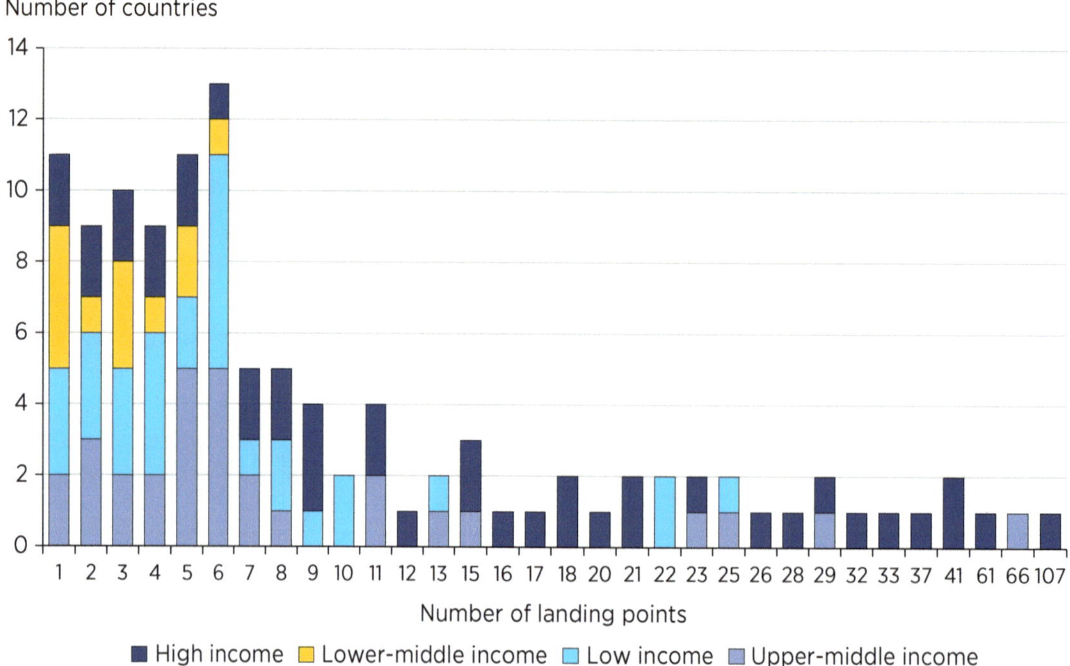

Source: Original figure for this publication.
Note: The figure includes only countries with populations over 1 million. Empty bins have been omitted from the horizontal axis for visual clarity. The data are for 2025.

Mobile networks help extend connectivity beyond these corridors, but the spatial mismatch between infrastructure density and population distribution highlights persistent gaps in continental digital access. Map 4.7 illustrates, for example, the expansion of digital infrastructure in Côte d'Ivoire since 2010.

MAP 4.6 Digital infrastructure in Africa, by type of technology, 2025

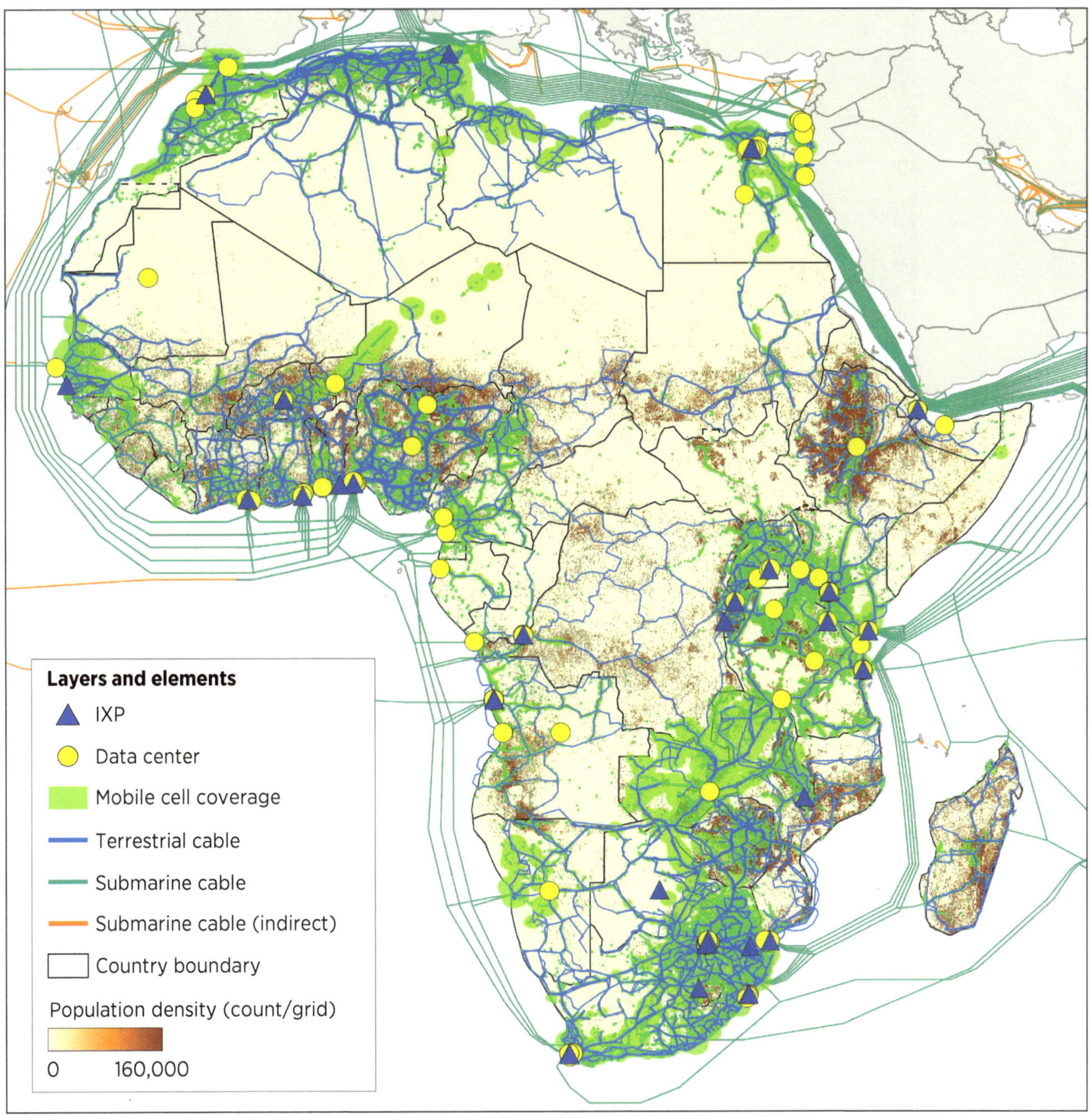

Source: Original map for this publication.
Note: IXP = internet exchange point.

MAP 4.7 **Expansion of digital infrastructure in Côte D'Ivoire, 2010 versus 2025**

a. 2010

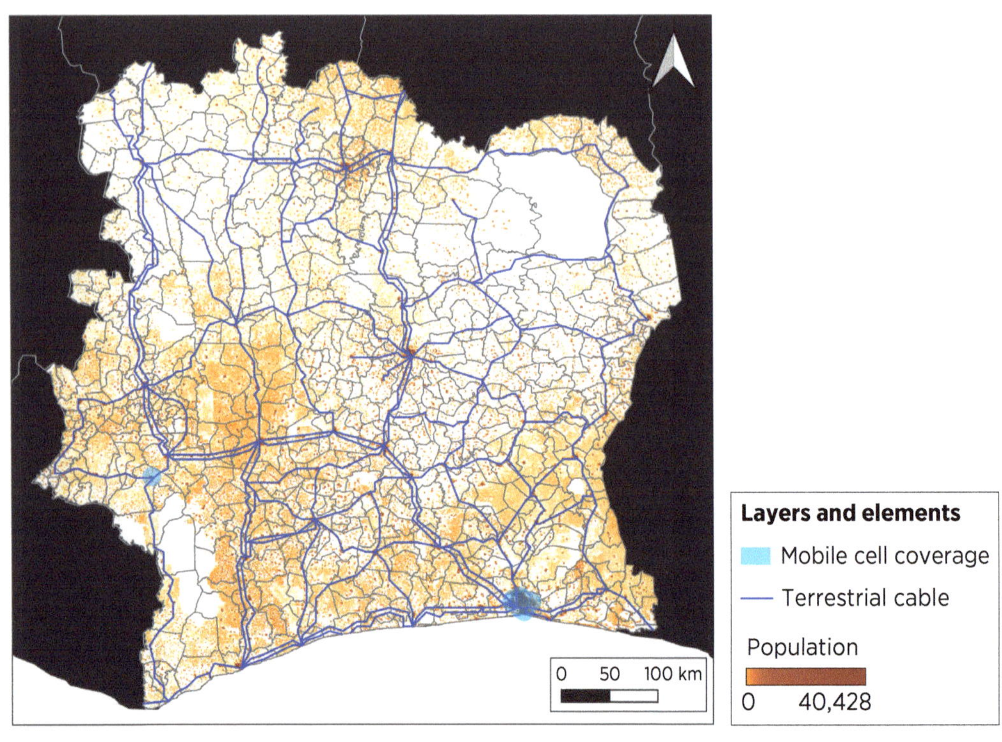

b. 2025

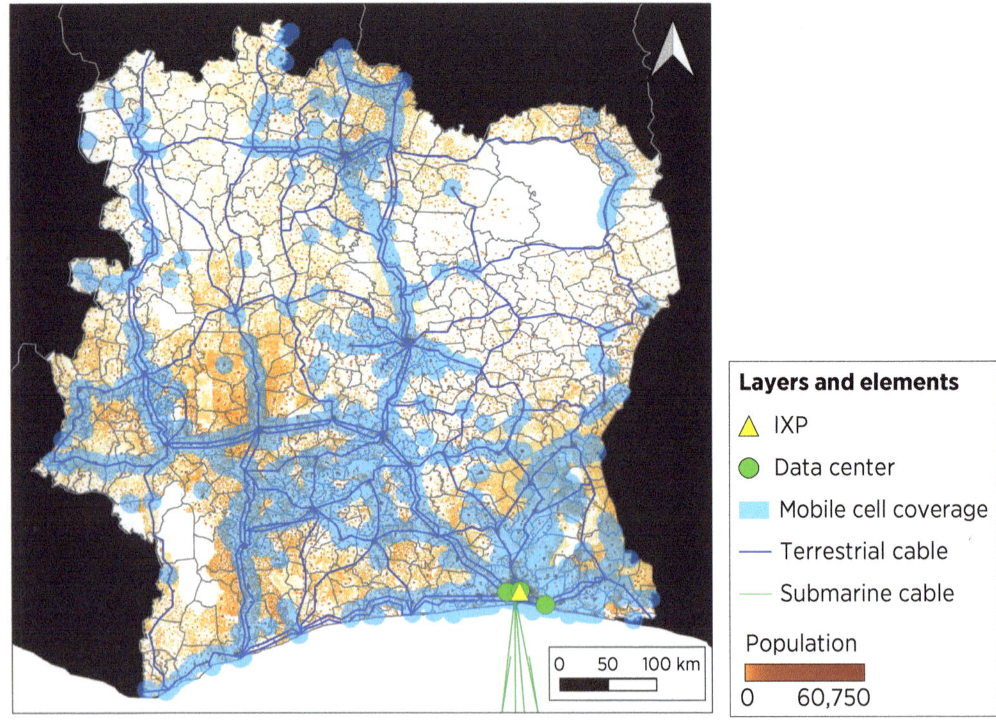

Source: Original figure for this publication.
Note: IXP = internet exchange point; km = kilometer.

ANNEX 4A. DATA SOURCES AND METHODOLOGY FOR MAPPING PHYSICAL STOCKS

TABLE 4A.1 Overview of data sources and methodology by sector

a. Energy				
Subsector	**Data source**	**Country coverage**	**Project coverage**	**Methodology note**
Generation	Global Energy Monitor World Resources Institute World Bank Electricity Planning Model GlobalData Construction Projects Database	196	8,851 GW 114,474 unique power plant records	Automated and manual matching processes were used to merge, add, and clean data sets.
Transmission and distribution	OpenStreetMap Energy Data GridFinder	200	11.8 million km	Automated and manual matching processes were used to merge, add, and clean data sets.

b. Transportation				
Subsector	**Data source**	**Country coverage**	**Project coverage**	**Methodology note**
Roads	OpenStreetMap	186	19.3 million km	Coverage includes all standard vehicular paved roads, but not restricted access or unpaved roads.
Railroads	OpenStreetMap	141	1.1 million km	Coverage includes urban, nonurban, passenger, and freight rail tracks, but not rolling stock. Country coverage includes only countries with rail infrastructure.

c. Digital				
Subsector	**Data source**	**Country coverage**	**Project coverage**	**Methodology note**
Data centers	TeleGeography Inc. Global Data Plc. DataCenters Map	122	8,232 total; refined to 7,863 unique entries	Automated and manual matching processes were used to merge, add, and clean data sets.
Radio access network[a]	OpenCellID Project by Unwired Labs	220	59m cells; approximately 10–20m macro sites[a]	Coverage includes estimated global stock of active mobile cells. Macro sites were estimated from the location of cells.
IXPs	TeleGeography Inc. Packet Clearing House, Inc.	175	1,200 IXPs	Coverage includes national and regional IXPs.
Terrestrial fiber-optic cables	International Telecommunication Union Africa Bandwidth	186	3.9 million km	Coverage includes core networks like long-haul, national, regional, and metro routes; it excludes last-mile.
Submarine cables	TeleGeography Inc. Global Data Plc. Online articles	185	628 cables; 1.8 million km	Coverage includes nearly all international connectivity routes.

Source: Original table for this publication.
Note: GW = gigawatt; IXP = internet exchange point; km = kilometer.
a. Covers second-generation through fifth-generation technologies.

ANNEX 4B. DETAILED DESCRIPTION OF THE METHODOLOGY FOR TRANSPORTATION

Table 4B.1 shows the OpenStreetMap (OSM) tags and corresponding values used to identify roads and railroads for the analysis. For roads, the surface tag is not consistently filled out across all roads, and those with missing values are not strictly paved or unpaved. Thus, including only those roads that were explicitly tagged as paved (or equivalent) would not yield an accurate assessment of the actual paved network extents. Instead, the analysis establishes reasonable upper and lower bounds for the network extent and, for the preferred estimate, takes the midpoint value.

TABLE 4B.1 OSM tags and values used to filter roads and railroads

Road		Rail	
Tag key	**Values**	**Tag key**	**Values**

highway	• motorway,
	• motorway_link,
	• trunk,
	• trunk_link,
	• primary,
	• primary_link,
	• secondary,
	• secondary_link,
	• tertiary,
	• tertiary_link,
	• unclassified,
	• residential
		railway	• tram,
			• tram_crossing,
			  tram_level_crossing,
			  tram_stop,
			• light_rail,
			• monorail,
			• subway,
			• rail,
			• narrow_gauge

surface[a]	• paved, • asphalt, • chipseal, • concrete, • concrete:lanes, • concrete:plates, • paving_stones, • paving_stones:lanes, • grass_paver, • sett, • unhewn_cobblestone, • cobblestone, • bricks, • metal	service	• main, • mainline, • highspeed, • freight, • regional, • commuter, • transport, • railway, • rail, • tram, • subway, • light_rail, • industrial, • monorail, • "N/A"
geom_type	• LineString, • MultiLineString	geom_type	• LineString, • MultiLineString
osm_type	• way		

Source: Original table for this publication.
Note: OSM = OpenStreetMap.
a. Used for initial identification of paved roads. Analysis was carried out for roads of all surface types. Refer to the description in the text.

For the lower bound, the roads tagged as paved (or equivalent) serve as a convenient conservative estimate. In other words, the lower bound is established by assuming that all the roads with missing surface information are unpaved. For the upper bound, applying the inverse assumption—that is, that all roads with missing surface information are paved—would be straightforward but likely yields too lax an estimate. In general, OSM roads data are more complete the more significant the road is. Thus, those roads with missing pavement information are broadly smaller roads, which are also more likely to be unpaved. Assuming that all roads with missing pavement information are paved can grossly overestimate network lengths, especially in low-income countries with a prevalence of unpaved roads and incomplete OSM data. Instead, for the upper bound, the analysis assumes that the share of roads that are paved (or equivalent) among the roads missing surface information is the same as that for which surface information is not missing, conditional on country and "highway" tag classification.

ANNEX 4C. ESTIMATION OF PHYSICAL SITES FROM MOBILE CELLS DATA

The estimation of physical sites for mobile coverage (for example, cell towers) consisted of analyzing and clustering approximately 59 million raw mobile cell records from Oracle Cloud Infrastructure, a global crowdsourced database. Each record represents a unique mobile cell or sector, defined by its coordinates, network operator, and radio technology (for example, GSM). The process began by cleaning and normalizing the coordinates, projecting them into country-specific planar coordinate systems, typically azimuthal equidistant or Universal Transverse Mercator projections, to ensure that distance calculations in meters were geographically meaningful.

Once spatially standardized, the algorithm used a density-based clustering method to group nearby cells belonging to the same operator into clusters interpreted as individual physical sites. The clustering parameters were regionally tuned, setting the neighborhood radius between 70 meters (m) in Europe and 120 m in Africa, and requiring at least three points per cluster to qualify as a site. This calibration reflected differences in tower density, topography, and urban morphology.

After initial clustering, additional spatial filters were applied to refine and consolidate sites. Clusters located within 50–100 m were merged to account for shared or multioperator towers, and a stricter 25–35 m deduplication radius was used to eliminate redundant records within the same operator, particularly in dense urban areas where antennas on a single mast might appear as separate entities because of Global Positioning System jitter. The resulting sites were enriched with technical attributes such as the number of sectors, radio technologies, median and 90th-percentile signal ranges, and first-seen year (approximating the installation date).

Each cluster was then classified as either a macro tower or a micro site on the basis of quantitative thresholds combining coverage radius and technical complexity. Specifically, a site was labeled macro if it exhibited (1) at least two sectors and a 90th-percentile signal range above 1.0 km, (2) two or more distinct radio technologies and a 90th-percentile range above 1.2 km, or (3) a maximum range above 2.0 km with multiple sectors.

Sites not meeting these thresholds were considered micro, typically representing small cells, rooftop nodes, or indoor installations. To avoid false positives, any site flagged as macro but with only one sector and range below 1.8 km was reassigned as micro.

Finally, each site's earliest time stamp was used to build cumulative country-year series of macro and micro sites, providing a temporal profile of network expansion from 2007 to 2025. To correct for systematic under- or overestimation due to OpenCellID's crowdsourced nature, regional adjustment multipliers were derived by comparing 2020 tower counts with TowerXchange benchmarks, then applied to scale non-HICs' totals. Although the results for micro sites were not validated because of the lack of reliable reference data, the estimates for macro sites (the only passive infrastructure component of the radio access networks computed for the capital stock, as defined in chapter 6) were validated against independent industry benchmarks. For example, according to EY-Parthenon (2024), Europe had approximately 500,000 cell towers by 2024, closely matching the estimated 446,107 macro sites. In Latin America, TowerXchange (2025a) reports about 245,587 telecom towers as of the first quarter of 2025, compared with 290,331 macro sites in this study. In Sub-Saharan Africa, TowerXchange (2025b) estimates 188,000 towers, whereas the model for this report yields 166,426 macro sites.

NOTES

1. IRENA (2025) estimates total off-grid capacity at 14.3 gigawatts, or approximately just 0.16 percent of total global installed power capacity as of 2024. Africa holds the second largest share of global off-grid capacity, surpassing even China in off-grid installations. The continent expanded its capacity mainly through decentralized solar solutions, supporting rural access and reliability; however, the same source estimates that Africa's off-grid generation capacity is only 0.9 percent of the total.
2. According to Fares and King (2016), for US investor-owned utilities, 30 percent of total capital expenditure is attributable to substations; the rest of the expenses go to transmission lines and towers. This share is likely an upper bound when compared to emerging markets figures.
3. The road and rail sectors combined made up between 81 percent and 93 percent of the total value in countries with complete data on transportation infrastructure capital value across all transportation subsectors in OECD Data Explorer, "Transport Infrastructure Investment and Maintenance Spending" (accessed November 21, 2025), https://data-explorer.oecd .org/vis?lc=en&pg=0&snb=62&vw=tb&df[ds]=dsDisseminateFinalDMZ&df[id]=DSD _INFRINV%40DF_INFRINV&df[ag]=OECD.ITF&df[vs]=1.0&dq=.A.INV.EUR..V&lom =LASTNPERIODS&lo=5&to[TIME_PERIOD]=false.
4. For more on OSM, refer to https://www.openstreetmap.org/#map=5/38.01/-95.84. This report is based on the July 1, 2025, snapshot, but the activities can be replicated with ease on an updated data set.
5. OSM data capture a greater average paved road network extent in low-income countries compared to data from the *CIA World Factbook* (CIA 2024, accessed on November 21, 2025, but no longer available) and the International Road Federation's *IRF World Road Statistics* (accessed November 21, 2025), https://worldroadstatistics.org/data/.
6. Refer also to National Oceanic and Atmospheric Administration, International Section, "Submarine Cables," https://www.noaa.gov/submarine-cables.
7. Coverage is nearly complete for submarine cables and IXPs (about 100 percent), high for core data centers and mobile cells (about 95 percent), and more limited for terrestrial fiber networks (between 40 percent and 80 percent) because of data constraints.

8. Based on data from OpenCellID, which covers about 59 million mobile cells across 220 countries.
9. Europe and Central Asia and North America show mature and dense LTE coverage, whereas South Asia and Sub-Saharan Africa remain dependent on GSM with limited LTE and New Radio rollout. East Asia and Pacific and Latin America and the Caribbean display transitional structures, where GSM and Universal Mobile Telecommunications System coexist with expanding LTE, and the Middle East, North Africa, Afghanistan, and Pakistan region shows gradual modernization within heterogeneous systems.
10. Macro sites are large, high-power installations, such as lattice towers or rooftop masts, that provide wide-area coverage, typically exceeding 1 km. Micro sites are low-power nodes that boost capacity and fill coverage gaps over shorter ranges, including pole-mounted antennas, distributed antenna systems, and indoor 4G/5G nodes. Because newer 4G and 5G networks operate at higher frequencies with shorter propagation ranges, they rely more heavily on dense deployments of micro cells; earlier 2G and 3G systems use lower frequencies, such as 800–900 megahertz, which propagate farther and penetrate buildings better.
11. Latin America and the Caribbean and the Middle East, North Africa, Afghanistan, and Pakistan occupy a middle ground, showing balanced but still macro-heavy networks.
12. IXP characteristics show clear differences in scale and performance, with Europe and Central Asia hosting the largest number of IXPs (276), followed by East Asia and Pacific (132) and North America (128), and wide differences in participation levels (East Asia and Pacific leads with 32) and traffic capacity (North America is at the top with 470,000 Mbps).
13. Submarine cable systems and their lengths and capacities are matched to countries on the basis of the presence of cable landings or base stations. When a single cable passes through multiple countries (for example, a system crossing five countries), each of those countries is assigned the full cable system and its total length and capacity. Therefore, country-level totals reflect territorial presence of cable infrastructure rather than a physical partitioning of the asset.

REFERENCES

CIA (US Central Intelligence Agency). 2024. "Roadways." *The World Factbook (2024 Archive).* https:// www.cia.gov/the-world-factbook/about/archives/2024/field/roadways/. Accessed November 21, 2025.

EY-Parthenon. 2024. "The Economic Contribution of the European Wireless Infrastructure Sector." Report for the European Wireless Infrastructure Association, EYGM Ltd. https://www.ey .com/content/dam/ey-unified-site/ey-com/en-gl/insights/strategy/documents/ey-parthenon -european-wireless-infrastructure-report-05-2024.pdf.

Fares, Robert L., and Carey W. King. 2016. "Trends in Transmission, Distribution, and Administration Costs for U.S. Investor Owned Electric Utilities." White Paper UTEI/2016-06-01, University of Texas at Austin Energy Institute.

IRENA (International Renewable Energy Agency). 2025. *Renewable Capacity Statistics 2025.* IRENA.

Mauldin, A. 2023. "Do Submarine Cables Account for Over 99% of Intercontinental Data Traffic?" *TeleGeography*, May 4, 2023. https://blog.telegeography.com/2023-mythbusting-part-3.

Meijer, Johan R., Mark A. J. Huijbregts, Kees C. G. J. Schotten, and Aafke M. Schipper. 2018. "Global Patterns of Current and Future Road Infrastructure." *Environmental Research Letters* 13 (6).

TowerXchange. 2025a. "TowerXchange's LATAM Guide: A Country-by-Country Guide of the Central and Latin American Tower Industry." TowerXchange. https://contents.comms.delinian.com /rs/462-OQR-635/images/Regional%20Guide.pdf?version=0.

TowerXchange. 2025b. "TowerXchange's Sub-Saharan African Guide: A Country-by-Country Guide to the African Tower Industry." TowerXchange. https://capacityglobal.com/news/telecom -tower-industry-towerxchanges-sub-saharan-african-guide/.

5

Unit Replacement Costs

KEY MESSAGES

Infrastructure provision costs vary widely across countries, sectors, and project types. Unit replacement costs for energy, transportation, and digital infrastructure display large dispersion across countries and within sectors, implying that similar physical investments can entail very different fiscal burdens depending on technology, location, and implementation context.

Technology choices are the primary driver of cost differences in the energy sector. Energy infrastructure is highly capital intensive, with unit costs varying substantially by generation technology. Modular renewable technologies such as solar photovoltaic and onshore wind have experienced sharp, sustained cost declines over time, reflecting learning effects and supply chain efficiencies, whereas fossil, hydro, and nuclear systems remain more capital intensive. Transmission costs are comparatively more uniform and driven mainly by voltage and geography.

Transportation construction costs exhibit extreme dispersion and strong sensitivity to scale, complexity, and context. Unit costs of roads and railways vary by more than an order of magnitude across projects. Economies of scale are evident for large, programmatic investments, and costs rise sharply with engineering complexity—such as bridges, tunnels, urban settings, and difficult terrain—and with more fragmented project structures. Road and rail construction costs are strongly correlated with gross domestic product (GDP) per capita, likely reflecting higher labor and material prices, stricter standards, and quality and regulatory requirements in richer countries.

Digital infrastructure costs are shaped by scale effects and market concentration. Across radio access networks, data centers, fiber, and submarine cables, unit costs display strong economies of scale. Large portfolios and hyperscale projects account for a disproportionate share of total investment; smaller, high-specification deployments drive up observed average costs, particularly in high-income markets.

A reproducibility package is available for this book in the Reproducible Research Repository at https://reproducibility.worldbank.org/catalog/536.

INTRODUCTION

This chapter estimates how much it costs to build the fundamental infrastructure that delivers energy, transportation, and digital services across countries. It describes a systematic effort to compile and analyze detailed data on construction costs. The central objective is to use these unit costs as building blocks to estimate how much it would take to replace existing infrastructure. Combined with the physical stocks in each country, and factoring in depreciation, the total value of these vital assets can be estimated.

Understanding the factors that drive variation in unit costs has important policy implications. When high costs arise from sources that can be influenced by policy, they can be directly addressed through targeted interventions. For example, if elevated railway construction costs reflect markups in concrete and steel production, freight transportation, or construction services, strengthening competition in these upstream sectors and improving procurement practices could help reduce costs. By contrast, when higher costs are driven by factors beyond immediate control, such as conflict or natural disasters, these conditions must be carefully accounted for in infrastructure investment decisions (Bosio et al. 2022; Liscow et al. 2025).

Wide disparities in road project expenditures across countries underscore the urgency of richer data and a deeper grasp of unit cost determinants—especially as fiscal pressures intensify (Collier et al. 2016). Past research has shown that underestimating construction costs and timelines can have serious consequences for project planning and delivery, for example in the power sector (Bacon and Besant-Jones 1998). Although the literature remains sparse, efforts to collect and explore data on construction costs of infrastructure have gradually expanded (Brooks and Liscow 2023; Link et al. 2016; Turner et al. 2023). This report aims to contribute meaningfully to this growing body of empirical knowledge.

The results show that energy infrastructure is highly capital intensive, and that technology choices strongly shape costs. Unit costs vary substantially across technologies, and renewable options such as solar photovoltaic and onshore wind are becoming increasingly cost competitive over time, reflecting learning effects and supply chain efficiencies. The results also show that transportation construction costs exhibit clear economies of scale, with larger programmatic investments associated with lower unit costs. Meanwhile, complex assets such as bridges and tunnels—as well as difficult construction environments including rugged terrain, dense urbanization, and heavy rainfall—are systematically linked to higher costs. Higher GDP per capita is also associated with higher unit costs, likely reflecting differences in labor, materials, equipment, and regulatory requirements. Finally, the results show that digital infrastructure costs display strong scale effects and marked regional disparities, with investment highly concentrated in large tower portfolios and hyperscale data centers. Unit costs are consistently higher in high-income markets, and fiber and internet exchange point (IXP) costs are elevated in project data because these investments often reflect short, high-specification deployments rather than the bulk of network rollouts.

OVERVIEW OF METHODOLOGY

To estimate the unit costs of constructing and maintaining various types of energy, transportation, and digital infrastructure projects, this chapter draws on a wide array of data sources. The methodological choices are guided by both the availability of reliable data and empirical evidence regarding the degree of cost variation observed in comparable construction activities.

In the energy sector, research finds that technology and learning effects are the most influential determinants of installation costs for power plants, although geographic, institutional, and macro-socioeconomic factors also play important roles. Fossil, hydro, and nuclear technologies remain the most capital intensive, whereas modular, mass-produced renewables (such as solar photovoltaic and onshore wind) exhibit the lowest capital intensity.[1] These renewables have benefited the most from learning effects and supply chain efficiencies. Notably, installation costs for transmission lines tend to be more uniform across countries than costs for power plants, with variations primarily driven by voltage requirements and geographic conditions (IEA 2021; IRENA 2023).

To ensure that the analysis reflects the latest developments, this chapter leverages the most current data from leading international agencies on the installation costs required to produce 1 megawatt of electricity-generating capacity across fossil, nuclear, and renewable technologies, accounting for countries' diverse energy mixes (IEA 2024; IRENA 2024). Empirical models and machine learning techniques are also applied to validate these estimates. For transmission networks, this chapter relies on World Bank project data to estimate the capital costs of constructing 1 kilometer (km) of transmission lines across six different voltage levels (World Bank 2026). For time coverage and other details for energy, refer to annex 5A.

In the realm of transportation infrastructure, the literature documents substantial variation in unit replacement costs both across and within countries. For roads and railways, factors such as project design, labor costs, input prices, and geographic conditions are all critical. Even after accounting for these determinants, however, significant residual cost dispersion remains—often correlating with local institutional factors (including corruption, sponsor characteristics, and procurement capacity) and broader macro-socioeconomic conditions such as conflicts (Collier et al. 2016; Faber 2014; Liscow et al. 2025).

Building on that body of research, this chapter develops empirical models to estimate the unit costs of linear transportation projects, specifically the costs to construct 1 km of paved roads or railways (annex 5A). The approach incorporates the key cost drivers identified in the literature and leverages a comprehensive global project-level database—encompassing more than 5,000 road projects and over 3,000 rail projects across 139 countries from 1980 to 2025. The estimated coefficients are applied to predict construction costs for the corresponding physical infrastructure stocks.

In the digital sector, unit replacement costs vary widely because each subsector responds to different technical, geographic, and economic drivers. For example, costs for radio access network (RAN) are shaped by physical conditions such as terrain, by settlement patterns such as population density and urbanization, by the availability of supporting infrastructure, and by technology and labor costs. IXP costs reflect the sophistication of the exchange, ranging from small university-hosted setups to carrier-grade installations. Data center costs are driven by technology requirements, land and energy prices, labor market conditions, supply chain depth, and site remoteness, which are often less favorable in developing economies (Cushman and Wakefield 2023; Oughton 2023; Oughton et al. 2022; Rahkonen et al. 2020; World Bank 2021, 2022).

Using a consistent data-driven approach, the analysis integrates project-level and benchmark information across subsectors. Overall, the data set includes more than 4,000 projects with cost data. For RAN, the analysis uses 301 tower sale transactions across 75 countries, covering about 1.24 million macro sites from 2007 to 2025. Data center estimates draw on 2,259 construction records from 58 countries (2003–25). Terrestrial fiber relies on 128 projects from 37 countries (2009–28), and submarine systems on 288 projects worldwide (1993–2025). Because of the absence of direct cost data, IXP costs were derived using an engineering table approach based on capacity and number of participants (annex 5A).

ENERGY

This section presents the steps taken to derive unit costs for energy projects, covering both power generation by specific technology and transmission lines. It details the main sources and the methodology, and presents some general stylized facts on the unit costs used in this report.

Power generation

To estimate the capital costs of power plants, the analysis draws on two authoritative sources, the International Energy Agency (IEA 2024) and the International Renewable Energy Agency (IRENA 2024). Both organizations compile cost estimates relying on a mix of utility surveys; submitted cost data from governments, utilities, and industry; reported project data; and market intelligence. For each source, the chapter applies the most detailed unit cost estimates available, combining variations across location, technology subtype, and plant size.[2]

IEA publishes 2023 unit costs for coal, gas, oil, and nuclear power plants in nine regions and countries, including major countries such as Brazil, China, India, Japan, and the United States. Figure 5.1 presents the available information, broken down by specific technologies. Gas-fired or oil-fired power plants are typically less capital intensive in terms of construction costs; for example, because of their compact and modular turbine design, gas-fired power plants' unit costs averaged US$1,000 per kilowatt. Coal-fired plants are more expensive, given their larger physical footprint and the need for extensive boiler and emissions-control systems. Among coal-based generation technologies, capital costs increase with technological sophistication. Combined-cycle power plants report unit costs of about US$1,500 per kilowatt. For all technologies, adding carbon capture and storage technology increases the capital cost by 50 percent.

FIGURE 5.1 Unit cost of fossil and nuclear technologies, by type of technology, selected countries and regions

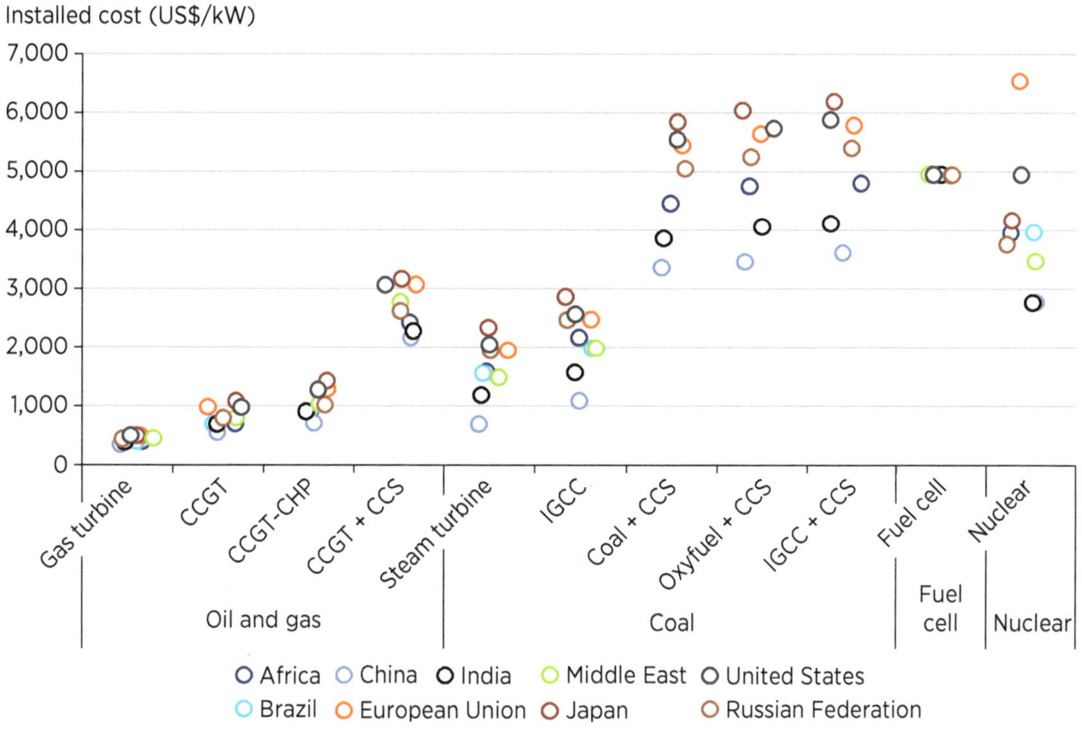

Source: Original calculations based on IEA 2024.
Note: CCGT = combined cycle gas turbine; CCS = carbon capture and storage; CHP = combined hear and power; IGCC = integrated gasification combined cycle; kW = kilowatt.

Because not all power plants report their specific technologies, the compiled data set relies on the following assumptions. For oil and gas plants that don't mention their technologies, the data set uses the installed (that is, overnight construction) cost of combined-cycle gas turbine as the default value. For coal-fired power plants, the chapter assumes that power plants built 20 years ago use subcritical coal technology and that those built less than 20 years ago use supercritical coal technology. Because the unit cost of fossil fuels remains relatively stable over time, the GDP deflator is used to adjust price changes in previous years. To address spatial data gaps, the methodology applies country-level cost differentials derived from machine learning–based construction cost estimates using a global project-level data set covering fossil fuel power generation in 152 countries. Predicted project costs are aggregated to the country level, and deviations from the global average are used to construct relative cost ratios that are applied to unit cost estimates. For countries without IEA-reported fossil fuel cost data, the implied country-level differentials are applied; for countries lacking information in both the IEA and project data sets, unit costs are imputed using the global average. Additional details on the machine learning–based construction cost validation are provided in box 5.1.

BOX 5.1

Power generation unit cost: Benchmarking with machine learning validation

Estimating the unit cost of power generation projects typically relies on international benchmarks such as averages from the International Energy Agency (IEA) and International Renewable Energy Agency (IRENA). These averages provide a consistent global reference basis but can mask wide variations in project-level costs—especially in data-sparse developing countries.

To test the robustness of these benchmarks, a background paper for this report (Li, Lyu, and Steinbuks 2025) applies a suite of machine learning models to 4,358 completed power plant projects across 152 countries from the GlobalData Construction Database. The models relate unit costs to project-specific characteristics (capacity, technology, financing), geographic variables (location, terrain, night-light intensity), and national factors (governance, labor costs, market structure). This approach follows a parsimonious theoretical framework analogous to that used for linear transportation investment in this chapter.

A broad suite of machine learning algorithms is applied, including Ridge and Lasso (least absolute shrinkage and selection operator) regressions, generalized additive models, tree-based learning models, and nonlinear techniques (support vector machine and neural network). Simple averages of regression, tree-based, and other nonlinear families are also computed as ensemble baselines.

Results show that machine learning methods—particularly tree-based algorithms—reduce median prediction error by about 30 percent compared to the world average benchmark and achieve about 20 percent lower root mean square error. Approximately 60 percent of the time, the machine learning models predict a more accurate estimate with smaller absolute error compared to the world average. The accuracy of unit cost estimates relying on the IEA and IRENA global averages can thus be improved using weights generated by the machine learning methods based on project capacity, location, and technology configurations. However, these gains come at a cost: implementing such models requires extensive data preparation and computational resources.

Overall, although machine learning offers valuable validation and refinement, the internationally accepted IEA and IRENA benchmarks remain a reliable and interpretable basis for assessing power generation costs, especially in the case of limited project-level data.

IRENA reports annual installed costs for renewable generation technologies with varying levels of disaggregation. To illustrate the data coverage, figure 5.2a presents solar facility costs for 15 countries and figure 5.2b presents wind farm costs for 45 countries. Solar installation costs, dominated by solar photovoltaic technology,[3] have declined consistently over time, with cross-country disparities narrowing, indicative of technological maturation and spillovers. Wind installation costs show comparable trends: onshore costs have fallen steadily since the 1980s, and offshore costs have experienced a sharper decline since the late 2000s, likewise reflecting accelerated deployment and maturation and technology spillovers. The unit cost of hydropower generation varies significantly depending on generation capacity and regional factors, as indicated in figure 5.3. To account for these variations, this chapter assigns the global average installed unit cost based on capacity, adjusting for time trends using the GDP deflator. Given significant technological progress driving the capital costs of modern renewables, it further refines the unit cost over the period from 2010 to 2023 by incorporating more recent time and regional variations. More details are available in annex 5B.

FIGURE 5.2 Installed unit cost of selected renewable technologies, by year

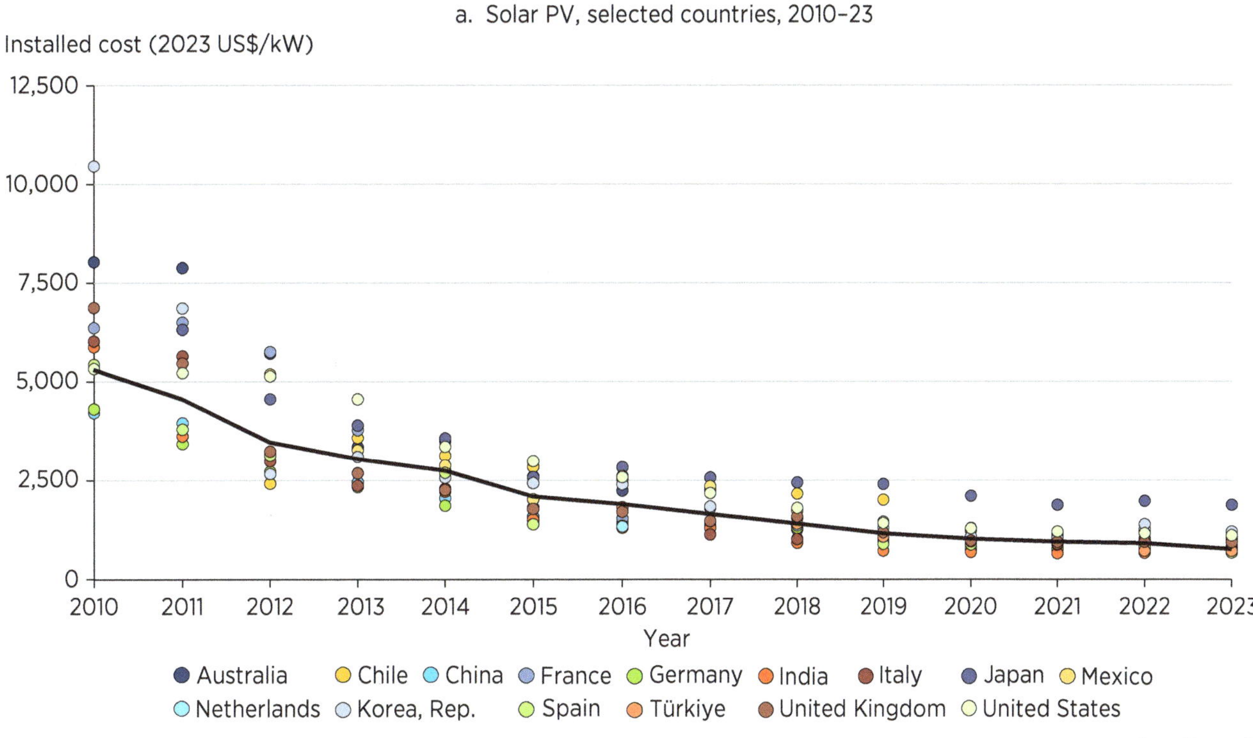

a. Solar PV, selected countries, 2010–23

(continued)

FIGURE 5.2 Installed unit cost of selected renewable technologies, by year *(continued)*

b. Onshore and offshore wind power, by region, 1984–2023

Installed cost (2023 US$/kW)

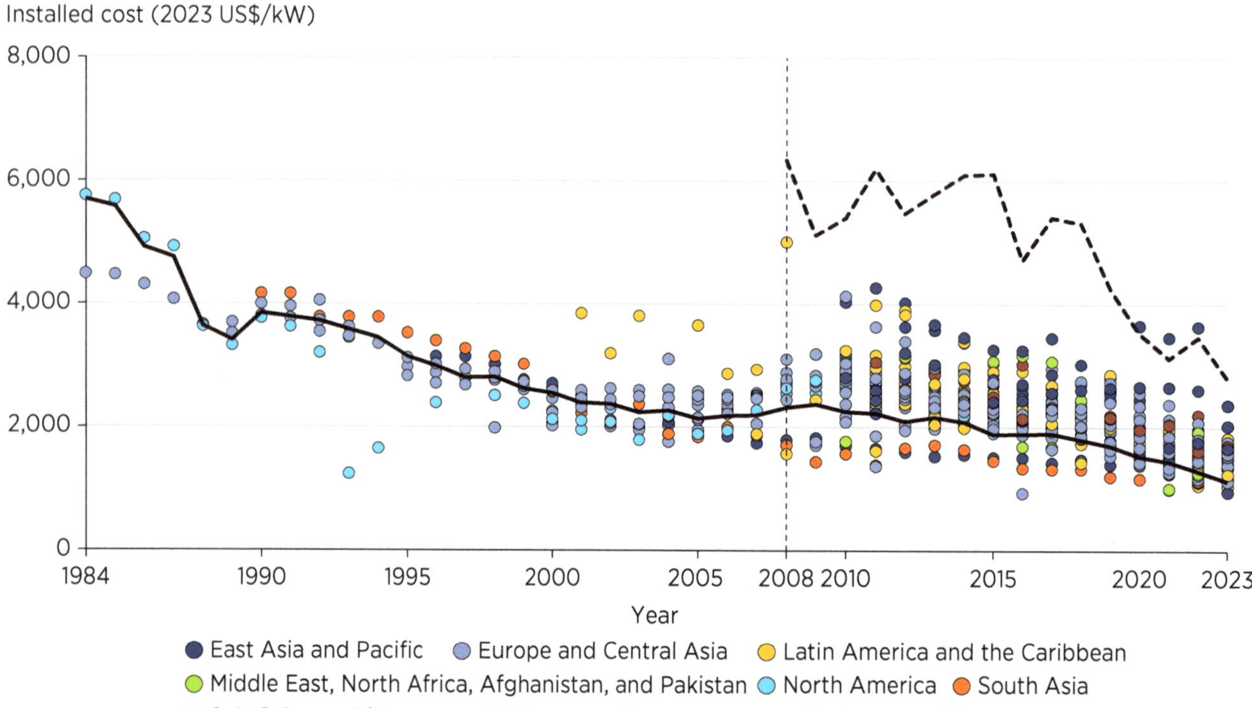

Source: Original calculations based on IRENA 2024.
Note: kW = kilowatt; PV = photovoltaic.

FIGURE 5.3 Installed cost of hydro power, 2016–23

Installed cost (2023 US$/kW)

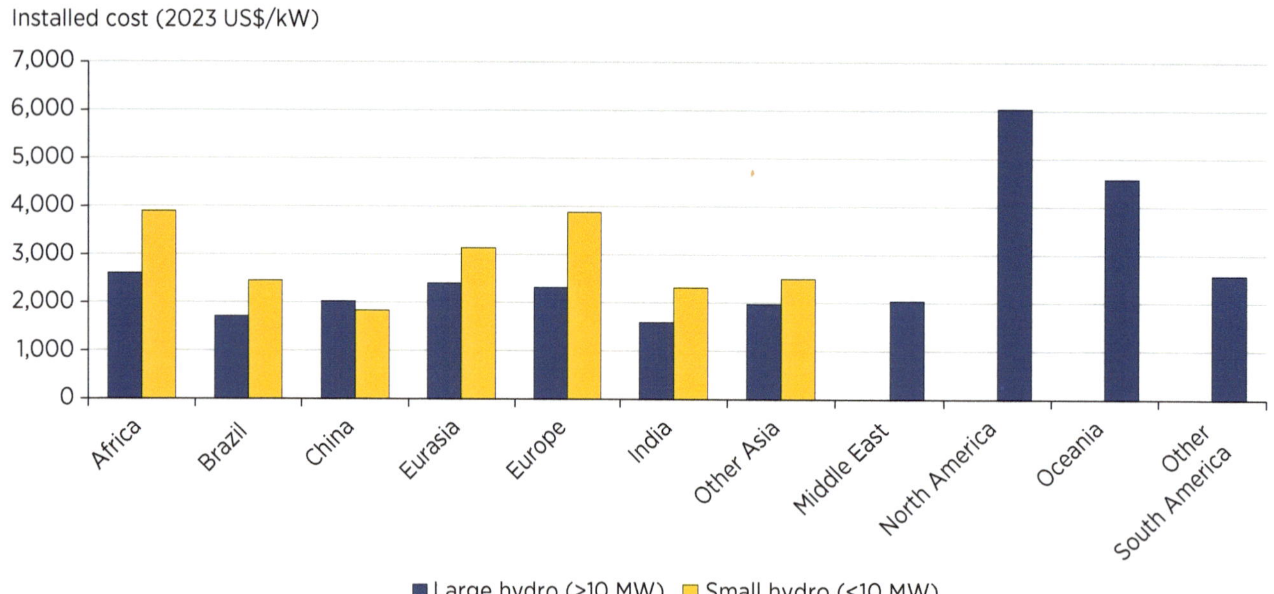

Source: Original calculations based on IRENA 2024.
Note: Region names in figure 5.3 are based on treatment in the source and differ from World Bank region names. kW = kilowatt; MW = megawatt.

Transmission and distribution lines

The report estimates the capital cost of transmission lines using unit cost information derived from past World Bank project documents. The data are drawn from a systematic review of World Bank–financed projects initiated between 2003 and 2025. The sample for transmission lines includes 75 projects, with an average completion period of seven years. Figure 5.4 presents the average unit costs for transmission lines. As expected, unit costs rise with voltage, reflecting the higher construction and material requirements of lines that transmit electricity.[4]

The sample for distribution lines includes nine projects initiated between 2008 and 2021. Because of the limited sample size, a single representative unit cost is estimated at US$0.125 million/km (in constant 2024 prices). To assign costs, each line in the data set of physical transmission infrastructure described in chapter 3 is matched to its voltage-specific unit cost whenever voltage data are available.[5]

TRANSPORTATION

This section adopts a well-known framework and derives a simple empirical model to explain and predict the unit cost of linear transportation projects, including railways and roads (box 5.2). The framework builds on intuitive results from a standard production function: unit cost rises with input prices, declines with implementation efficiency, and can

FIGURE 5.4 Unit cost for transmission lines, selected regions and subregions

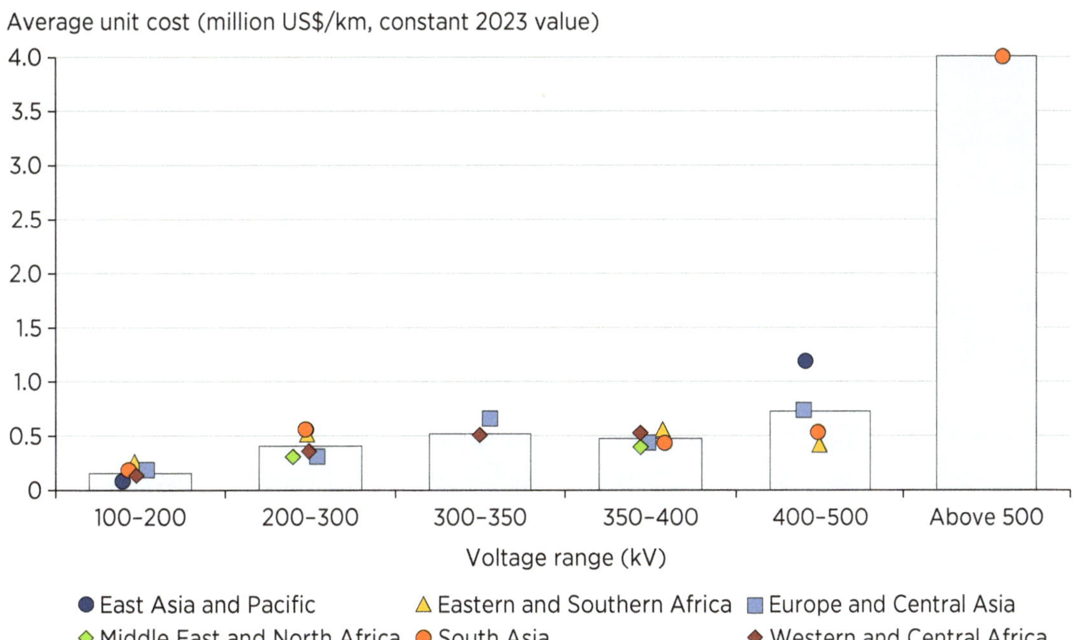

Source: Original calculations based on World Bank 2026. Region names are based on the review of past projects, which used the previous World Bank regional classification.
Note: km = kilometer; kV = kilovolt.

vary with project capacity, depending on the existence of economies of scale. The derived empirical model captures the variations of project design, location factors, time-varying country characteristics, and other macro-socioeconomic shocks.

BOX 5.2

Transportation sector unit cost: Framework and empirical modeling

Think of constructing a linear transportation project—say, a two-track commuter rail line. Let x_1 denote the size of the project (measured as track length in kilometers). A firm chooses labor (x_2) and other inputs such as capital services and materials (q) to deliver w_1 at the lowest possible cost, given input prices w_1 and w_2:

$$\min w_1 x_1 = w_2 x_2 \text{ subject to } q = f(x_1, x_2)$$

Without losing generality, assume a Cobb–Douglas production function: $f(x_1, x_2) = A^{-\delta} x_1^{\alpha} x_2^{\beta}$, where A summarizes the efficiency of the broader environment in which firms operate: procurement quality, institutions, and so on. The parameters α and β capture how responsive construction output is to labor and other inputs.

Solving the firm's problem yields a compact expression for average (unit) cost:

$$\frac{C(w_1, w_2, q)}{q} = \theta(\alpha, \beta) A^{\frac{\delta}{\alpha+\beta}} q^{\frac{1-(\alpha+\beta)}{\alpha+\beta}} w_1^{\frac{\alpha}{\alpha+\beta}} w_2^{\frac{\beta}{\alpha+\beta}}.$$

This formula is intuitive. Unit cost rises with input prices, increases with efficiency, and varies with project size. The exponent on q reveals whether economies of scale exist.

For empirical modeling, let $c = C/q$ and take logarithmic transformations. Adding project type (technology) and time fixed effects plus an error term gives

$$lnc_{psct} = D_{ps} + D_t + \gamma A_{ct} + \phi_0 lnq_{psct} + \phi_1 lnw_{1psct} + \phi_2 lnw_{2psct} \in_{psct}$$

for project p, type (technology) s, country c, and announced year t.

The fixed effects D_{ps} absorb systematic differences across work types, technology complexity, and funding and implementation models—that is, public versus private; D_t nets out global shocks that elevate costs across all projects.

Clearly, two margins are central for investment decisions. First is scale: ϕ_0 indicates whether building longer railway lowers unit costs, which informs sizing decisions. Second is prices: ϕ_1 and ϕ_2 capture how strongly wages, rental costs of equipment, and material prices feed into unit costs.

Because detailed project-level wage and input prices are not observed, country-level variables are used as proxies. Time-variant construction sector wages, construction

(continued)

> **BOX 5.2** **Transportation sector unit cost: Framework and empirical modeling**
> **(continued)**
>
> sector market concentration levels, and prices of key materials (cement, steel),
> alongside gross domestic product per capita are relied on as a broad input price
> anchor. Local factors along the alignment of the linear infrastructure project are also
> considered because they may determine input prices. Particularly, geographic and
> environmental covariates include terrain ruggedness, mean annual rainfall, luminosity,
> and built-up volume.
>
> Finally, unit costs are not determined by technology and input prices alone, but are
> embedded in an institutional context. Motivated by Collier et al. (2016) and Liscow,
> Slattery, and Nober (2025), efficiency is measured using the World Governance
> Indicators and regional fixed effects, which capture procurement integrity, regulatory
> quality, and broader government capacity. Putting these elements together, the final
> empirical specification is
>
> $$lnc_{psct} = \lambda_1 X_{psct} + \lambda_2 Z_{ct} + D_{ps} + D_t + \epsilon_{psct},$$
>
> where X_{psct} represents project-level geographic and environmental characteristics that
> influence input prices, and Z_{ct} denotes country-level time-varying proxies for input
> prices and market structure, as well as measures on inefficiency. The final analysis relies
> on gross domestic product per capita and regional dummies because of collinearity
> among country-level variables.
>
> *Source:* Based on Collier et al. 2016 and Link et al. 2016.

The models are estimated using a comprehensive database of real-world construction
projects compiled by GlobalData Plc. The cleaned data set contains 5,327 road
projects and 3,341 rail projects announced between 1980 and 2025, with a significant
concentration in the period after 2010. Each project entry includes detailed characteristics,
such as the type of work, physical components, funding and implementation modality,
and, crucially, the project's value. This project-level information is complemented with
an array of publicly available data to capture location- and country-level characteristics.
For the subsequent analysis and modeling, all project values have been inflated to 2024
US dollars.

Consistent with the literature, unit costs exhibit considerable variation across the projects.
For example, the 5th–95th percentile range of cost per kilometer of road spans from
US$0.6 million to US$38.3 million. Consequently, using naïve average costs can yield
grossly inaccurate estimates of construction costs and asset valuations. Figure 5.5 shows
the distribution of unit costs by income group for roads and railways. The modes of
both distributions sit below US$1 million per kilometer but have very long right tails.
Furthermore, costlier projects tend to be constructed in higher-income countries.

FIGURE 5.5 Count and unit cost of linear transportation projects, by income group

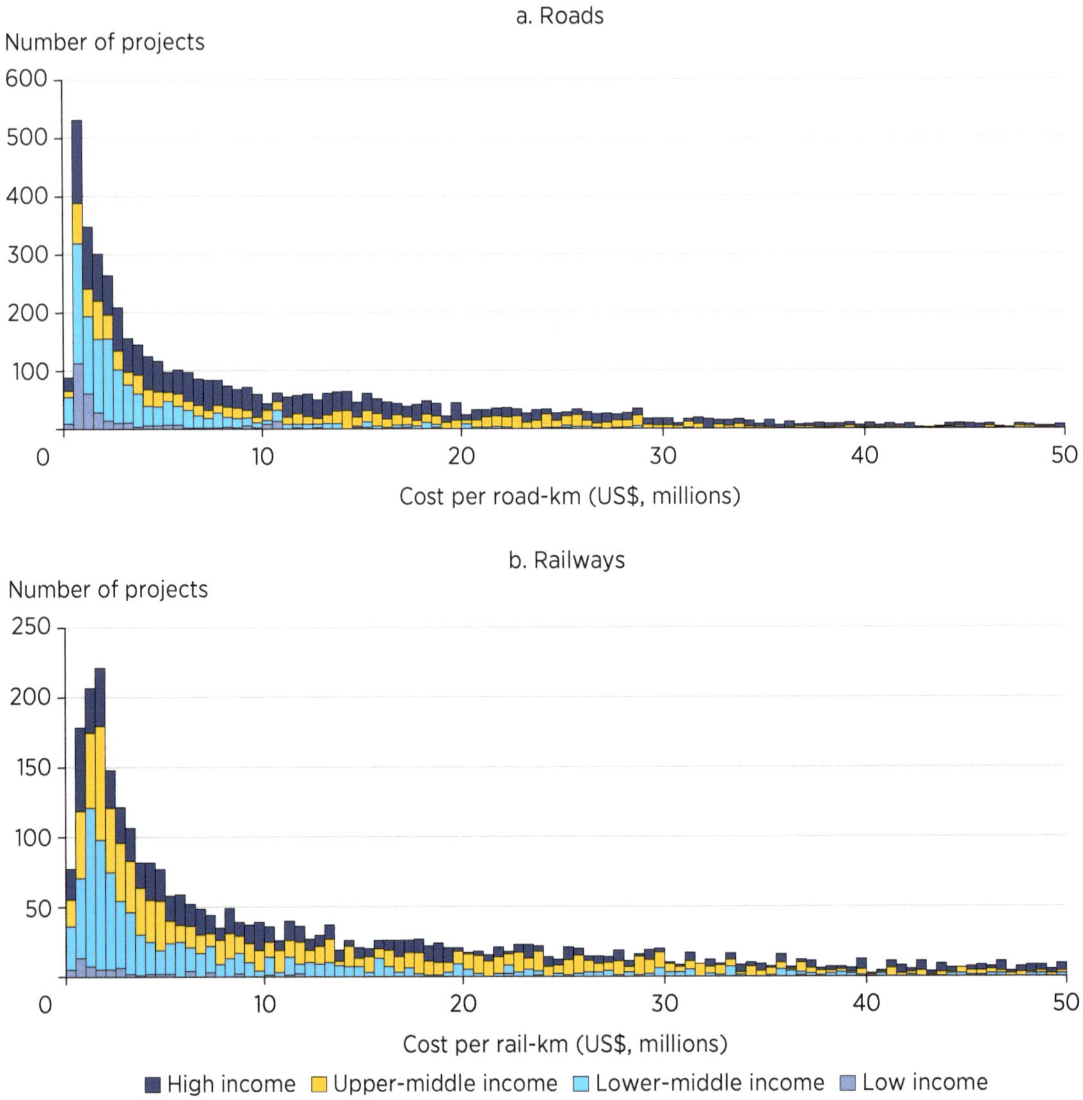

a. Roads

b. Railways

Source: Original calculations based on GlobalData Plc.
Note: km = kilometer.

The box-and-whisker plots in figures 5.6 and 5.7 show distributions of unit costs for road and rail grouped by specific attributes. The top and bottom whiskers indicate the maximum and minimum unit costs in the sample data (excluding outliers), and the three lines within the box show the first, second, and third quartiles.

Figure 5.6a examines the difference in unit costs for road projects with and without bridges and tunnels. Unsurprisingly, projects involving more complex infrastructure tend to be more expensive. Figure 5.6b shows unit cost differences by work type for road projects. As expected, new construction is costlier than redevelopment, upgrade, and renovation.

FIGURE 5.6 Unit cost of roads, by project characteristics

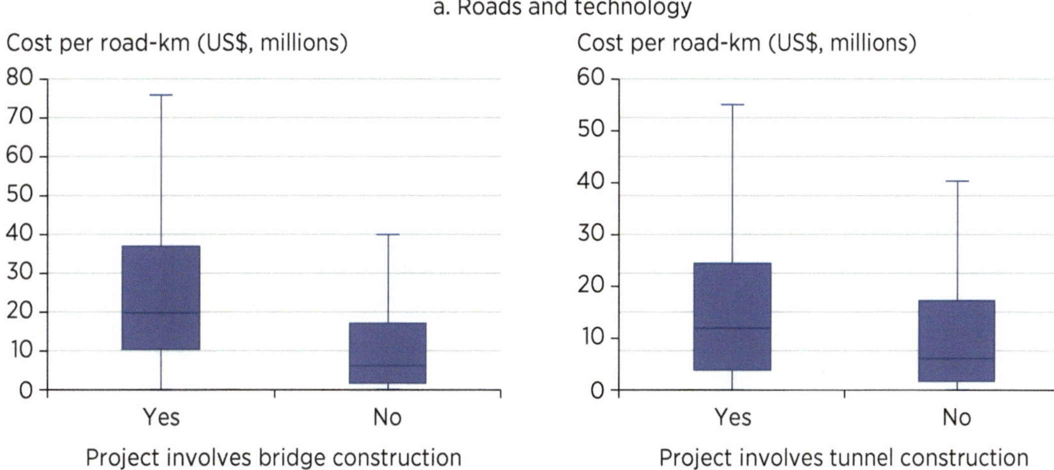

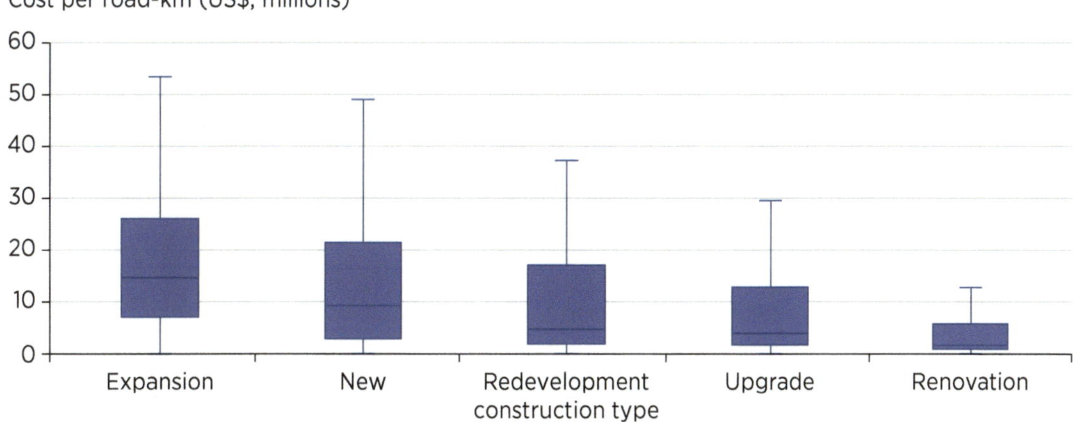

Source: Original calculations based on GlobalData Plc.
Note: km = kilometer.

However, expansion projects in the data set are generally more expensive on a per-kilometer basis than new projects, likely reflecting the composition of expansion projects that intrinsically comprise more lanes, tend to be in high-demand areas, and more often involve construction of highways or other high-quality roads.

Figure 5.7a shows the distribution of unit costs for rail projects by rail type. Evidently, urban rail projects tend to be more expensive than nonurban ones, emphasizing the importance of controlling for spatial context. Similarly, Figure 5.7b shows the distribution of unit costs for rail projects by project type (programmatic, parent, sub, sub-sub). As project components are divided and subcontracted, unit costs increase, on average, which could be a result of more complex components being subcontracted and an indication of economies of scale in project organization.

FIGURE 5.7 Unit cost of railways, by project characteristics

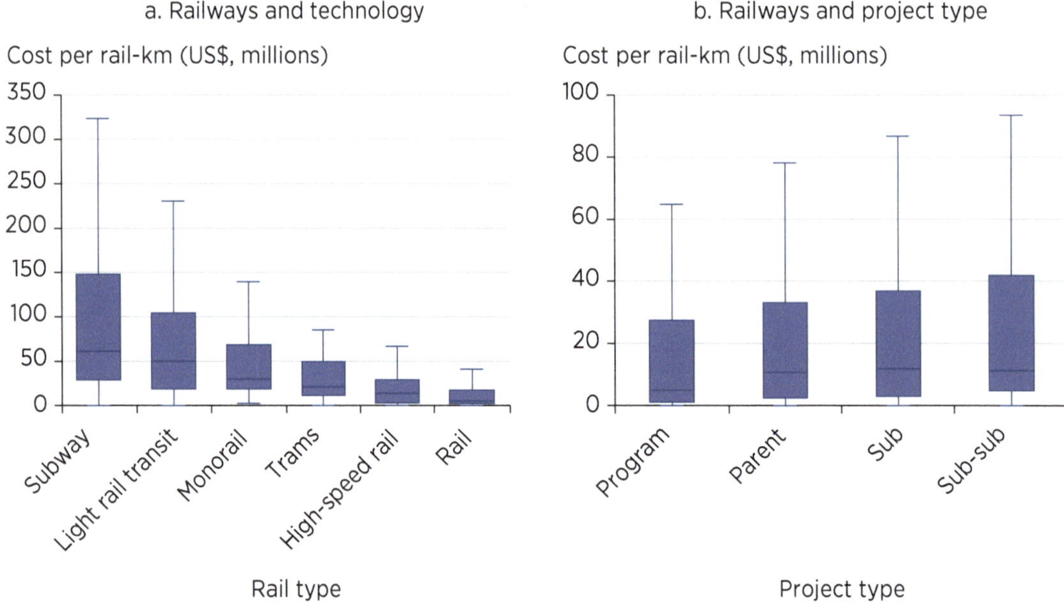

Source: Original calculations based on GlobalData Plc.
Note: km = kilometer.

Taking a more systematic approach to addressing the variation in unit costs, figures 5.8 and 5.9 show the results of the empirical analysis for roads and rail, respectively. For ease of interpretation, the figures report standardized coefficients. Across both road and rail construction projects, a negative association with the announcement year suggests that construction has become cheaper in real terms, all else equal. Economies of scale are evident for road construction projects: unit costs change inelastically with the number of lanes, and large-scale programmatic projects are associated with lower unit costs. For railway projects, programmatic projects are also associated with a negative coefficient, which is, however, not significant at a 95 percent confidence level. Interestingly, the public funding mode is associated with lower unit costs for rail projects but higher unit costs for road projects—although the association is only marginally significant for the latter. For both sectors, new construction is more expensive than upgrading, renovation, redevelopment, and even expansion once other factors have been controlled for.

Infrastructure type, environment, and country income are all associated with higher costs. In general, more complex infrastructure, such as bridges, tunnels, and stations, is associated with larger project unit costs. Similarly, more challenging construction environments, including terrain ruggedness, dense surrounding buildup, and heavy precipitation, are associated with larger project unit costs for both subsectors. GDP per capita is strongly correlated with high construction costs for both road and rail projects, reflecting the effects of underlying factors, such as labor costs, material and equipment costs, social and environmental regulation, and capacity.

FIGURE 5.8 Modeling results for the unit cost of roads, by project characteristics, income level, and region

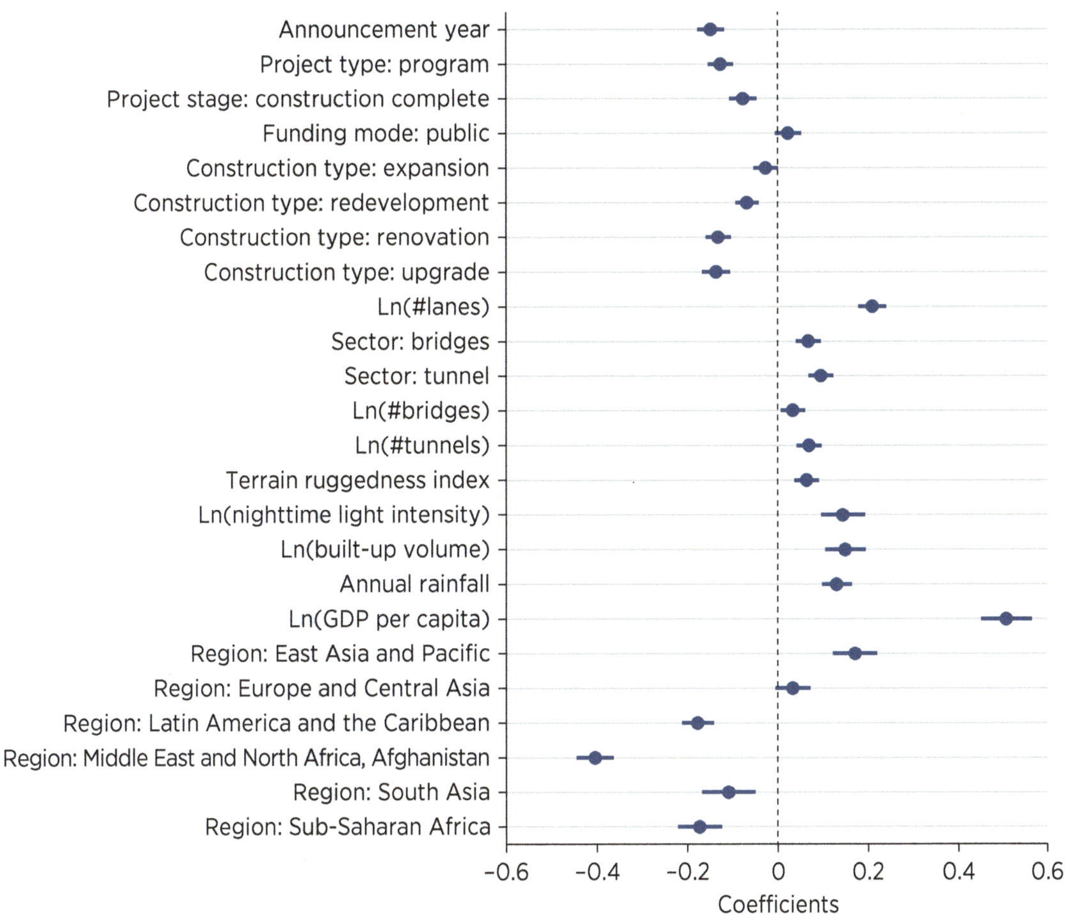

Source: Original calculations for this publication.
Note: All estimates are standardized for visual display and plotted with 95 percent confidence intervals. Estimations used dummy variables based on previous World Bank regional classification. Base category for Project type is Parent, Sub, or Sub-sub. Base category for Project stage is Canceled, Design, EPC award, Execution, On-hold, Planning, Pre-design, Pre-tender, Study, or Tender. Base category for Funding mode is Public/Private or Private. Base category for Construction type is New. Base category for Region is North America. EPC = engineering, procurement, and construction.

Unit costs vary across regions. They appear to be highest in East Asia and Pacific for both road and rail, but generally appear lower in Latin America and the Caribbean. The remaining regions show no common pattern between the two subsectors; however, regional variation is broadly more pronounced for the road sector. In general, the regional effects serve as catchalls for residuals that have not otherwise been controlled for, such as quality. Consequently, it appears sensible that more local heterogeneity occurs in road quality and construction methods, whereas railways perhaps require more uniform standards.

FIGURE 5.9 Modeling results for the unit cost of railways, by project characteristics, income level, and region

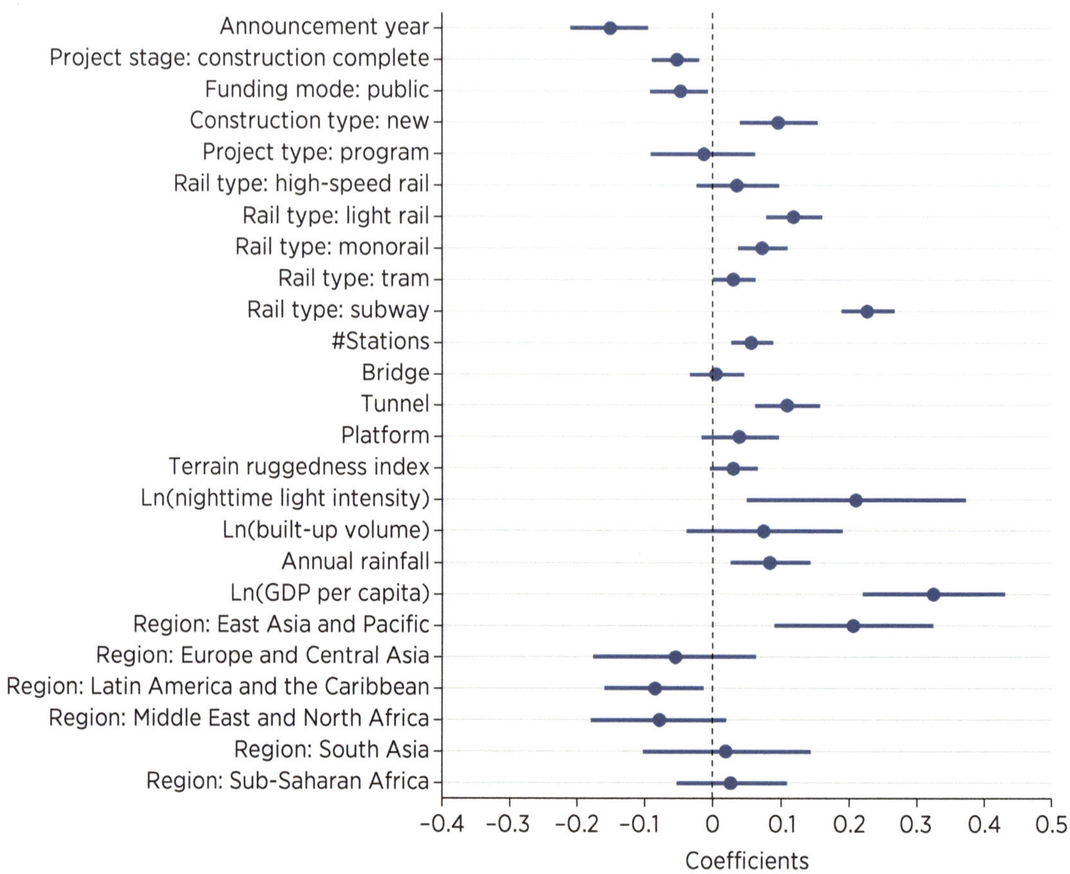

Source: Original calculations for this figure.
Note: All estimates are standardized for visual display and plotted with 95 percent confidence intervals. Estimations for figure 5.9 used dummy variables based on previous World Bank regional classification. Base category for Project stage is Canceled, Design, EPC award, Execution, On-hold, Planning, Pre-design, Pre-tender, Study, or Tender. Base category for Project Type is Parent, Sub, or Sub-sub. Base category for Funding Mode is Public/Private or Private. Base category for Construction type is Expansion, Redevelopment, Renovation, or Upgrade. Base category for Region is North America. EPC = engineering, procurement, and construction.

DIGITAL

This section presents the steps taken to derive unit cost for the different digital components covered in the report, namely RAN (cell towers), data centers, IXPs, and terrestrial fiber-optic and submarine cables. It details the main sources and the methodology, and presents some general stylized facts on the resulting unit costs.

Radio access network

The report derived cost per macro site (tower) from transaction data reported by TowerXchange (annex 5A). The data set includes 301 tower sale transactions across 75 countries between 2007 and 2025, representing roughly 1.24 million cell towers

FIGURE 5.10 Costs of cell towers, by region

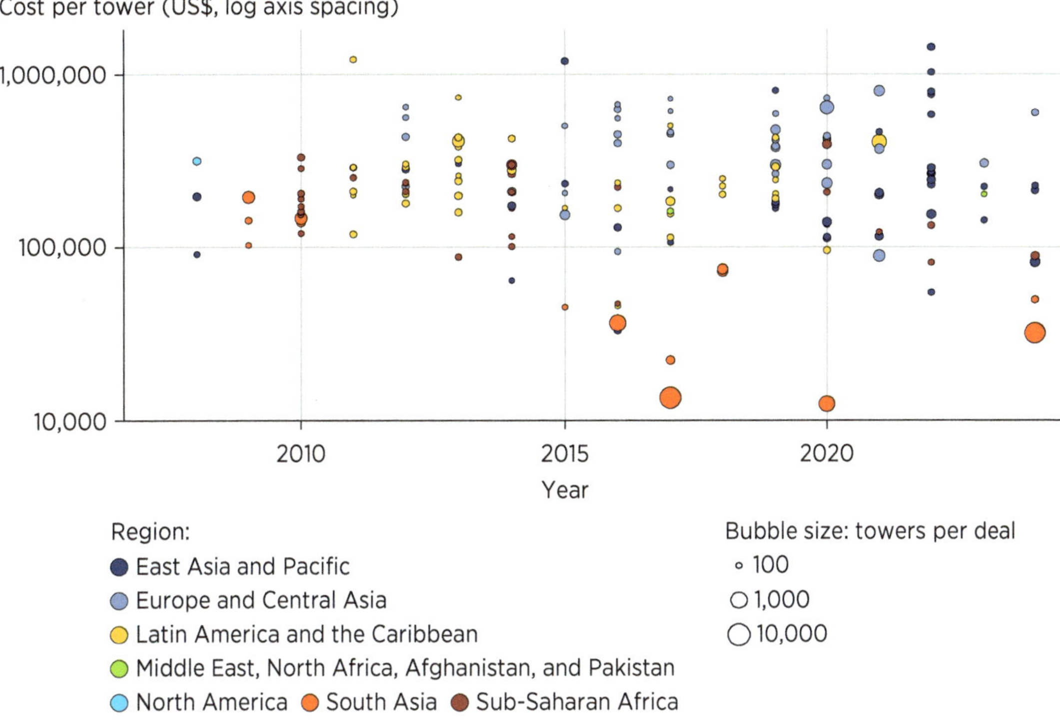

Source: Original calculations based on data from TowerXchange.

worldwide (figure 5.10). On average, each observed deal involved about 4,300 towers, with an estimated mean cost of US$308,746 per tower and an average total transaction value of about US$1.5 billion, indicating a concentrated market structure in which a few large-scale acquisitions account for most of the global tower stock traded.[6] The estimation of the cost per micro site followed an engineering table approach calibrated using the distribution of the cost per macro site.

Across income groups, unit costs and transaction sizes vary. High-income countries account for 107 deals in the sample, showing the highest average unit costs (about US$465,000 per tower, with a standard deviation of US$259,000) and the largest deal sizes (about 6,400 towers per transaction). Upper-middle-income countries follow with average costs near US$253,000 and smaller transactions (about 3,000 towers). Low-income and lower-middle-income countries record the lowest per-tower costs (US$246,000 and US$183,000, respectively), although lower-middle-income countries stand out for their larger-scale deals (about 7,500 towers).

To impute macro site costs for markets without observed transactions, national averages were first computed for countries in the sample using a weighted mean, with each deal's per-tower cost weighted by its tower count to give greater influence to large-scale transactions. For countries lacking data, tower costs were then estimated through a weighted nearest-neighbor approach that identified the three most comparable countries based on geographic proximity, GDP per capita, land area, and urbanization rate. Each missing value was calculated as an inverse-distance weighted average of these reference countries, ensuring that estimated tower costs reflect both regional and economic conditions, including differences in construction, land, and labor costs.

For micro sites, given the lack of project-level data, the calculation of the unit cost followed a methodology based on an engineering table. First, a benchmark unit cost was anchored in a 2024 estimate of US$20,000 based on an analysis of industry reports (Accenture Strategy 2018; Gieske 2024; Mordor Intelligence 2025).[7] To extend this benchmark globally, the model applied a country-specific scaling factor that reflects relative differences in macro site construction across countries. Specifically, it obtained each country's micro site unit cost by multiplying the US 2024 benchmark by the ratio of its average per-tower value to that of the United States. This approach assumes that the cost of deploying micro sites varies proportionally with macro site costs, providing a data-driven estimate independent of the underlying radio technology.

Data centers

The estimation of the costs of data centers started with the collection of project cost data for 2,259 data centers or about one-fourth of the universe of core data centers in the world, built between 2003 and 2025, plus a few planned projects up to 2040. The average observed real project cost is approximately US$530 million (in 2024 terms) with a standard deviation of US$1,503.5 million, showing a strong right skew pushed by the newer and higher-capacity data centers (figure 5.11). The distribution suggests that, although most facilities cost less than US$200 million, a few very large hyperscale builds push the mean above half a billion.

The estimation of the cost of data centers relied on a random forest regression model with 500 trees that was trained to predict the logarithm of project costs using attributes such as installed capacity (megawatts), facility area (square feet), GDP per capita at the time of announcement, completion year, and regional or income classification. The model achieved an R^2 of 0.5 and a root mean square error of 0.89, equivalent to an average absolute prediction error of about US$2.44. Missing explanatory variables were imputed using predictive mean matching, ensuring realistic replacements drawn from observed distributions. The trained model was then applied to projects lacking cost data, with results showing a slight underestimation tendency. Each predicted cost reflected both information on technology–related components (computing, storage, and networking equipment) and supporting physical systems (power, cooling, and structural fit-out). Predicted costs were brought to present value using a 5 percent annual discount rate based on the project's completion year, and country-level aggregates were computed to estimate the total replacement value of data center infrastructure in 2024 US dollars.

Internet exchange points

Project costs for IXPs were unavailable, so unit replacement costs were estimated using participants and peak traffic as proxies for capacity and value. Missing data on these

FIGURE 5.11 Costs of data centers, by country income level

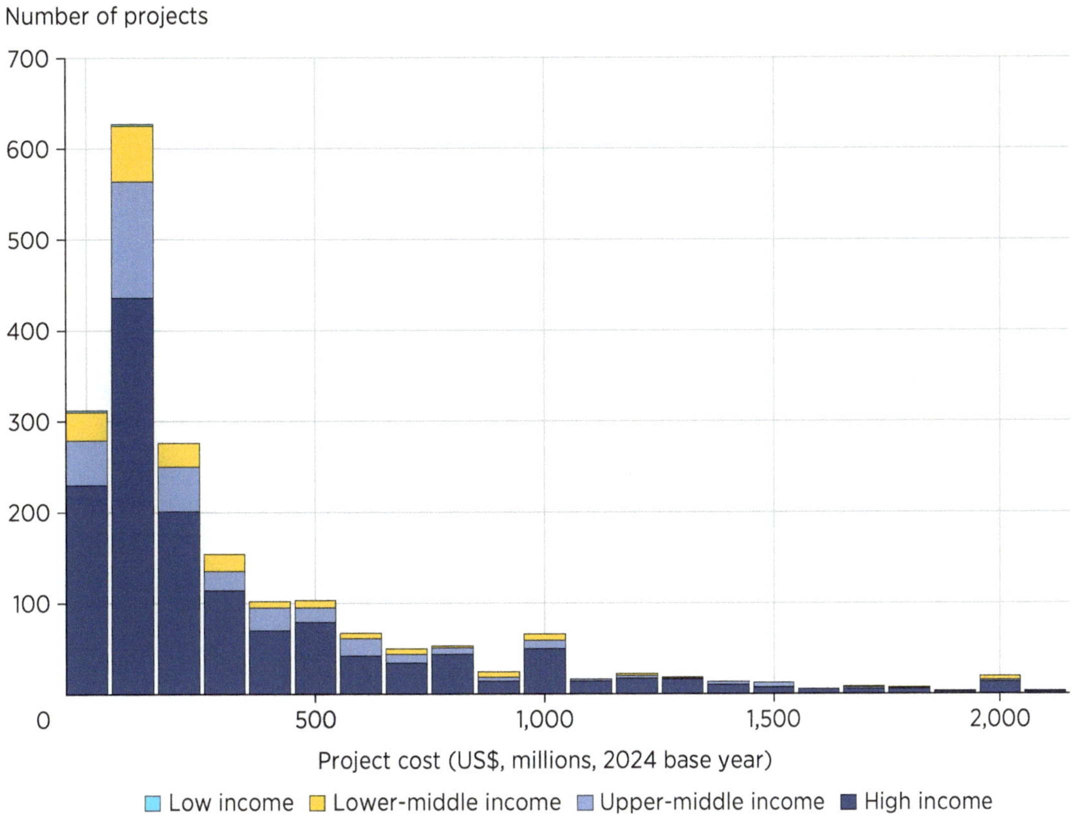

Number of projects

Source: Original calculations based on data from GlobalData and Data Centers Map.
Note: Distribution truncated at US$35 billion.

two indicators, present in roughly 57 percent of observations, were imputed using income group averages to ensure cross-country consistency. Thus, the imputation relied on the following means: high-income countries averaged about 41 participants and 473,000 megabits per second (Mbps), upper-middle-income countries 49 participants and 351,000 Mbps, lower-middle-income countries 19 participants and 161,000 Mbps, and low-income countries 8 participants and 7,000 Mbps. The completed data set was then used to classify IXPs into three capacity tiers: the 33rd and 67th percentiles of participants and peak traffic defined low, medium, and high tertiles, with each IXP receiving scores (0–2) on both dimensions. These scores were averaged to produce an overall capacity level. Each level was assigned an estimated literature-based replacement unit cost of US$30,000 for low capacity, US$150,000 for medium capacity, and US$1 million for high capacity (Internet Society 2014; Lee and Son 2021).

Terrestrial fiber-optic and submarine cables

The data set for costing terrestrial fiber-optic cables (FOCs) comprises 128 FOC projects spanning 37 countries and five regions over 2009–28, with total reported investment of roughly US$71.8 billion and an aggregate route length near 3.10 million km.

Projects are large on average (about US$561 million and 24,248 km) but much smaller at the median (US$124.5 million and 1,267 km), indicating a strong right skew from a few mega-backbones. The average cost per km observed in this sample data is roughly US$4.61 million/km, whereas the km-weighted mean is approximately US$23,142/km, highlighting how short, high-cost builds inflate unweighted averages relative to the cost associated with most deployed kilometers (figure 5.12).

A supervised machine learning pipeline was used to estimate replacement costs of terrestrial FOC as a function of route length. The sample was split (80/20) to evaluate alternative models with total project cost as the dependent variable and route length as the predictor. Three specifications were fitted and compared using out-of-sample R^2, mean absolute error, and root mean square error: (1) random forest (500 trees), (2) tuned regression tree, and (3) ordinary least squares. The random forest was retained for prediction because of its superior accuracy and flexibility to capture nonlinearity and scale effects. The trained model was applied to Geographic Information System inventories from other sources (for example, Africa Bandwidth and the International Telecommunication Union) to compute country-level total km with replacement cost. Unit costs were then derived as predicted investment (US dollars) divided by total route-km. A key limitation is the exclusion of last-mile networks, likely causing an underestimate of total fiber stock.

FIGURE 5.12 Costs of terrestrial FOC, by region

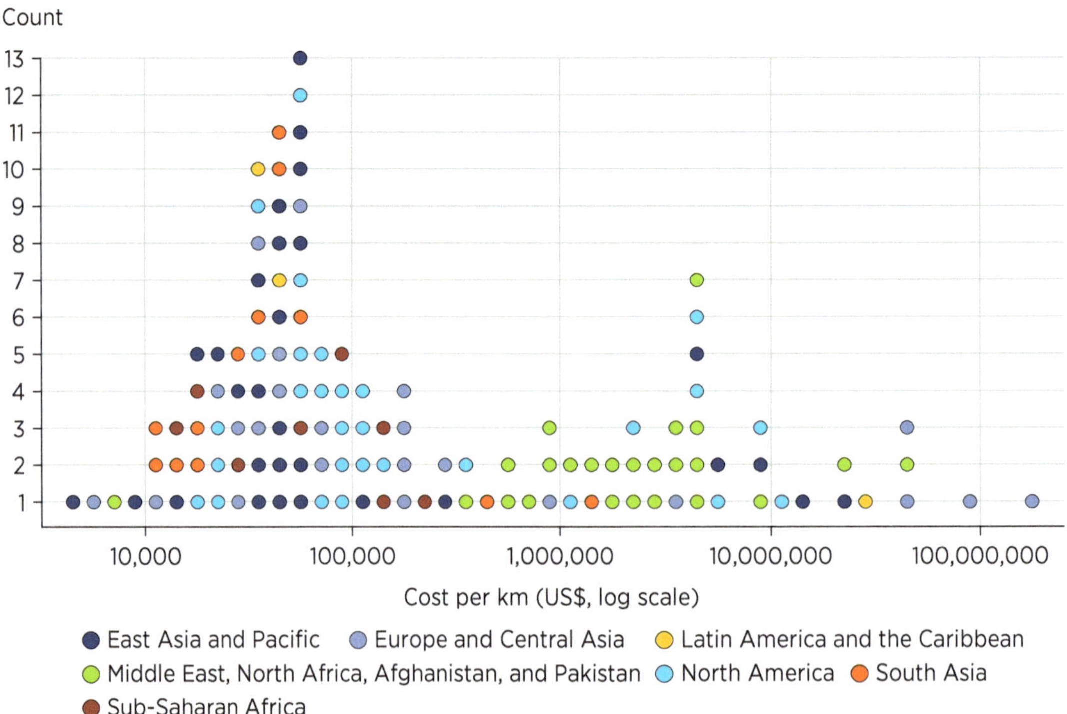

Source: Original calculations based on data from GlobalData Plc.
Note: FOC = fiber-optic cable; km = kilometer.

The unit cost of submarine cables was estimated from a near-global data set covering almost the entire installed base, with cost data for 288 projects (47 percent of recorded builds). Observed replacement cost totals about US$67.24 billion (figure 5.13), with an average project length of approximately 3,000 km and a median of 770 km. Supplier totals are led by Alcatel Submarine Networks (US$29.23 billion) and SubCom (US$18.43 billion), whose weighted average costs per km are about US$37,571/km and US$35,294/km, respectively.

For those submarine cables with missing cost data, the estimation relied on a random forest regression model developed by Leo Breiman (2001). Before modeling, all relevant predictors—such as the year the cable entered into service, total length (km), number of fiber pairs, total design capacity (in gigabits per second), and number of countries directly connected—were reviewed, and missing values for these variables were imputed using the median of the available data. Three regression models were tested: random forest, linear regression, and decision tree, each trained using fivefold cross-validation to compare accuracy and robustness. The random forest model was ultimately selected because of its superior predictive performance and its ability to avoid overfitting when additional trees are added. The model passed its characteristics through all trees, and each tree returned a predicted cost based on similar cases found in its training subset. The final predicted construction cost for each cable was then obtained by averaging the predictions across all 500 trees, producing a stable estimate of cost. Once total project costs were either observed or imputed, the cable-level estimates were converted into country-level values. For each submarine system, both the total length (km) and total project cost (US dollars) were distributed evenly across all countries directly connected to the cable system. An annual depreciation rate of 5 percent was then applied to all projects to reflect the gradual decline in asset value over time.

FIGURE 5.13 Costs of submarine cables, by decade

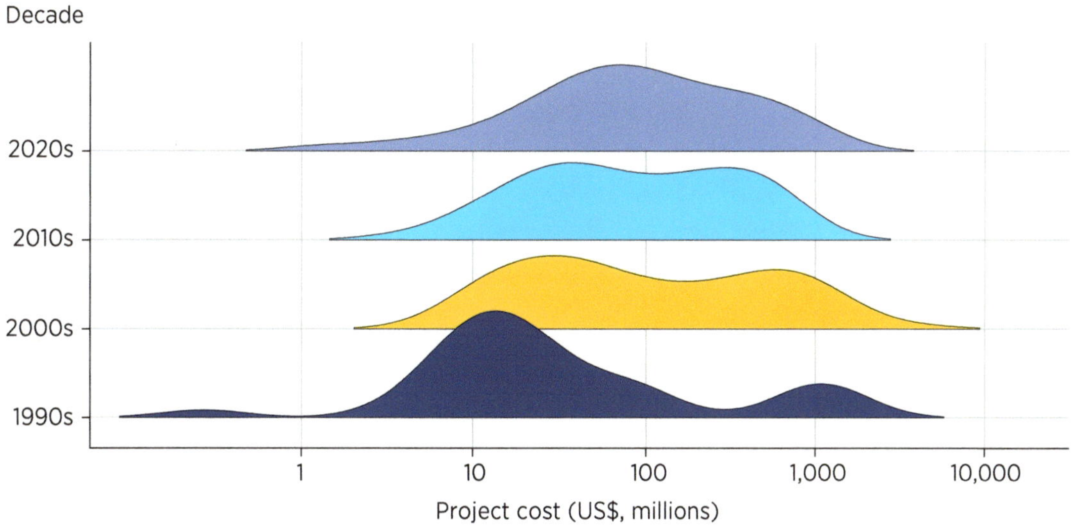

Source: Original calculations based on data from GlobalData Plc and TeleGeography.

ANNEX 5A. DATA AND METHODOLOGY FOR UNIT COST ESTIMATION

Subsector	Data source	Data type	Year coverage	Country and project coverage	Method type	Method details
a. Energy						
Power generation: nonrenewable	IEA	Country/ regional level	2024	9 countries/ regions	Reported value Weighted averages	Countries covered: reported value Other countries: apply country-variance inferred from random tree model forecast, by country and technology
Power generation: renewable	IRENA	Country/ regional level	Wind: 1984–2024 Solar: 2010–24 Hydropower: averages of 2010–15 and 2016–23	Wind: 45 countries Solar: 15 countries Hydropower: global average	Reported value Weighted averages	Countries covered: reported data Countries not covered: weighted averages, by region and technology
Power generation: forecasting model	GlobalData Plc.	Project level	1970–2025	152 countries 4,358 projects	Random forest	Covariates: project details (generation capacity, technology, funding source) Country income, labor costs, competitiveness, governance score, region fixed effect, and year trend Geographic characteristics (terrain, rainfall, density, luminosity)
Transmission lines	World Bank	Project level	2003–25	50 countries 75 projects	Weighted averages	Weighted averages, by region and technology
Distribution lines	World Bank	Project level	2008–21	9 countries 9 projects	Weighted averages	Weighted averages, by region and technology
b. Transportation						
Roads	GlobalData Plc.	Project level	1980–2025	160 countries 5,327 projects	OLS regression	Covariates: project design (type, technology), implementation modality Country income, region fixed effect, and year trend Geographic characteristics (terrain, rainfall, density, luminosity)
Railways	GlobalData Plc.	Project level	1980–2025	139 countries 3,341 projects	OLS regression	Covariates: project design (type, technology), implementation modality Country income, region fixed effect, and year trend Geographic characteristics (terrain, rainfall, density, luminosity)

(continued)

ANNEX 5A. DATA AND METHODOLOGY FOR UNIT COST ESTIMATION *(continued)*

Subsector	Data source	Data type	Year coverage	Country and project coverage	Method type	Method details
c. Digital						
RAN: macro sites	TowerXchange	Transaction level	2007–25	75 countries 301 transactions 1.24 million macro sites	Weighted averages and weighted nearest-neighbor	Comparable countries were chosen by geographic proximity, GDP per capita, land area, and urbanization rate.
RAN: micro sites	Industry estimates[a]	Benchmark values	2018–23	US and global benchmarks	Engineering table	Industry estimates were set to a US benchmark of US$20,000, which was converted to country-specific values by applying a scaling factor based on each country's ratio of its average per-macro site value to that of the United States.
Data centers	Data Center Map TeleGeography GlobalData Plc.	Project level	2003–25	58 countries 2,259 projects	Random forest	Predictors included project capacity (MW), country, region, income group, and project completion year.
IXPs	Jensen (2009) Lee and Son (2021)	Benchmark values	2009 and 2021	Theoretical benchmarks obtained from the literature	Engineering table	Unit replacement costs were estimated using participants and peak traffic as proxies for capacity and value.
Terrestrial fiber-optic cables	GlobalData Plc.	Project level	2009–28	37 countries 128 projects	Random forest	Predictor: cable length.
Submarine cables	TeleGeography GlobalData Plc. Online articles	Project level	1993–2025	178 countries 288 projects	Random forest	Predictors included service year, length, fiber pairs, capacity, and number of countries connected.

Source: Original table for this publication.
Note: IEA = International Energy Agency; IRENA = International Renewable Energy Agency; IXP = internet exchange point; MW = megawatt; OLS = ordinary least squares; RAN = radio access network; TowerXchange = TowerXchange—The Independent Community for Tower Professionals.
a. Industry estimates for micro sites include Accenture Strategy (2018), which estimates the deployment cost of a small cell at US$33,500, 30 percent of which corresponds to US-specific regulatory expenses; Gieske (2024), who estimates generic fifth-generation hardware pricing at US$10,000; CellTeks, "Private LTE" (accessed November 13, 2025), https://cellteks.com/private-lte/, which estimates capital expenditure at US$5,000–US$15,000 per small cell; and Mordor Intelligence (2025), which estimates small cell costs globally at US$10,000–US$50,000.

ANNEX 5B. POWER GENERATION: SOURCE AND LEVEL OF DISAGGREGATED INFORMATION BY TECHNOLOGY

Type	Source	By region	By technology	By size
Gas and oil	IEA (2024)	✓	✓	
Coal	IEA (2024)	✓	✓	
Hydropower	IRENA (2024)	✓	✓	✓
Wind	IRENA (2024)	✓	✓	
Solar	IRENA (2024)	✓	✓	
Nuclear	IEA (2024)	✓	✓	
Geothermal	IRENA (2024)			
Bioenergy	IRENA (2024)	✓		✓

Sources: IEA 2024 and IRENA 2024.

NOTES

1. Note that the reverse holds for fixed versus marginal costs, with renewables having a higher share of fixed costs versus variable costs than other technologies.
2. For further details on the level of disaggregated information used in the estimation by technology, refer to annex 5A.
3. Eighty-three percent of the installed solar capacity in the data set uses solar photovoltaic technology.
4. Note that the category above 500 kilowatts has only one project.
5. For lines without voltage information, the following assumptions are applied: (1) all low-voltage lines identified from the GridFinder tool (refer to chapter 4) are classified as distribution lines, and (2) transmission lines lacking voltage data are assumed to be 110-kilovolt transmission lines.
6. Most of the tower deals entail sale and leaseback construction, and do not include the actual active network equipment.
7. Value estimation also used information from CellTeks, "Private LTE" (accessed November 13, 2025), https://cellteks.com/private-lte/.

REFERENCES

Accenture Strategy. 2018. "Impact of Federal Regulatory Reviews on Small Cell Deployment." Accenture. https://api.ctia.org/docs/default-source/default-document-library/small-cell -deployment-regulatory-review-costs_3-12-2018.pdf.

Bacon, Robert W., and John E. Besant-Jones. 1998. "Estimating Construction Costs and Schedules." *Energy Policy* 26 (4): 317–33.

Bosio, Erica, Simeon Djankov, Edward Glaeser, and Andrei Shleifer. 2022. "Public Procurement in Law and Practice." *American Economic Review* 112 (4): 1091–117.

Breiman, L. 2001. "Random Forests." *Machine Learning* 45 (1): 5–32.

Brooks, Leah, and Zachary Liscow. 2023. "Infrastructure Costs." *American Economic Journal: Applied Economics* 15 (2): 1–30.

Collier, Paul, Martina Kirchberger, and Måns Söderbom. 2016. "The Cost of Road Infrastructure in Low- and Middle-Income Countries." *World Bank Economic Review* 30 (3): 522–48.

Cushman and Wakefield. 2023. "2023 Global Data Center Market Comparison." Cushman and Wakefield. https://cushwake.cld.bz/2023-Global-Data-Center-Market-Comparison/38/.

Faber, Benjamin. 2014. "Trade Integration, Market Size, and Industrialization: Evidence from China's National Trunk Highway System." *Review of Economic Studies* 81 (3): 1046–70.

Gieske, John. 2024. "What Are 5G Small Cells? We Explain Everything!" Nybsys, June 12, 2024. https://nybsys.com/what-are-5g-small-cells/.

IEA (International Energy Agency). 2021. *World Energy Outlook 2021*. IEA. https://doi.org/10.1787/14fcb638-en.

IEA (International Energy Agency). 2024. World Energy Outlook 2024. IEA. https://www.iea.org/reports/world-energy-outlook-2024.

Internet Society. 2014. "The Internet Exchange Point Toolkit and Best Practices Guide: How to Maximize the Effectiveness of Independent Network Interconnection in Developing Regions and Emerging Markets." Collaborative draft, Internet Sociey. https://www.internetsociety.org/wp-content/uploads/2021/04/Global-IXPToolkit_Collaborative-Draft_Feb-24.pdf.

IRENA (International Renewable Energy Agency). 2023. *Renewable Capacity Statistics 2023*. IRENA.

IRENA (International Renewable Energy Agency). 2024. *Renewable Power Generation Costs in 2024*. Abu Dhabi: IRENA.

Jensen, Mike. 2009. "Promoting the Use of Internet Exchange Points: A Guide to Policy, Management, and Technical Issues." Internet Society. https://www.internetsociety.org/wp-content/uploads/2012/12/promote-ixp-guide.pdf.

Lee, Yeong Ro, and Chang Yong Son. 2021. "In-Depth Study on the Design and Implementation Plan of Internet Exchange Points in CLMV Countries." ESCAP Working Paper Series No. 04/2021, ICT and Disaster Risk Reduction Division, United Nations Economic and Social Commission for Asia and the Pacific.

Li, Yue, Xinxin Lyu, and Jevgenijs Steinbuks. 2025. "Benchmarking Energy Infrastructure Costs with Machine Learning." Background paper for this report, World Bank.

Link, Heike, Chris Nash, Andrea Ricci, and Jeremy Shires. 2016. "A Generalized Approach for Measuring the Marginal Social Costs of Road Transport in Europe." *International Journal of Sustainable Transportation* 10 (2): 105–19.

Liscow, Zachary, Cailin Slattery, and Will Nober. 2025. "State Capacity and Infrastructure Costs." *Yale Law & Economics Research Paper*, August 23, 2025.

Mordor Intelligence. 2025. *5G Infrastructure Market Size & Share Analysis*. Mordor Intelligence. https://www.mordorintelligence.com/industry-reports/5g-infrastructure-market.

Oughton, Edward J. 2023. "Policy Options for Broadband Infrastructure Strategies: A Simulation Model for Affordable Universal Broadband in Africa." *Telematics and Informatics* 76: 101908. https://doi.org/10.1016/j.tele.2022.101908.

Oughton, Edward J., Niccolò Comini, Vivien Foster, and Jim W. Hall. 2022. "Policy Choices Can Help Keep 4G and 5G Universal Broadband Affordable." *Technological Forecasting & Social Change* 176 (March): 121409. https://doi.org/10.1016/j.techfore.2021.121409.

Rahkonen, T., A. Lawrence, and R. Ascierto. 2020. *Best-in-Class Data Center Provisioning*. Uptime Institute Intelligence. https://uptimeinstitute.com/best-in-class-data-center-provisioning.

Turner, Matthew, Neil Mehrotra, and Juan Pablo Uribe. 2023. "Does the US Have an Infrastructure Cost Problem? Evidence from the Interstate Highway System." NBER Working Paper 30989, National Bureau of Economic Research.

World Bank. 2021. *World Development Report 2021: Data for Better Lives*. World Bank.

World Bank. 2022. "Using Geospatial Analysis to Overhaul Connectivity Policies: How to Expand Mobile Internet Coverage and Adoption in Sub-Saharan Africa." World Bank.

World Bank. 2026 (forthcoming). *Cost of Transmission: Insights from World Bank-Financed Transmission Projects*. ESMAP Technical Report, Energy Sector Management Assistance Program, World Bank.

6

Infrastructure Capital Stocks

KEY MESSAGES

This chapter presents capital stock estimates for selected energy, transportation, and digital sectors. It does so by combining the physical stock inventories of chapter 4 with the unit cost estimates discussed in chapter 5, and then adjusting for depreciation.

Global infrastructure capital stocks are large in aggregate, but highly unequal across countries and regions. The results reveal vast global infrastructure wealth, yet capital stocks remain heavily concentrated in high-income countries. Many low-income economies—especially in Sub-Saharan Africa—hold very small asset bases relative to population and development needs.

Energy capital stocks are highly concentrated and display stark per capita disparities. Global energy infrastructure capital—estimated at over US$9 trillion—is concentrated in East Asia and Pacific, Europe and Central Asia, and North America. Per capita energy capital in high-income regions exceeds that of Sub-Saharan Africa by more than an order of magnitude, reflecting different stages of electrification and network maturity.

Transportation infrastructure dominates global infrastructure capital by value. Transportation assets—valued at almost US$25 trillion—account for most of global infrastructure capital, with roads alone representing about 86 percent of transportation value and railways the remainder. As with energy, larger stocks are found in high-income countries in North America and Europe and Central Asia, as well as in East Asia.

Digital infrastructure capital—estimated at US$1.6 trillion—is smaller in aggregate, and presents an extremely skewed distribution. Data centers and radio access networks dominate digital capital, with infrastructure characterized by a deep cross-country divide in capacity and service quality.

A reproducibility package is available for this book in the Reproducible Research Repository at https://reproducibility.worldbank.org/catalog/536.

INTRODUCTION

This chapter presents capital stock estimates for selected energy, transportation, and digital sectors.

The results show that global infrastructure capital stocks are large in aggregate but highly unequal across countries and regions. Global energy infrastructure, estimated at US$9.27 trillion, is heavily concentrated in East Asia and Pacific, Europe and Central Asia, and North America; many low-income economies, particularly in Sub-Saharan Africa, remain severely undercapitalized. Transportation infrastructure is substantially larger, with road and railway assets totaling US$24.6 trillion (US$21.1 trillion in roads, or 86 percent; and US$3.5 trillion in rail, or 14 percent). Global digital capital stock is estimated at roughly US$1.59 trillion, concentrated mainly in data centers and radio access networks.

METHODOLOGY

To estimate infrastructure capital stocks, this chapter discusses the outputs of two main processes. First, the unit cost estimates described in chapter 5 are multiplied by the physical inventory of each sector discussed in chapter 4. These sector valuations are then aggregated to obtain the sector's total replacement cost at current prices.[1] Second, these replacement costs are adjusted for depreciation over time, with depreciation applied in two ways depending on data availability (box 6.1). Together, these two steps produce an evidence-driven estimate of the current value of infrastructure assets, reflecting both their physical extent and the inevitable effects of aging, technological progress, and cost evolution.

BOX 6.1

Estimating capital depreciation

Valuing the entire existing capital stock at replacement cost does not provide an accurate estimate of the current value. Replacement costs represent the value of the infrastructure in its "new" state, immediately following the completion of construction. Determining the correct value of infrastructure asset stocks thus ideally involves depreciating the replacement costs according to the age and vintage of the assets. This report deals with that requirement in two ways depending on the data available.

With Time Series Data Available

The first case, and the most satisfactory one, is when time series data on the amount of physical assets are available, thus allowing for application of a depreciation rate based

(continued)

BOX 6.1   **Estimating capital depreciation *(continued)***

on the age of the assets. This is the case for energy generation, and for three of the five digital assets, namely data centers, submarine cables, and cell towers.

For power generation assets, depreciation was calculated using the recorded construction year of each power plant and applying a standard straight-line depreciation method based on the technology's expected lifespan. A lifespan of 40 years is assumed for all power plants, except for hydropower and nuclear facilities, which are assigned an 80-year lifespan. It is further assumed that 5 percent of the original capital value remains as the salvage value at the end of the plant's operational life. Nuclear power plants are treated as an exception, with no residual value upon retirement.

In the case of digital, an annual depreciation rate of 5 percent was then applied to all projects to reflect the gradual decline in asset value over time.

With No Time Series Data Available

In the second case, information on past values of the stocks is not available, making it impossible to determine the age composition of the assets inventory and requiring application of an adjustment to the aggregate stock. This is the case for transportation, roads and railroads, energy transmission and distribution lines, and internet exchange points and terrestrial fiber-optic cables. This report uses country-specific ratios of replacement to depreciated value, which are applied to the current figures.

For transportation, to approximate the ratio between replacement costs and present asset values, this report uses data from national accounts.[a] Specifically, for each country it calculates the ratio of general government capital stock to the cumulative gross fixed capital formation over the average service life of roads, taken to be 58 years. This average service life is computed using road service lives in Australia, Belgium, Canada, Chile, Cyprus, the Czech Republic, Denmark, Estonia, Finland, France, Germany, Hungary, Israel, the Republic of Korea, Italy, Latvia, Lithuania, Malta, Mexico, the Netherlands, Portugal, Slovakia, Slovenia, the United Kingdom, and the United States (Bennet et al. 2020; Eurostat and OECD 2015).

For growing economies with considerable recent infrastructure investment, the ratio will be closer to 1, because the value of the capital investments will not yet have depreciated much. Conversely, in mature economies, the ratio will be considerably lower—typically about 0.5 for economies in a steady state. In countries with incomplete national accounts data, this report uses the average ratio (0.562), which applies to 1.53 percent of roads (by length). Although this methodology captures the state of general government capital stock, it is a reasonable approximation for the transportation sector.

(continued)

BOX 6.1   **Estimating capital depreciation *(continued)***

For energy transmission and distribution lines, depreciation follows the same methodology as roads and railways. In the digital sector, the report applies the country-specific ratio of depreciated to replacement value as calculated for data centers to internet exchange points, and that of radio access network to terrestrial fiber-optic cables.

a. Using 2021 data from International Monetary Fund, "IMF Investment and Capital Stock Dataset, 1960–2019" (accessed November 21, 2025), https://infrastructuregovern.imf.org/content/dam/PIMA/Knowledge-Hub/dataset /IMFInvestmentandCapitalStockDataset2021.xlsx.

ENERGY

A total of 216 economies is included in the estimation of the energy capital asset value, derived by multiplying the unit installation cost with the corresponding amount of physical stock for power generation, transmission, and distribution. The replacement cost is subsequently adjusted to account for depreciation over time (box 6.1).

The global energy stock, estimated at US$9.27 trillion in 2024, shows wide disparities across regions and countries (map 6.1). In aggregate terms, stock values are concentrated in East Asia and Pacific, Europe and Central Asia, and North America, reflecting decades of capital accumulation in power generation and networks (figure 6.1). China stands out with the single largest national stock, whereas many low-income economies—particularly in Sub-Saharan Africa—register very small asset bases. The global distribution is highly skewed: a handful of countries holds the majority of the world's energy capital, and most low- and lower-middle-income economies remain undercapitalized. Overall, power generation assets represent the majority of total energy capital stock, with transmission and distribution accounting for a smaller yet important share.

The comparison of total and per capita energy capital stocks highlights the stark divergence in infrastructure accumulation across regions. North America remains dominant in per capita terms: energy capital exceeds US$3,000 per person, nearly 15 times the per capita stock in Sub-Saharan Africa (figure 6.2). Latin America and the Caribbean and the Middle East, North Africa, Afghanistan, and Pakistan occupy the middle ground, with relatively balanced shares of generation and transmission-distribution assets. In contrast, South Asia and Sub-Saharan Africa lag far behind in both aggregate and per capita stock, underscoring persistent underinvestment relative to demographic and economic growth. The composition of assets also differs: richer regions show a higher share of transmission and distribution capital—signifying mature, service-dense systems—whereas poorer regions' stock remains dominated by generation assets, signaling earlier stages of electrification and network build-out. These disparities point to a widening infrastructure gap that mirrors differences in income, reliability, and access across regions.

MAP 6.1 Spatial distribution of energy capital assets

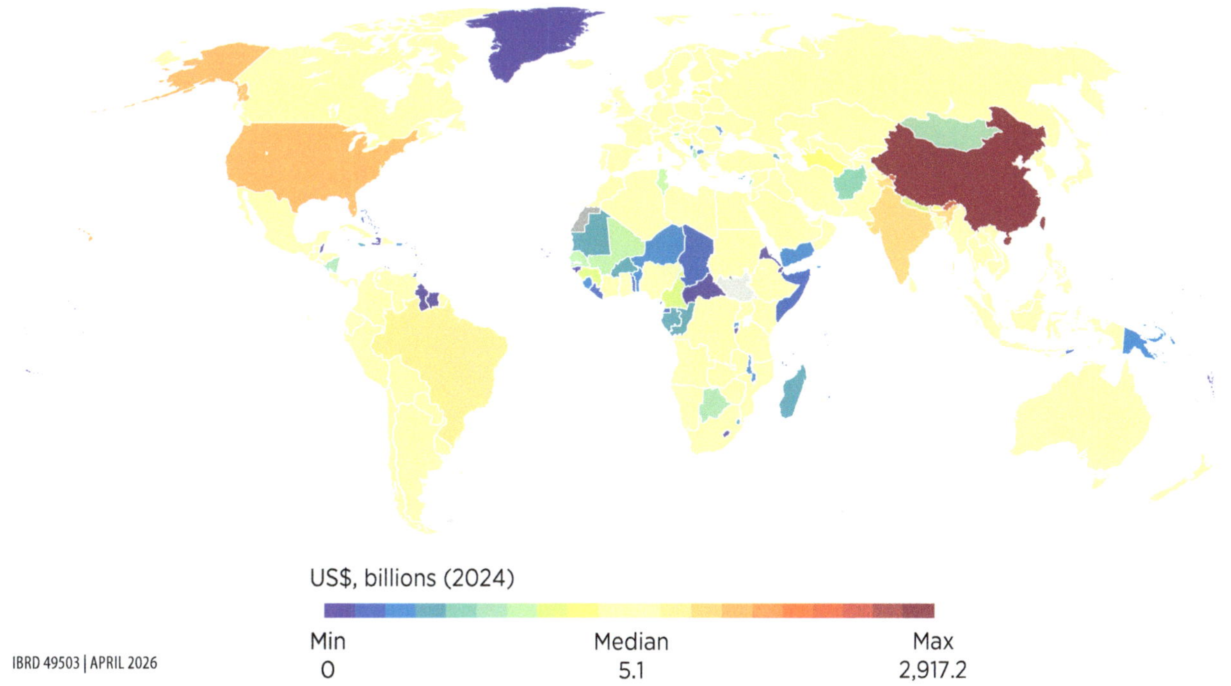

Source: Original map for this publication.
Note: The map illustrates the depreciated total capital value of the global energy infrastructure stock using 2024 data.

FIGURE 6.1 Energy capital assets, by region

Total stock value (US$, trillions)

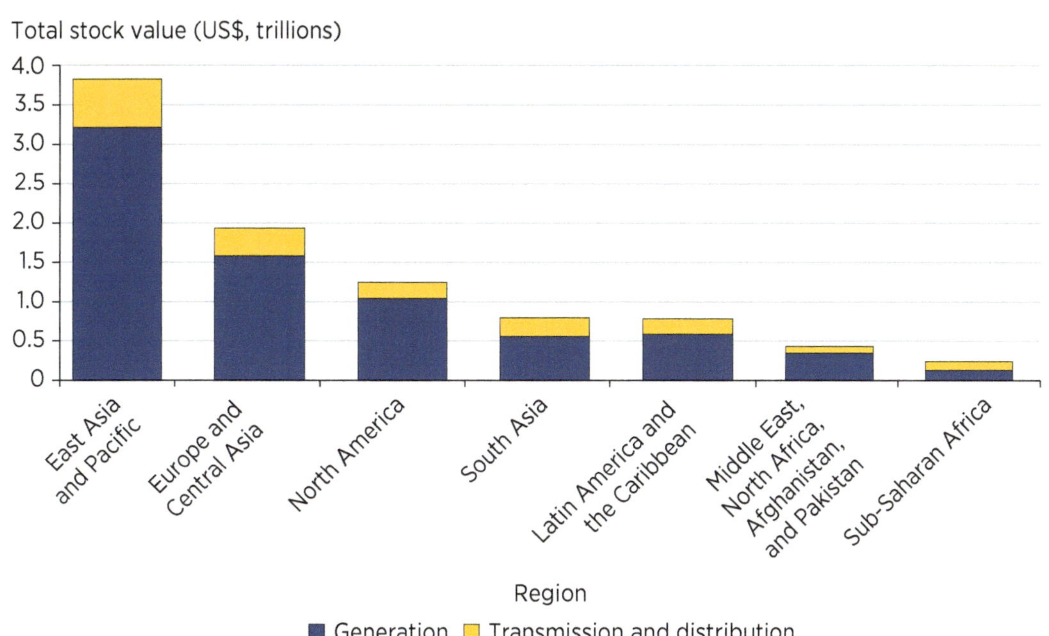

Source: Original figure for this publication.
Note: The figure illustrates the depreciated total capital value of the global energy infrastructure stock using 2025 physical assets data and 2024 unit cost data.

FIGURE 6.2 Energy capital assets per capita, by region

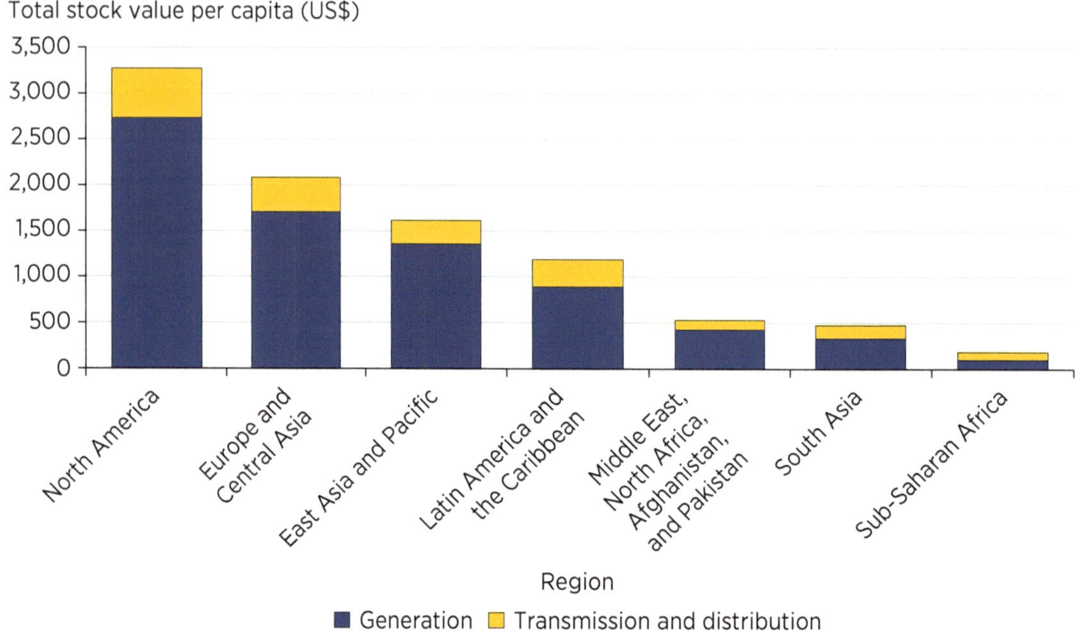

Source: Original figure for this publication.
Note: The figure illustrates the depreciated total capital value of the global energy infrastructure stock using 2025 physical assets data and 2024 unit cost data.

At the subnational level, map 6.2 illustrates differences between Argentina and Brazil, two large, geographically adjacent economies in Latin America and the Caribbean with similar levels of economic development and comparable energy sector structures. Both are upper middle-income economies with extensive hydro and thermal generation. However, the scale and spatial distribution of energy capital assets exhibit marked differences between the two countries.

Brazil displays very high aggregate intensity and deep territorial penetration: at the state level, energy capital density reaches almost US$400,000 per square kilometer (km²) at the upper end, with a median of about US$45,000–US$50,000/km². At the municipal level, peak values exceed US$15 million/km² and the median remains at US$17,000/km², indicating widespread diffusion beyond a small set of hubs. This pattern reflects a dense national power system in which large-scale assets coexist with extensive transmission and secondary generation infrastructure across municipalities. At the same time, large portions of the Amazon basin stand out for their persistently low energy capital densities, underscoring the deliberate absence of large-scale generation and transmission investment in ecologically sensitive and sparsely populated areas.

MAP 6.2 Subnational-level energy capital assets, Argentina and Brazil, 2024

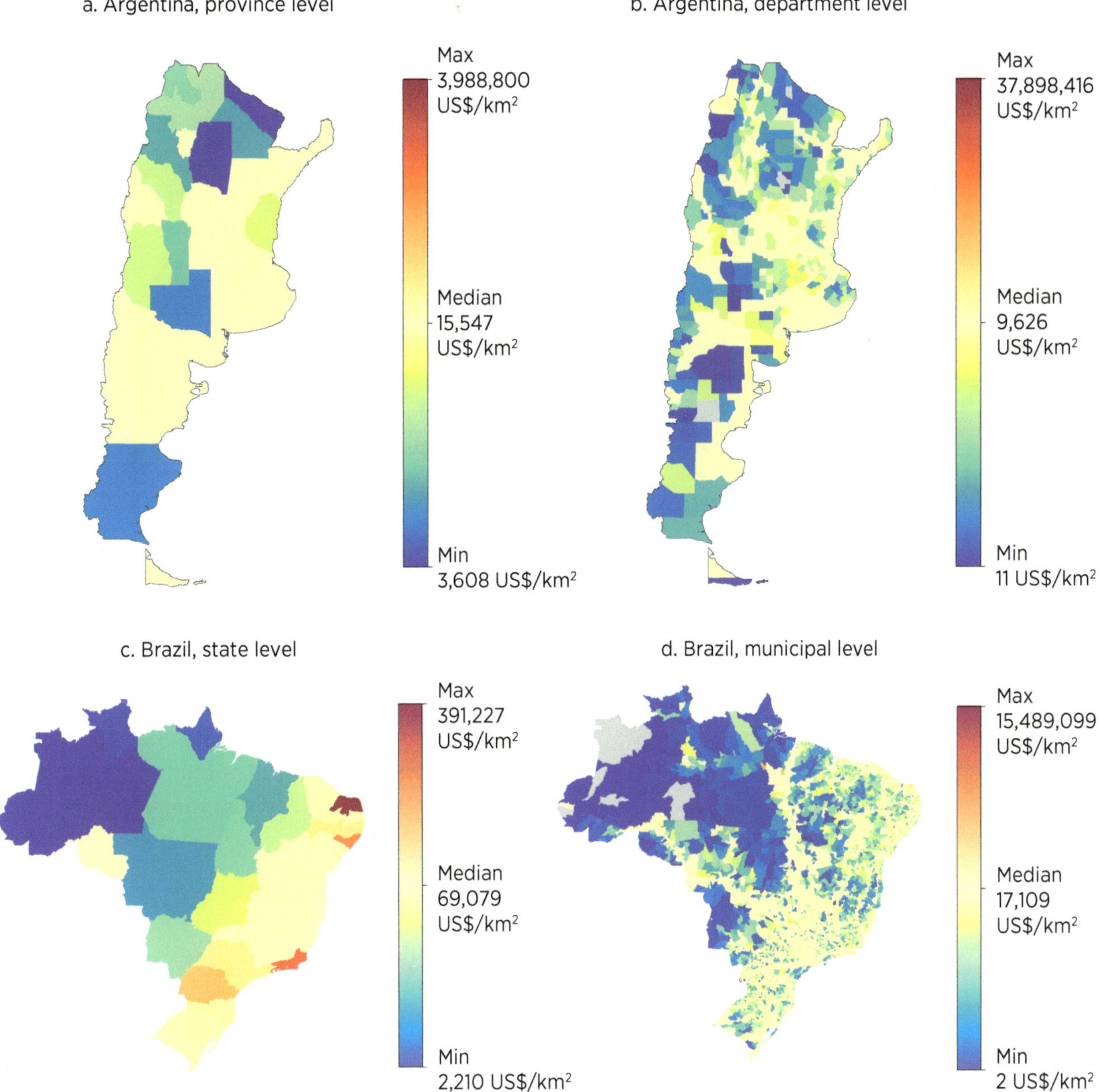

Source: Original map for this publication.
Note: The figure shows the depreciated capital stock value of energy generation, transmission, and distribution based on 2024 data. km² = square kilometer.

Argentina, by contrast, exhibits a far more uneven spatial profile. The province-level maximum is similarly high in absolute terms (approaching US$4 million/km²), but the median is substantially lower (about US$15,000–US$16,000/km²). At the department level, the median falls to below US$10,000/km², with large swathes of territory clustered near the minimum. High-intensity assets are concentrated in a limited number of departments and corridors, and much of the country remains weakly capitalized. All in all, unlike Brazil's energy capital, which functions as a territorial system, generating broad spatial spillovers and resilience, Argentina's energy capital remains more nodal and enclave-like, limiting its capacity to support balanced regional development.

TRANSPORTATION

By combining physical stock estimates from OpenStreetMap with the predictive cost models, this chapter quantifies the total replacement cost of each country's road and railway network—that is, how much it would cost to construct these linear transportation infrastructures from scratch. The evaluation follows a four-step process:

1. For each road and railway segment in the physical stock database, extract the relevant tags associated with each road and railway segment from OpenStreetMap (for example, number of lanes, bridges, and tunnels) and merge with the relevant spatial and socioeconomic variables, such as nighttime lights, terrain ruggedness, and GDP per capita.

2. Apply the respective predictive cost model presented in chapter 5 to estimate the unit cost per kilometer for each road and railway segment,[2] then multiply by the segment length to arrive at the replacement cost for each segment.

3. Aggregate replacement cost values within each national and subnational jurisdiction.

4. Adjust for depreciation (box 6.1).

The transportation capital stock estimates include 186 countries and territories (map 6.3). By 2024, the combined cumulative asset value across the road and rail sectors amounts to US$24.6 trillion. Of this amount, roads account for US$21.1 trillion (86 percent) and railways for US$3.5 trillion (14 percent).

The distribution of transportation infrastructure and asset values shows stark inequalities (figures 6.3 and 6.4). The East Asia and Pacific, Europe and Central Asia, and North America regions make up the bulk of the world's transportation infrastructure by value with 38 percent, 29 percent, and 24 percent, respectively. The remaining four regions make up less than 9 percent combined, with the least endowed region, Sub-Saharan Africa, associated with merely 0.7 percent of the world's transportation infrastructure. In terms of asset values, on average, each person worldwide is associated with US$3,079 worth of transportation infrastructure; however, in Sub-Saharan Africa that value is only US$133 compared to US$15,537 in Canada and the United States—a 117-fold difference.

The high-resolution geo-coded asset data also enable investigations at a far more granular scale. Map 6.4 shows transportation asset density at the state level in Nigeria. Panels a and b show the density of road and rail assets, measured in meters per square kilometer;

MAP 6.3 **Spatial distribution of transportation capital assets**

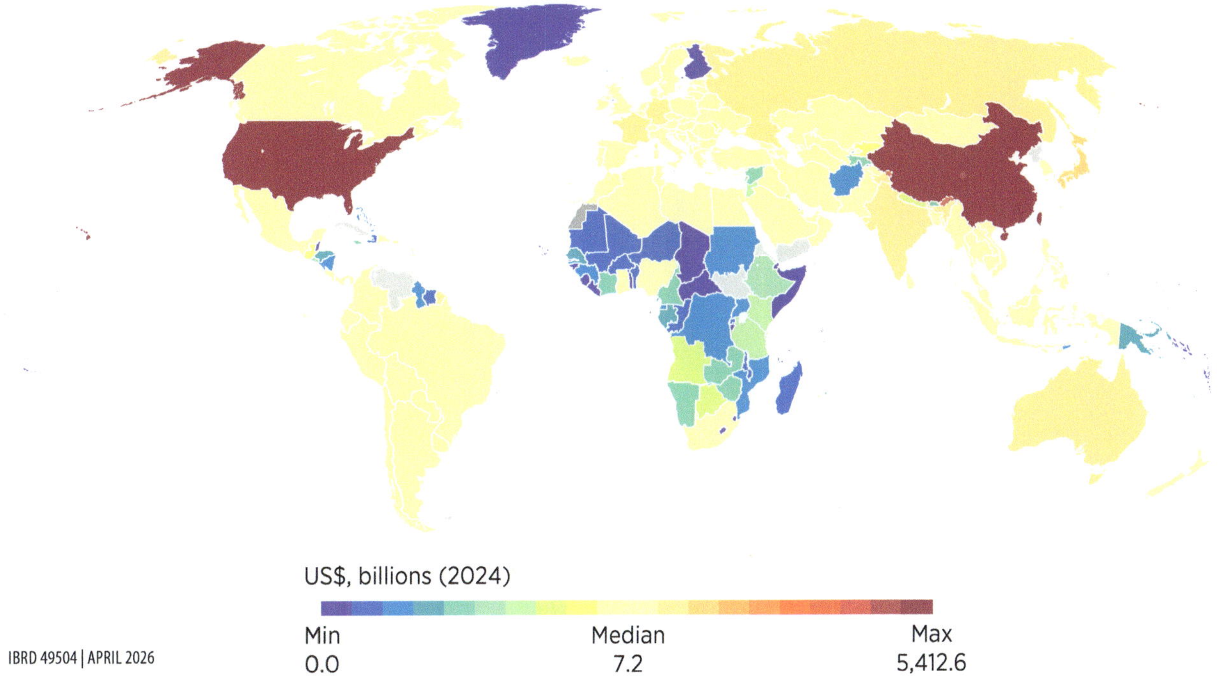

Source: Original map for this publication.
Note: The map illustrates the depreciated total capital value of the global transportation infrastructure stock using 2024 data.

panel c shows their combined value, measured in US dollars per square kilometer. Whereas the physical asset density maps show some variation and highlight some of the urban areas, the capital asset density map shows a stark contrast between the north and south. In terms of capital value, the vast majority of transportation assets are found near the coastal states in the south and near a few major cities, namely Abuja in the center and Kano in the north. The difference between the physical and capital asset density maps suggests that, although transportation infrastructure exists in the northern states, it is on average of lower value on a per-kilometer basis—because of, for example, fewer lanes or less complex infrastructure.

Similarly, map 6.5 shows the disparate per capita value of road assets at the district level in the Dominican Republic and Haiti. Although the two countries share the island of Hispaniola and have comparable geography and climate, the border between the two countries stands out as a sharp discontinuity. Whereas the Dominican Republic has experienced decades of tourism-focused investment, Haiti remains among the poorest countries in the region.

FIGURE 6.3 Transportation capital assets, by region

Total stock value (US$, trillions)

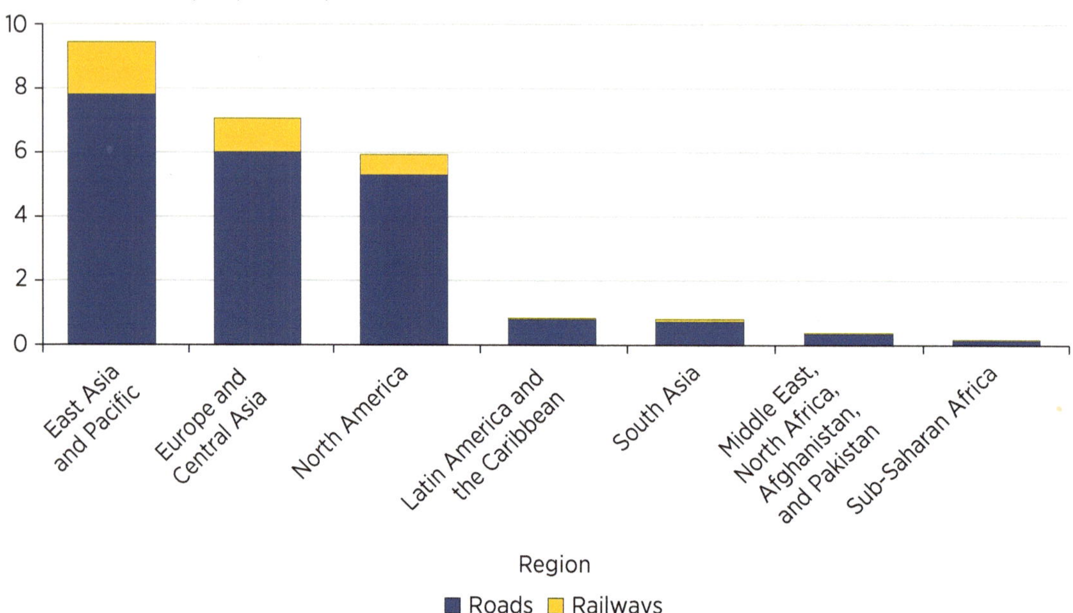

Source: Original figure for this publication.
Note: The figure illustrates the depreciated capital value of the transportation infrastructure stock using 2024 data.

FIGURE 6.4 Transportation capital assets per capita, by region

Total stock value per capita (US$)

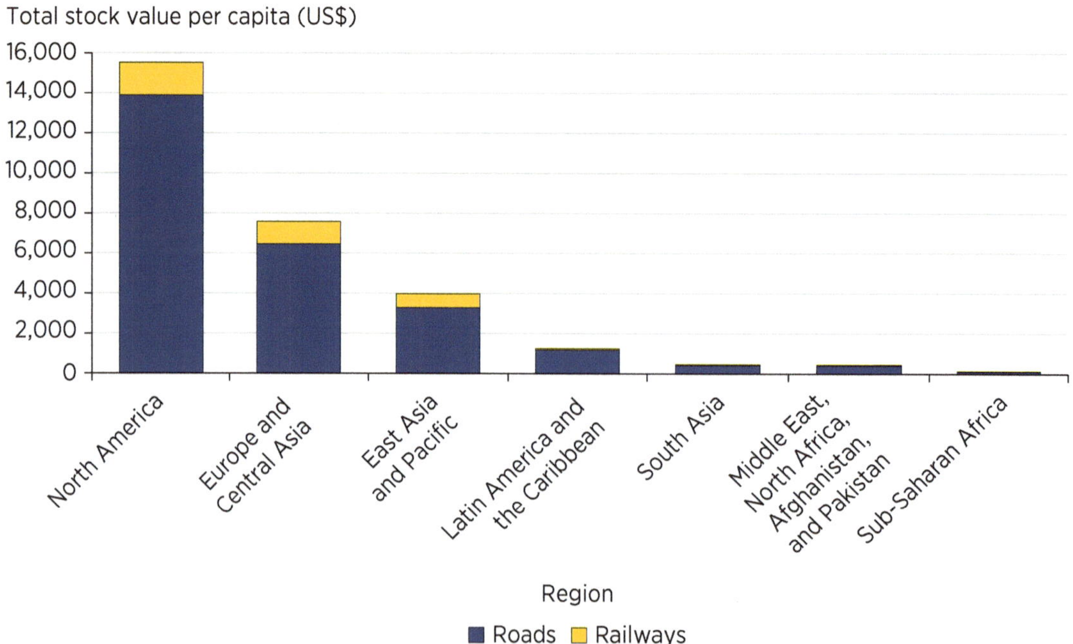

Source: Original figure for this publication.
Note: The figure illustrates the depreciated capital value of the transportation infrastructure stock, using 2024 data.

MAP 6.4 **Subnational distribution of transportation physical and capital assets at the state level, Nigeria**

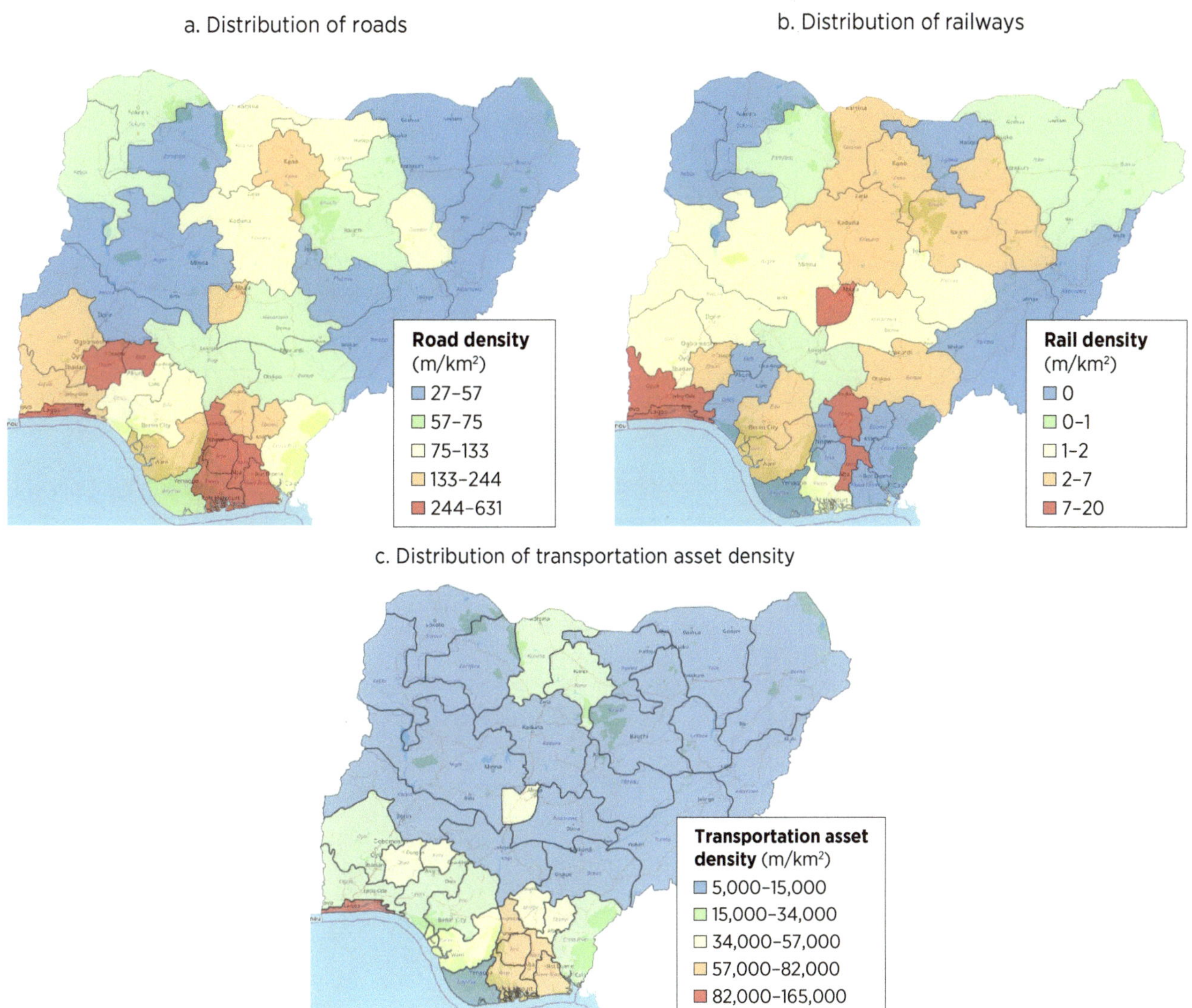

Source: Original map for this publication.
Note: Panel c illustrates the depreciated capital value of the transportation infrastructure stock using 2024 data.
km² = square kilometer; m = meter.

DIGITAL

The digital capital stock estimates include a total of 217 countries. By 2024, global digital capital stock had reached about US$1.59 trillion in real depreciated value (US$2.43 trillion in real replacement value). This amount corresponds to an average of roughly US$7.3 billion per country. The median, however, is only about US$737 million, indicating that most countries fall below the global average. At the extremes, depreciated digital capital ranges from as little as US$22,000 and US$188,000 in the smallest cases like Kosovo and San Marino, respectively, to nearly US$305 billion in the United States (map 6.6).[3]

MAP 6.5 **Subnational distribution of road capital assets per capita value at the district level, Dominican Republic and Haiti**

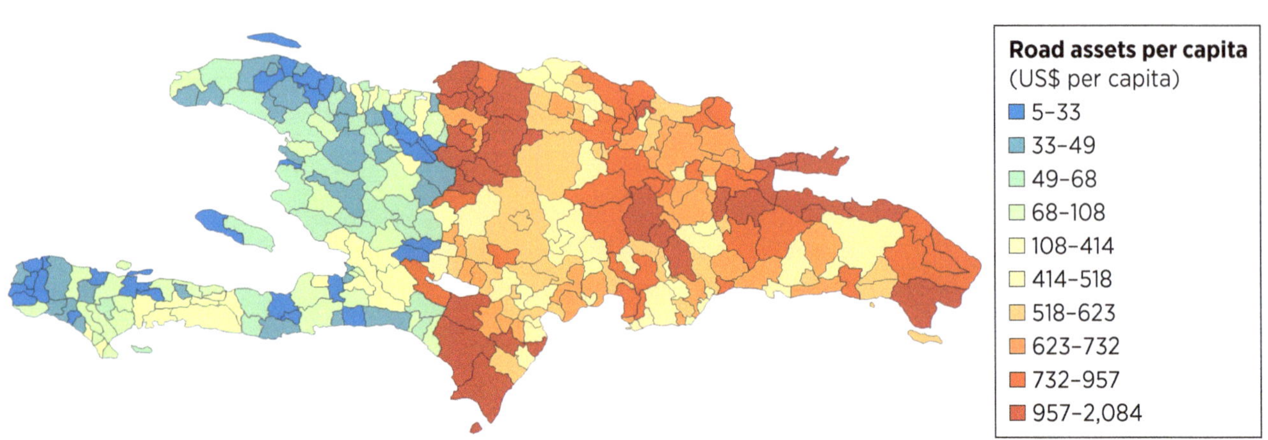

Source: Original map for this publication.
Note: The map illustrates the depreciated road capital assets per capita value using 2024 data. The Dominican Republic is the country on the right and Haiti is the country on the left.

MAP 6.6 **Spatial distribution of digital capital assets**

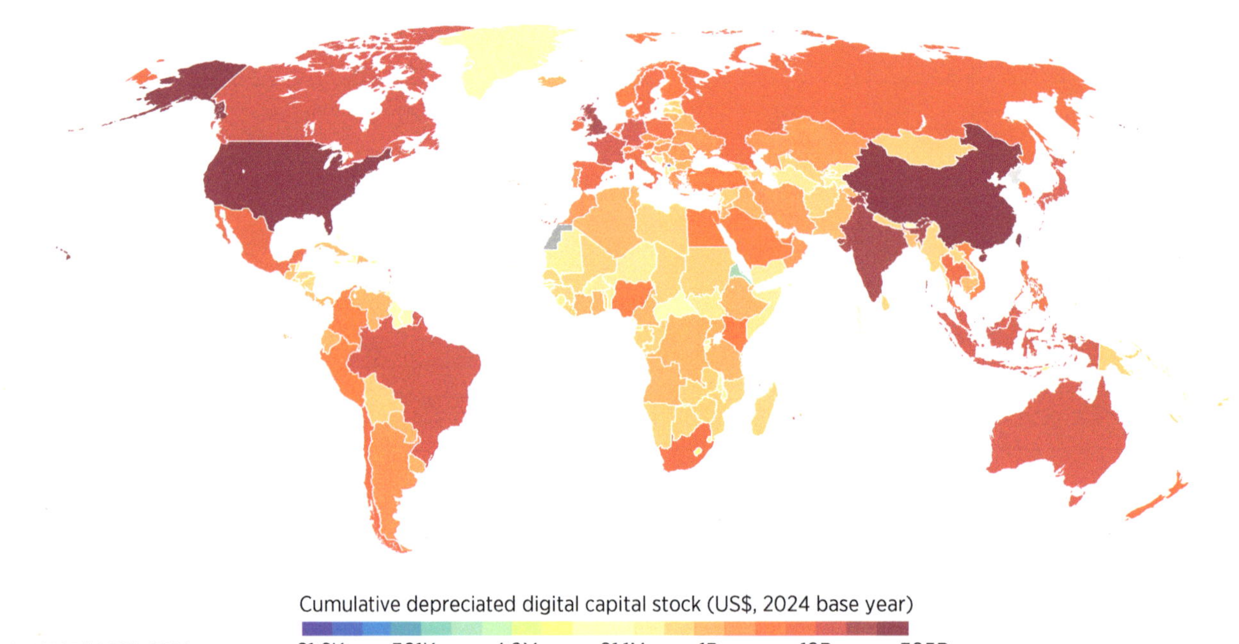

Source: Original map for this publication.
Note: The map illustrates the depreciated total capital value of the global digital infrastructure stock using 2024 data.

After accounting for depreciation, the global composition shows a clear concentration of the digital capital stock in data centers and radio access networks. Data centers represent the largest share, at about US$875 billion (55 percent of the global total), followed by radio access networks with roughly US$580 billion (36.5 percent). In contrast, the transmission backbone contributes far smaller amounts: submarine cables account for about US$78 billion and terrestrial fiber-optic networks for roughly US$56 billion, together making up less than 9 percent of the total.[4] Internet exchange points remain small in capital terms, at roughly US$0.1 billion globally, highlighting the comparatively modest investment needs of interconnection infrastructure relative to the large data center and radio access network systems.

Global digital capital stock is also concentrated by country income level and by region. High-income countries account for 57 percent of the global digital capital stock.[5] By region, 78 percent of this stock is concentrated in East Asia and Pacific, Europe and Central Asia, and North America. In contrast, Latin America and the Caribbean and South Asia hold about 7 percent each; the Middle East, North Africa, Afghanistan, and Pakistan region holds about 3.6 percent; and Sub-Saharan Africa has only 3.4 percent (figure 6.5).

FIGURE 6.5 Digital capital assets, by region and component

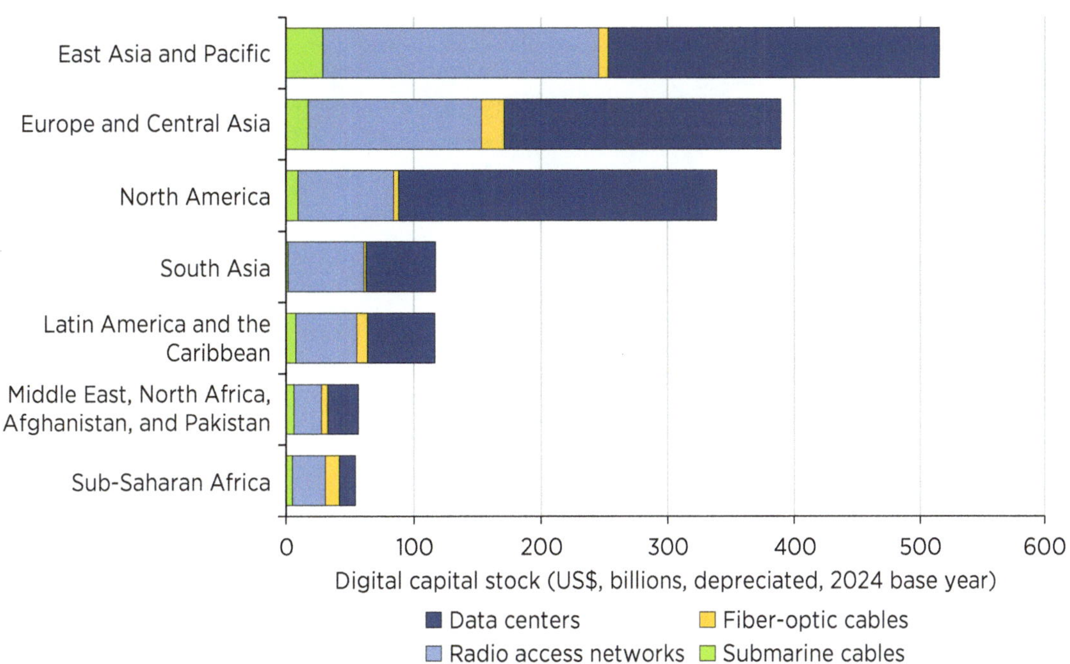

Source: Original figure for this publication.
Note: Because of data unavailability, the figure does not include full radio access network stocks for China and India. Internet exchange points are not included because the figure measures costs in billions of US dollars. The figure illustrates the depreciated capital value of the digital infrastructure stock using 2024 data.

The level of inequality of digital capital stock per capita across countries is higher than global income inequality, with a Gini coefficient of about 0.75 compared to a coefficient of 0.67 for income inequality in 2020 (Chancel et al. 2021).[6] North America stands far ahead globally, with about US$904 in digital capital stock per person, a value driven mainly by extremely high levels of data center infrastructure and radio access network assets. The Europe and Central Asia region follows at roughly US$422 per person, with balanced investments in data centers and radio access networks. Sub-Saharan Africa has the lowest level, at about US$43 per person (figure 6.6).

While differences in digital capital are evident across countries, they are also present within them. Ecuador's canton-level distribution of digital infrastructure capital stock illustrates the extent of these estimations (map 6.7). The per capita distribution of digital capital in Ecuador shows a sharp contrast between major urban corridors and the country's rural periphery. Quito and Guayaquil still anchor the highest total asset concentrations, but adjusting for population reveals smaller cantons, especially in parts of the northern Andean–Amazon foothill and the southern highlands, with comparatively high digital capital intensity. These pockets could suggest targeted investments, likely linked to strategic infrastructure investments and extractive activities.

FIGURE 6.6 Digital capital assets per capita, by region and component

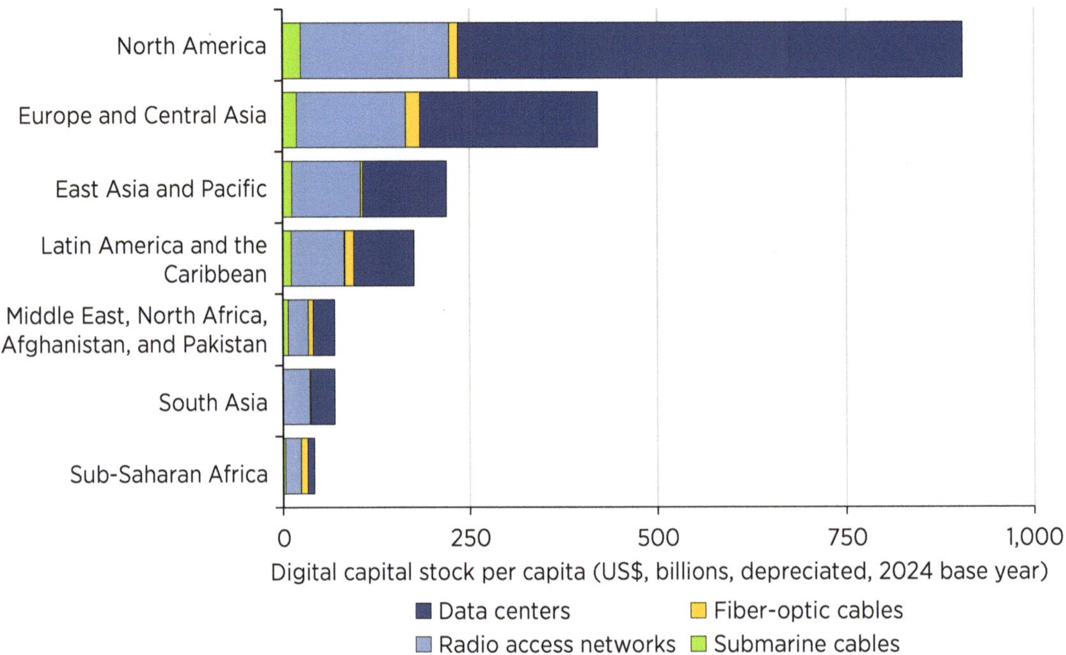

Source: Original figure for this publication.
Note: Because of data unavailability, the figure does not include full radio access network stocks for China and India. Internet exchange points are not included because the figure measures costs in billions of US dollars. The figure illustrates the depreciated capital value of the digital infrastructure stock per capita using 2024 data.

MAP 6.7 Subnational distribution of digital capital assets, Ecuador

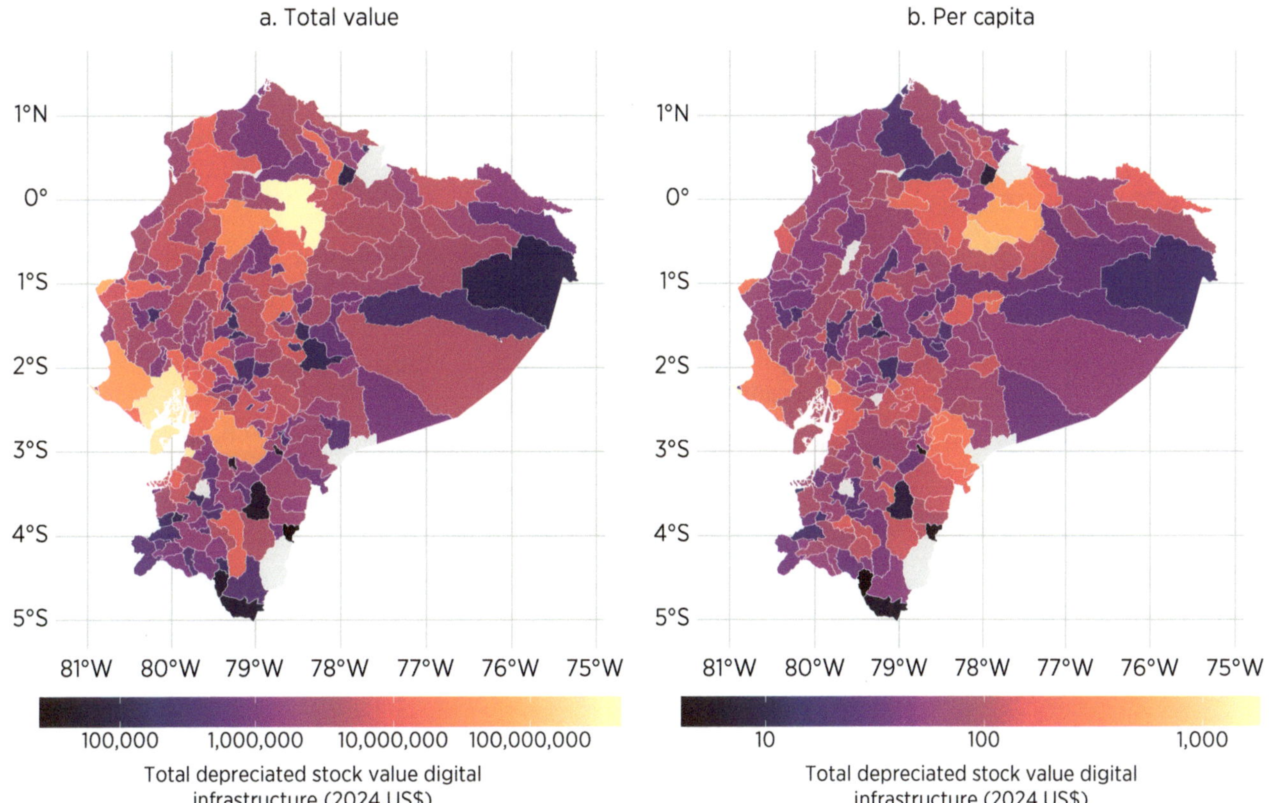

Source: Original map for this publication.
Note: The map covers continental Ecuador only. It illustrates the depreciated total capital value of the digital infrastructure stock in Ecuador using 2024 data.

NOTES

1. Replacement cost represents the value of an asset in its pristine, newly constructed state; it does not fully capture the economic worth of assets that have been in service for several years.
2. To apply the predictive cost model, the estimation assumed the following project characteristics: AnnouncementYear = 2025, ProjectType = Program, FundingMode = Public. For railway, ConstructionType = New. For roads, replacement costs were calculated twice, once with ConstructionType = New and once with ConstructionType = Upgrade. The average value was used to account for (1) new road construction often following existing alignments, thus lowering costs; and (2) GlobalData capturing only large-scale projects (greater than US$25 million), meaning the sample likely skews toward motorways and other higher-quality roads, which cannot adequately be controlled for in the regression modeling. Where data exist, validation suggests that the mixed New-Upgrade approach yields more accurate replacement cost values.
3. The total replacement cost of the digital sector was calculated by combining two components: the reported project values for assets with available cost information, and the estimated unit costs multiplied by the physical stock for assets without valuation data. For obtaining the depreciated capital stock, a 5 percent depreciation rate was applied to assets with time-series information. For assets without ready-for-service dates (internet exchange points and terrestrial fiber-optic cables), country-specific ratios of depreciated to replacement value were applied, using analogs from subsectors with similar rollout patterns: the data center ratio for internet exchange points and the radio access network ratio for fiber-optic cables (box 6.1).

4. The relatively low estimated capital stock for terrestrial fiber-optic networks largely reflects gaps in available physical infrastructure data, rather than the true economic importance of fiber in the transmission backbone.
5. Upper-middle-income countries contribute 30.1 percent, lower-middle-income countries 12.0 percent, and low-income countries less than 1.0 percent.
6. The average of the per capita digital capital stock is US$770, and the median is US$194.

REFERENCES

Bennett, Jennifer, Robert Kornfield, Daniel Sichel, and David Wasshausen. 2020. "Measuring Infrastructure in BEA's National Economic Accounts." NBER Working Paper 27446, National Bureau of Economic Research.

Chancel, Lucas, Thomas Piketty, Emmanuel Saez, and Gabriel Zucman. 2021. *World Inequality Report 2022*. World Inequality Lab.

Eurostat and OECD (Organisation for Economic Co-operation and Development). 2015. *Eurostat-OECD Compilation Guide on Land Estimation*. European Union and OECD. https://www .oecd.org/content/dam/oecd/en/publications/reports/2015/07/eurostat-oecd-compilation-guide -on-land-estimations_g1g554ee/9789264235175-en.pdf.

7

Measuring Benefits

KEY MESSAGES

A large and increasingly rigorous empirical literature finds positive causal effects of infrastructure investment, with impacts varying by sector and context. The evidence base has evolved from aggregate public capital correlations to sector-specific studies using microdata, spatial variation, and quasi-experimental methods. These more recent studies have strengthened causal identification while highlighting systematic heterogeneity across energy, transportation, and digital infrastructure.

Meta-analysis of 606 estimates confirms moderate but robust output elasticities of infrastructure. After correcting for publication bias and model selection, estimated output elasticities cluster at about 0.03 for energy, 0.03–0.05 for transportation, and 0.03–0.04 for digital infrastructure. These elasticities are stable across outcome definitions and broadly consistent between developed and developing economies. Values are larger for transportation in developing contexts, whereas the reverse is true for digital, potentially because of network effects.

Sector-specific elasticities are smaller than earlier public capital estimates but remain economically meaningful. The elasticities derived from sector-level measures are below those in earlier public capital meta-analyses; however, because they relate more directly to usable capacity or access, they provide a more appropriate basis for computing differentiated social rates of return by sector.

Impact heterogeneity is expected, but current evidence supports bounded ranges rather than finely differentiated elasticities. Although infrastructure impacts tend to be larger in infrastructure-scarce settings—particularly in Sub-Saharan Africa—the number of credible studies is insufficient to support systematic estimation by region or income group. This report therefore relies on central elasticities from the meta-analysis, with regional estimates used as robustness bounds.

A reproducibility package is available for this book in the Reproducible Research Repository at https://reproducibility.worldbank.org/catalog/536.

THE CURRENT STATE OF THE ART

As argued in chapter 1, accumulated evidence over the years provides strong evidence that infrastructure services—such as transportation, energy, water and sanitation, and digital infrastructure—are essential elements in the development process. No country has developed without growing its energy infrastructure, providing basic services, and ensuring connectivity for its people and productive units.

Of course, these correlations need not imply causation. Over the last three or four decades, extensive literature has considered this issue. Foster et al. (2023) provide a systematic qualitative review of over 300 studies published between 1983 and 2022, examining how investments in infrastructure—specifically digital, energy, and transportation—affect development outcomes in low- and middle-income countries. Their paper highlights that, despite wide recognition of infrastructure as a prerequisite for economic development, rigorous measurement of its causal impact has been challenging. Recent advances in data and methodology have enabled more granular analyses, revealing the specific channels through which infrastructure influences household welfare, productivity, employment, human capital, and trade.

The literature has evolved from a narrow focus on public capital and macroeconomic output to sector-specific studies using microlevel and spatial data, reflecting increased methodological sophistication and diversification of research questions, and yielding an overall positive message. The review finds robust evidence that energy infrastructure, particularly electrification, supports structural transformation by enabling migration to higher-value-added activities and increasing labor force participation, especially among women. Electrification also contributes to the establishment of nonfarm businesses, better health and education outcomes, and improved indoor air quality. Transportation infrastructure, especially rural roads, is found to reduce poverty and raise household welfare by increasing income, consumption, and employment opportunities. Improved market access leads to higher agricultural production, greater adoption of modern techniques, and lower price dispersion. Investments in highways, railways, and ports further support manufacturing output, exports, and regional convergence. Urban transportation systems facilitate city decentralization and access to employment, and efficient ports are vital for international competitiveness. Finally, digital infrastructure, such as broadband internet and mobile phones, significantly boosts firm productivity, employment, and household welfare. In developing countries, access to digital technologies is linked to higher consumption, reduced poverty, and improved labor market outcomes, even among poorer and less-skilled populations. Mobile phones also enhance market efficiency by reducing price dispersion and improving coordination between producers and traders, with additional effects on education and political mobilization. Overall, the overwhelming balance of evidence suggests that infrastructure improvements play a vital role in supporting the development process.

The story has nuances, however. Regarding electrification, for example, studies using experimental methods sometimes find smaller short-term impacts, especially in dispersed rural populations (Lee et al. 2020). Reliability of power supply emerges as a critical factor for firm productivity and household income, with frequent outages undermining the benefits of electrification (Gertler et al. 2017).

In transportation, depending on features of the environment such as the degree of mobility of capital and labor, large-scale corridor investments may shift activity over space rather than generate growth, or they may concentrate economic activity in primate cities (Redding and Turner 2015). In the digital space, Aker and Cariolle (2023) and Hjort and Tian (2025) point to significant heterogeneity in the impact of mobile phones and internet technology depending on the context.

Similar variation may occur in macroeconomic studies. In advanced economies, research consistently finds that public capital investment by governments tends to generate a positive multiplier effect, with estimates typically ranging between 0.6 and 1.0 (Ramey 2019). In contrast, sparser and more varied evidence from developing countries shows both negligible and beneficial impacts (Vagliasindi and Gorgulu 2021). Although part of this inconsistency stems from challenges related to data availability and measurement, more fundamental issues include misaligned investment priorities, limited absorptive capacity, and shortcomings in project design and execution (Straub 2011).

Given this varied evidence, it is a challenge to come up with reliable figures capturing the expected benefits from infrastructure investments. Although a few well-identified studies may provide evidence in specific contexts and under specific implementation protocols, caution is in order because issues of external validity may prevent generalizability. Traditional cross-country studies, by contrast, provide assessments over a large and diverse number of settings but have well-known methodological shortcomings and thus may have weaker internal validity. Faced with this question, Foster et al. (2025) chose to aggregate the results in the literature using meta-analysis. That approach has several advantages (for an overview, refer to Stanley and Doucouliagos 2012). First, some have argued that relying on a broader set of underlying studies, rather than on a selected set of estimates deemed robust, led to better policy decisions (Pritchett 2024). Second, meta-analysis purges the average impact from publication bias, which leads to estimates deviating from true underlying values and has been shown to be pervasive in the literature.[1]

META-ANALYSIS RESULTS

Foster et al. (2025) present a comprehensive meta-analysis of over 1,000 estimates from infrastructure studies, examining the effects of infrastructure investments—across the transportation, energy, and digital (information and communication technology) sectors—on a wide range of development outcomes (box 7.1).[2] They review literature spanning several decades, focusing on outcomes such as economic output, employment, wages, inequality, poverty, trade, human capital, population, and environmental impacts. To apply the meta-analysis toolbox, those authors focus on studies reporting elasticities or semi-elasticities only, so they are directly comparable. Their paper finds that infrastructure investments generally have a positive and significant impact on development outcomes, but the magnitude and nature of these effects vary considerably by sector and country context. Notably, digital and energy infrastructure tend to have larger estimated effects in developed countries, whereas transportation investments show higher elasticities in developing countries. The study also finds evidence of systematic publication bias favoring positive results.

A meta-analysis approach to estimating infrastructure average impacts

Foster et al. (2025) conduct a quantitative meta-analysis of over 1,000 elasticity estimates from 221 studies covering transportation, energy, and digital infrastructure. The authors aim primarily to derive summary estimates of the "true" effect of infrastructure on development outcomes, explain observed heterogeneity, and assess the extent of publication bias in the literature. To do so, they analyze both sector-level and sector-outcome-level subsamples, combining homogeneous categories of dependent and independent variables to reduce sample heterogeneity.

A central methodological feature is the use of the FAT-PET-PEESE approach, as proposed by Stanley and Doucouliagos (2012). This three-step process begins with the Funnel Asymmetry Test (FAT), which visually and econometrically assesses publication bias by examining the relationship between effect sizes and their precision (standard errors). The Precision-Effect Test (PET) then evaluates whether a genuine effect exists beyond publication bias, and the Precision-Effect Estimate with Standard Error (PEESE) refines the estimate by accounting for a quadratic relationship between effect sizes and their variance. All regressions are estimated using weighted least squares, and standard errors are clustered at the study level to account for within-study correlation.

To address heterogeneity across studies, the analysis includes a wide range of moderator variables capturing differences in study design (such as aggregation level, data type, econometric technique, and treatment of endogeneity) and context (sector, country, time period, and so on). Given the large number of potential moderators and the risk of multicollinearity, these variables are chosen employing rigorous model selection techniques: two variants of Lasso (least absolute shrinkage and selection operator)—one with theoretically grounded penalization and one with cross-validation—and Bayesian model averaging. These methods help identify the most relevant controls and produce more robust estimates by averaging across plausible models.

The methodology is further supported by robustness checks, including exclusion of outliers, restriction to studies reporting elasticities, and subsampling by identification strategy (for example, ordinary least squares versus instrumental variables). The supplementary appendix (S4) of Foster et al. (2025) provides technical details on estimating equations and implementation of these procedures. Overall, the approach is designed to yield credible, policy-relevant estimates of infrastructure's impact while transparently accounting for bias and heterogeneity in the underlying literature.

The present report builds on Foster et al. (2025) and derives new estimates to inform the analysis of social rates of return done in chapter 3. In keeping with the framework outlined in chapter 1, this chapter focuses on the subset of studies that use output, productivity, or some measure of income as the dependent variable—that is, the dimension to be explained. Doing so provides values for the output elasticity of infrastructure development (mostly in terms of access or investment in capacity). To derive more granular estimates differentiated across contexts and outcomes, it also expands the set of papers initially covered by adding more recent contributions. Overall, the exercise collected 606 observations from 157 studies. Table 7.1 provides a breakdown across the three sectors.

Using the most appropriate estimation techniques, which control for publication bias and include moderators selected using Robust Lasso (least absolute shrinkage and selection operator), the analysis derives the elasticities across the three sectors, which gives a value for the percentage increase in gross domestic product implied by a 1 percent increase in either infrastructure access or capacity (refer to box 7.1 for technical details and annex 7A for a list of the papers included in the analysis). Table 7.2a shows generic elasticities, broken down across developed versus developing countries, using output as the explained variable. Panel b shows elasticities for a slightly larger sample of studies using both output and measures of income. Values are quite similar across the two panels. Note that, for energy, the lack of sufficient studies covering developed countries means that a separate estimator cannot be derived.

TABLE 7.1 Number of observations and studies used in the estimations

Sector	Observations	Studies
Energy	144	37
Transportation	299	69
Digital	163	51
Total	606	157

Source: Based on Foster et al. 2025.

TABLE 7.2 Meta-analysis estimates, by sector and country development level

a. Output	Energy	Energy	Transportation	Transportation	Digital	Digital
Main effect	0.0277***	0.0275***	0.0289***	0.0517***	0.0399***	0.0308***
	(0.004)	(0.004)	(0.007)	(0.003)	(0.009)	(0.003)
Observations	81	73	96	181	82	69
R-squared	0.351	0.348	0.673	0.107	0.797	0.621
Number of studies	28	26	27	35	26	26
Sample	All	Developing	Developed	Developing	Developed	Developing
Moderators	Yes	Yes	Yes	Yes	Yes	Yes

(continued)

TABLE 7.2 Meta-analysis estimates, by sector and country development level *(continued)*

b. Output + income	Energy	Energy	Transportation	Transportation	Digital	Digital
Main effect	0.0325***	0.0315***	0.0275***	0.0519***	0.0399***	0.0308***
	(0.004)	(0.005)	(0.007)	(0.003)	(0.009)	(0.003)
Observations	144	136	98	201	82	81
R-squared	0.352	0.217	0.675	0.104	0.797	0.621
Number of studies	37	35	28	41	26	28
Sample	All	Developing	Developed	Developing	Developed	Developing
Moderators	Yes	Yes	Yes	Yes	Yes	Yes

Source: Original calculation based on Foster et al. 2025.
Note: Significance for the main effect coefficient: *** = 1 percent.

As seen in table 7.2, elasticities are pretty consistent across outcomes and countries' level of development. In energy, elasticities are about 0.03, but they cover a slightly larger range in transportation and digital, 0.03–0.05 for the former and 0.03–0.04 for the latter. Notably, the elasticities coming out of sector-specific studies are generally smaller than those found in earlier research focused on public capital. As a point of comparison, a previous meta-analysis by Bom and Ligthart (2014) finds a short-run output elasticity of public capital supplied at the central government level of 0.083 and a long-run one of 0.122. Given that the public capital figures lump together all sectors, the implications in terms of social rates of return are likely to be comparable.[3] The advantage of the estimates used here is the ability to compute differentiated returns across sectors.

The analysis could not systematically derive a finer breakdown, for example by region, because of limited sample size; however, table 7.3 reports some results, although they are restricted to estimations with more than 20 observations. It is noteworthy, although not necessarily surprising, that the elasticities tend to be larger for Africa. Because the samples for Latin America and the Caribbean are systematically too small, the table does not report any value for that region. Similarly, reporting elasticities by income levels is not feasible because of the underrepresentation of low-income countries.

Beyond these global or regional averages, heterogeneity is expected across countries in terms of impact, making the use of differentiated elasticities desirable. However, the current lack of sufficient studies does not allow for such differentiation through the meta-analysis approach. The social rate of return computations in chapter 3 use estimates from table 7.2a and b, and table 7.3 as robustness checks, because these estimates provide lower and upper bounds on the range of available values. Spotlights 7.1 and 7.2 try to address this issue in the case of roads, using alternative estimation techniques and more granular geospatial information to estimate country-specific impacts of new road construction and energy investment, respectively. Reassuringly, the elasticity values obtained using alternative methodologies are broadly in line with those from the meta-analysis.

TABLE 7.3 Meta-analysis estimates, by sector, selected regions

Region	Africa	Africa	Africa	South Asia	South Asia	East Asia and Pacific	East Asia and Pacific	Europe and Central Asia	Europe and Central Asia
	Energy	Transportation	Digital	Transportation	Energy	Energy	Transportation	Transportation	Digital
Main effect	0.1314***	0.2637***	0.0812***	0.0465***	0.0333***	0.0369***	0.0207***	0.0631***	0.0269***
	(0.019)	(0.059)	(0.015)	(0.000)	(0.005)	(0.001)	(0.004)	(0.006)	(0.004)
Observations	22	135	27	31	58	49	25	56	52
R-squared	0.883	0.162	0.778	0.423	0.271	0.596	0.765	0.837	0.467
Number of studies	6	20	10	9	13	13	9	11	12
Moderators	Yes	Yes	Yes	Yes	Yes	Yes	Yes	Yes	Yes

Source: Original calculation based on Foster et al. 2025.

Note: Significance for the main effect coefficient: *** = 1 percent.

ANNEX 7A. PAPERS USED IN THE ANALYSIS

Article	Publication	Outcome	Treatment	Number of estimates
a. Africa: Energy				
Aevarsdottir et al. (2017)	IGC Working Paper	Household income per capita (log); household income (log)	Own solar lamp (0/1)	4
Iimi (2021)	World Bank Policy Research Working Paper	Sales (log)	Average duration of power outage (log)	2
Estache et al. (2005)	Working Paper	GDP per capita (log)	Electricity consumption per capita (log)	1
Iimi et al. (2015)	World Bank Policy Research Working Paper	Sales (log)	Electricity shortage days (log)	2
Fedderke and Bogetić (2009)	*World Development*	Per capita output	Electricity generation	1
Mensah (2018)	World Bank Policy Research Working Paper	TFP (log); value added (log); value added per worker (log)	Duration of outages in a month (log); number of outages in a month (log)	12
b. Africa: Transportation				
Russ et al. (2018)	*Journal of Development Studies*	GDP	Cost to market	2
Dorosh et al. (2012)	*Agricultural Economics*	Log total crop production (low input/subs); log total crop production (irrigated); log total crop production (high input)	Travel time to nearest city	9
Jedwab and Storeygard (2022)	*Journal of the European Economic Association*	Nightlight intensity	Market access	2
Fedderke and Bogetić (2009)	*World Development*	Per capita output	Total roads (km); paved roads (km); ports cargo handled; railroad (km); international passengers in airports	5
Nakamura et al. (2019)	World Bank Policy Research Working Paper	Amount of crop sold (log); household consumption (log)	Rural road (0/1)	2
Ali et al. (2015)	World Bank Policy Research Working Paper	GDP (log); nonagricultural income (log); wealth index (log); livestock sales (log); crop revenue (log)	Transportation cost to market (log)	10
Ali et al. (2015)	World Bank Policy Research Working Paper	GDP (log); wealth index	Transportation cost (log)	4
Gachassin (2013)	*Journal of African Economies*	Household per capita consumption (log)	Road upgrade (0/1)	2
Gachassin et al. (2015)	*Development Policy Review*	Household per capita consumption (log)	Access to nearest road (in hours)	2
Estache et al. (2005)	Working Paper	GDP per capita (log)	Paved roads per capita (km; log)	1

(continued)

ANNEX 7A. PAPERS USED IN THE ANALYSIS *(continued)*

Article	Publication	Outcome	Treatment	Number of estimates
Iimi et al. (2015)	World Bank Policy Research Working Paper	Crop produced (maize, coffee, rice, tea); sales (log)	Market access (transportation cost in US$/ton); distance to nearest road (km)	48
Iimi et al. (2018)	World Bank Policy Research Working Paper	Crop produced (rice)	Distance to nearest road (km); market access index	4
Iimi et al. (2015)	World Bank Policy Research Working Paper	Sales (log)	Transportation quality (inventory as days of production; logs)	2
Iimi (2021)	World Bank Policy Research Working Paper	Sales (log)	Market access index (log); transportation quality (inventory days; log); local market access (log); cost to port (log)	8
Iimi et al. (2018)	World Bank Policy Research Working Paper	Income (log); crop sales (log)	Dummy (0/1) main/feeder road rehabilitation	4
Iimi et al. (2017)	World Bank Policy Research Working Paper	Crop value (log)	Transportation cost to Djibouti (log)	4
Iimi et al. (2017)	World Bank Policy Research Working Paper	Crop value (log)	Transportation cost to port (log); road transportation cost to large/small city; road transportation cost to zonal capital (log)	8
Alder et al. (2023)	World Bank Policy Research Working Paper	Nightlight (log); cropland area (log)	Market access (travel time inverse; log); dummy (0/1) kebele (wards) within 5 km of improved road	8
Berg et al. (2016)	World Bank Policy Research Working Paper	Cropland area (log, log diff.); local GDP (log)	Lagged market access (log, log diff.); lagged market access due to road (log diff.)	8
Dumas and Jativa (2025)	*World Bank Economic Review*	Household income (log)	Dummy (0/1) living <30 km or 31–50 km from rehabilitated road	2
c. Africa: Digital				
Abreha et al. (2021)	World Bank Policy Research Working Paper	TFP (log); labor productivity (log)	Dummy (0/1) firm has 3G	2
Atangana Ondoa et al. (2023)	*Telecommunications Policy*	Monthly revenue (log)	Dummy (0/1) person uses mobile money	3
Bahia et al. (2020)	World Bank Policy Research Paper	Nonfood consumption; food consumption; total consumption	3G/4G for over 1 year	3
Chavula (2013)	*Information Technology for Development*	GDP per capita (log)	Internet users per 100 people (log); telephone subscriptions per 100 people (log); mobile subscriptions per 100 people (log)	3
Estache et al. (2005)	Working Paper	GDP per capita (log)	Telephone lines per 1,000 people (log)	1

(continued)

ANNEX 7A. PAPERS USED IN THE ANALYSIS *(continued)*

Article	Publication	Outcome	Treatment	Number of estimates
Fluckiger and Ludwig (2023)	*Journal of Economic Behavior and Organization*	Nightlight (log)	Dummy (0/1) if cluster has mobile internet coverage; lagged	2
Haftu (2018)	*Telecommunications Policy*	GDP per capita (log)	Cell phone subscription per 100 people; percentage of population using internet	2
Fedderke and Bogetić (2009)	*World Development*	Per capita output	Total phone lines	1
Kallal et al. (2021)	*Technological Forecasting & Social Change*	Value added (log)	ICT diffusion index (log)	1
Masaki et al. (2020)	World Bank Policy Research Paper	Food consumption, Nonfood consumption, total consumption	3G coverage (0/1); proximity to fiber-optic network (0/1)	9
d. South Asia: Transportation				
Abeberese and Chen (2022)	*Journal of Development Economics*	Labor productivity (log); TFP (log)	Distance from district center to highway	2
Binswanger et al. (1993)	*Journal of Development Economics*	Aggregate crop output (log)	Road density (log)	1
Donaldson (2018)	*American Economic Review*	Real agricultural income	Railroad in district (0/1)	2
Ghani et al. (2016)	*Economic Journal*	Output; output (young firms); labor productivity	0–10 km from GQ (0/1)	6
Eynde and Wren-Lewis (2021)	CEPR Discussion Paper	Land cropped during dry season	(0/1) village has road	1
Hulten et al. (2006)	*World Bank Economic Review*	TFP (manufacturing sector, log)	Road length (log)	1
Khanna and Sharma (2020)	*Quarterly Review of Economics and Finance*	TFP (log)	Total surfaced national highway (km; log); passengers carried (number; log); registered carrier departures (number; log); registered carrier departures per 10,000 people (number; log); air transportation, total freight (million/ton-km; log); total traffic at all major ports, 1,000 tons (log); railway goods transported (million ton-km; log); railway passengers carried (million/km; log); total road network length (km; log)	13
Naaraayanan and Wolfenzon (2019)	Working Paper	TFP (log)	Highway (0/1)	1
Khandker et al. (2009)	*Economic Development and Cultural Change*	Per capita expenditure	Road development project in village	4

(continued)

ANNEX 7A. PAPERS USED IN THE ANALYSIS *(continued)*

Article	Publication	Outcome	Treatment	Number of estimates
e. South Asia: Energy				
Binswanger et al. (1993)	*Journal of Development Economics*	Aggregate crop output (log)	Number of electrified villages in 10 km (log)	1
Corbett et al. (2019)	*Energy Policy*	Log value added; log revenue	Log total outages; log unexpected outages	4
Van de Walle et al. (2017)	*World Bank Economic Review*	Total consumption per capita; nonfood nonfuel expenditure per capita; food expenditure per capita	Access to electricity (0/1)	6
Eynde and Wren-Lewis (2021)	CEPR Discussion Paper	Land cropped during dry season (share of 1 km pixels)	Village is electrified (0/1)	1
Hulten et al. (2006)	*World Bank Economic Review*	TFP manufacturing sector (log)	Electricity capacity (MW; log)	1
Allcott et al. (2016)	*American Economic Review*	Log TFPR; log revenue	Shortages	6
Samad and Zhang (2017)	World Bank Policy Research Paper	Per capita expenditure; per capita income	Access to grid electricity (0/1)	4
Javid (2019)	*Sustainability*	GDP per worker (log)	Investment in energy sector (public and private); (log)	4
Khandker et al. (2012)	World Bank Policy Research Working Paper	Per capita expenditure (monthly; log); per capita food expenditure (monthly; log); per capita farm income (monthly; log); per capita nonfarm income (monthly; log); per capita nonfood expenditure (monthly; log); per capita total income (monthly; log)	Access to electricity (0/1); household demand for electricity (kWh/month; logs)	12
Khanna and Sharma (2020)	*Quarterly Review of Economics and Finance*	TFP (log)	Electric power generation (kW per capita; log)	2
Nagpal and Sovera (2022)	Working Paper	Productivity (EVI; log)	Dummy village electrified (0/1)	2
Rud (2012)	*Journal of Development Economics*	GDP manufacturing per capita (log); value added per capita of manufacturing sector (log)	Rural electrification (agricultural units connected to grid per 1,000 people)	3
Samad and Zhang (2016)	World Bank Policy Research Paper	Per capita total income; per capita farm income; per capita nonfarm income; per capita nonfood expenditure; per capita total expenditure; per capita food expenditure	Access to grid electricity (0/1)	12

(continued)

ANNEX 7A. PAPERS USED IN THE ANALYSIS *(continued)*

Article	Publication	Outcome	Treatment	Number of estimates
f. East Asia and Pacific: Energy				
Chakravorty et al. (2016)	Working Paper	HH expenditure (log); agricultural income (log); nonagricultural income (log); HH income (log)	Village electrified (0/1)	6
Fisher-Vanden et al. (2015)	*Journal of Development Economics*	Output (log)	Electricity scarcity (generation-capacity ratio; log)	1
Gao et al. (2023)	*Energy Policy*	Rural income (log); urban income (log)	Clean energy transition index (log)	2
Huang and Yao (2023)	*Energy Policy*	Rural income (log); agriculture productivity (log)	Transmission lines (km/m²; 0/1)	2
Kassem (2021)	Working Paper	Sales (log); TFPR (log)	Access to grid (0/1)	4
Khandker et al. (2013)	*Economic Development and Cultural Change*	Nonfarm income (log); farm income (log); total income (log); consumption expenditure (log)	Access to grid (0/1)	8
Wang et al. (2023)	*Energy Economics*	Green TFP (log)	Dummy UHV transmission in city (0/1)	1
Wang et al. (2023)	*Energy and Environment*	Regional GDP (log)	High-voltage grid density (log); dummy UHV(0/1); extra-high-voltage grid density (log)	6
Xiao et al. (2022)	*China Economic Review*	Agriculture income (log)	Electricity infrastructure (log)	2
Xiao et al. (2023)	*Energy Policy*	Wage income per capita (log); local GDP (log); transfer income per capita (log); income per capita (log)	Dummy village has PV power (0/1)	8
Xu et al. (2022)	*Solar Energy*	GDP per capita (log); GDP (log)	Dummy county has PV generation (0/1)	4
Yang et al. (2022)	*Sustainability*	GDP (log); GDP per capita (log)	Dummy county has UHV transmission (0/1)	4
Zhang and Ji (2017)	*Economic Modelling*	GDP per worker (log)	Electricity generation per worker (log)	1
g. East Asia and Pacific: Transportation				
Banerjee et al. (2020)	*Journal of Development Economics*	GDP per capita (log); GDP per capita growth (log); firm profit (log)	In distance to historical lines	3
Faber (2014)	*Review of Economic Studies*	Industrial gross value added; GDP (log); nonagriculture gross value added; agriculture gross value added	Connection to network (0/1)	4

(continued)

ANNEX 7A. PAPERS USED IN THE ANALYSIS *(continued)*

Article	Publication	Outcome	Treatment	Number of estimates
Emran and Hou (2013)	*Review of Economics and Statistics*	HH consumption per capita (log)	Distance to domestic market (log)	1
Fan and Chan-Kang (2005)	IFPRI Research Report	GDP per worker (log)	High-quality road length (km; log)	1
Gibbons and Wu (2020)	*Journal of Economic Geography*	Industrial output (log; long diff.); industry GDP (log; long diff.); industry value added (log; long diff.); GDP (log; long diff.); agriculture GDP (log; long diff.); services GDP (log; long diff.)	Index of air transportation access (log)	6
Baum-Snow et al. (2017)	*Review of Economics and Statistics*	Change in central city industrial GDP	Radial railroad indicator; ring road indicator	2
Baum-Snow et al. (2020)	*Journal of Urban Economics*	GDP (log)	Minimum port travel time (log); road efficiency units within 450 km (log)	2
Chen et al. (2018)	*Cambridge Journal of Regions, Economy and Society*	Real GDP (log)	Railway passenger traffic; highway density; highway passenger traffic	4
Zhang and Ji (2017)	*Economic Modelling*	GDP per worker (log)	Length of railway per worker (log); length of paved road per worker (km; log)	2
h. Europe and Central Asia: Transportation				
Andersson et al. (1990)	*Regional Science and Urban Economics*	Output	Length of railroads (km); length of roads (km); airport passengers	10
Iimi (2022)	World Bank Policy Research Working Paper	Sales (log)	Transportation cost to nearest border (log); market access based on transportation cost (log); transportation cost to nearest city (log)	3
Cadot et al. (2006)	*Journal of Public Economics*	Labor productivity (log)	Transportation infrastructure capital stock per worker (log)	2
Del Bo and Florio (2012)	*European Planning Studies*	GDP at PPP	Time to market; other roads; road PCA; multimodal access; motorways; railways	13
Bonaglia et al. (2000)	*Giornale degli Economisti e Annali di Economia*	TFP growth; value added per worker	Transportation public capital growth; railways public capital growth; roads public capital growth; transportation public capital per worker	4
Nombela (2005)	*Presupuesto y gasto público*	GDP per capita; productivity	Public capital: transportation	5
Creel and Poilon (2008)	*International Review of Applied Economics*	GDP	Transportation investment	1

(continued)

ANNEX 7A. PAPERS USED IN THE ANALYSIS *(continued)*

Article	Publication	Outcome	Treatment	Number of estimates
Cantos et al. (2005)	*Transport Reviews*	TFP; private sector output	Railroads capital stock; roads capital stock; airports capital stock; ports capital stock; infrastructure index	10
Bronzini and Piselli (2009)	*Regional Science and Urban Economics*	TFP	Railways public capital stock; roads public capital stock	2
Moreno and Lopez-Bazo (2007)	*Regional Science Review*	Output	Stock of transportation capital	2
Gibbons et al. (2019)	*Journal of Urban Economics*	Gross value added per worker; gross output per worker	Accessibility	4
i. Europe and Central Asia: Digital				
Arvanitis and Loukis (2009)	*Information Economics and Policy*	Value added per employee (log)	Employees use internet in daily work (0/1); employees use intranet in daily work (0/1)	8
Bertschek and Niebel (2016)	*Telecommunications Policy*	Labor productivity (log)	Employees use mobile internet (%)	4
Bertschek et al. (2013)	*Information Economics and Policy*	Sales per employee (log)	Firms use broadband (0/1)	2
Bloom et al. (2010)	Report	Output (log)	ICT per worker (number of laptops and PCs per worker; log)	3
Del Bo and Florio (2012)	*European Planning Studies*	GDP at PPP	Firms with e-commerce; digital PCA; firms with websites; telecom PCA; HH with broadband	9
Colombo et al. (2013)	*Information Economics and Policy*	Manufacturing firms value added (log); services firms value added (log)	Firms use broadband (0/1)	2
Czarnitzki et al. (2023)	*Journal of Economic Behavior & Organization*	Value added (log); sales (log)	AI intensity; dummy (0/1) if firm uses AI	9
DeStefano et al. (2018)	*Journal of Economic Behavior & Organization*	Output (log); TFP (log)	ICT capital stock (log)	2
Bonaglia et al. (2000)	*Giornale degli Economisti e Annali di Economia*	TFP growth	Communications public capital growth	1
Gruber et al. (2014)	*Telecommunications Policy*	GDP (log)	Broadband lines (millions; log)	1
Haller and Lyons (2015)	*Telecommunications Policy*	Labor productivity (log); TFP (log)	Firm has broadband (0/1)	2
Sen and Saray (2019)	*Journal of Economic Cooperation and Development*	GDP growth	Growth of internet users per 100 people; growth of fixed phones per 100 people; growth of mobile subscribers per 100 people	9

Source: Original table for this publication.

Note: 3G/4G = third generation/fourth generation; AI = artificial intelligence; diff = difference; EVI = Enhanced Vegetation Index; GQ = Golden Quadrilateral; HH = household; ICT = information and communication technology; IGC = International Growth Center; km = kilometer; kW = kilowatt; kWh = kilowatt-hour; m = meter; MW = megawatt; PC = personal computer; PCA = principal component analysis; PPP = purchasing power parity; PV = photovoltaic; TFP = total factor productivity; TFPR = total factor productivity revenue; UHV = ultra-high voltage.

NOTES

1. Publication bias arises from two main sources: the preference of editors and reviewers for statistically significant findings when selecting articles for publication, and the related "file-drawer" problem, whereby researchers are more likely to write up and submit studies with significant results, leaving nonsignificant findings unpublished.
2. A key contribution of the paper is its rigorous approach to addressing publication bias and heterogeneity in the literature to correct for biases and come as close as possible to "true" underlying effects. Refer to box 7.1 for details.
3. As explained in chapter 1, the marginal product of capital, referred to here as the social rate of return, is defined by the product of the benefit elasticity (the output elasticity of infrastructure investments) and the capital-output ratio. Because these ratios vary significantly across countries, with poorer ones generally having smaller stocks as a share of gross domestic product, the smaller elasticities reported here do not necessarily imply lower marginal returns.

REFERENCES

Aker, Jenny C., and Joël Cariolle. 2023. *Mobile Phones and Development in Africa: Does the Evidence Meet the Hype?* Palgrave Studies in Agricultural Economics and Food Policy. Palgrave Macmillan.

Bom, Pedro R., and Jenny E. Ligthart. 2014. "What Have We Learned from Three Decades of Research on the Productivity of Public Capital?" *Journal of Economic Surveys* 28 (5): 889–916.

Foster, Vivien, Nisan Gorgulu, Dhruv Jain, Stéphane Straub, and Maria Vagliasindi. 2025. "The Impact of Infrastructure on Development Outcomes: A Meta-Analysis." *World Bank Research Observer*, October 7, 2025. https://doi.org/10.1093/wbro/lkaf003.

Foster, Vivien, Nisan Gorgulu, Stéphane Straub, and Maria Vagliasindi. 2023. "The Impact of Infrastructure on Development Outcomes: A Qualitative Review of Four Decades of Literature." Policy Research Working Paper 10343, World Bank.

Gertler, Paul J., Kenneth Lee, and A. Mushfiq Mobarak. 2017. "Electricity Reliability and Economic Development in Cities: A Microeconomic Perspective." EEG State-of-Knowledge Paper Series 3.2, Oxford Policy Management, Center for Effective Global Action, and Energy Institute @ Haas.

Hjort, Jonas, and Lin Tian. 2025. "The Economic Impact of Internet Connectivity in Developing Countries." *Annual Review of Economics* 17: 99–124.

Lee, Kenneth, Edward Miguel, and Catherine Wolfram. 2020. "Does Household Electrification Supercharge Economic Development?" *Journal of Economic Perspectives* 34 (1): 122–44.

Pritchett, Lant. 2024. "'Rely (Only) on the Rigorous Evidence' Is Bad Advice." *Review of Development Economics* 28 (4): 2034–58.

Ramey, Valerie A. 2019. "Ten Years after the Financial Crisis: What Have We Learned from the Renaissance in Fiscal Research?" *Journal of Economic Perspectives* 33 (2): 89–114.

Redding, Stephen J., and Matthew A. Turner. 2015. "Transportation Costs and the Spatial Organization of Economic Activity." In *Handbook of Regional and Urban Economics*, Vol. 5, edited by Gilles Duranton, J. Vernon Henderson, and William C. Strange, 1339–98. Elsevier.

Stanley, T. D., and Hristos Doucouliagos. 2012. *Meta-Regression Analysis in Economics and Business.* Routledge Advances in Research Methods. Routledge.

Straub, S. 2011. "Infrastructure and Development: A Critical Appraisal of the Macro-Level Literature." *Journal of Development Studies* 47(5): 683–708.

Vagliasindi, Maria, and Nisan Gorgulu. 2021. "What Have We Learned about the Effectiveness of Infrastructure Investment as a Fiscal Stimulus? A Literature Review." Policy Research Working Paper 9796, World Bank.

Spotlight 7.1. Highways and Local Growth: A Comparative Perspective

A meta-analysis of studies employing the FAT-PET-PEESE framework[1] yields robust, bias-adjusted estimates of the impact of infrastructure investment. By correcting for publication bias and reconciling methodological heterogeneity, these pooled results provide a credible global benchmark. Nonetheless, the aggregate evidence cannot fully capture the potential heterogeneity of impacts across developing economies, because of the limited availability of country-specific data and studies.

To illuminate this heterogeneity, a background paper for this report undertakes a systematic, cross-country comparison of the effects of highways on growth (Gerrits et al. 2025). It first harmonizes open-source road network data sets to pinpoint highway extensions at a grid-cell level, and merges them with the newly released gridded gross domestic product (GDP) series for the whole world. It then applies a consistent identification strategy across the harmonized expansion map, and estimates impact elasticities using the synthetic difference in differences (SDID) methodology—an approach that strengthens causal inference while accommodating investments that are staggered in time. The resulting country-level elasticity estimates function as a robustness check on the meta-analytic findings, verifying whether the aggregate returns remain under a more granular and harmonized lens. Additionally, they can reveal the extent of impact heterogeneity across countries and regions, providing policy makers with nuanced, evidence-based guidance.

The comparative analysis relies critically on the rigorous harmonization of the two underlying data sets at a common resolution. Output is measured with a newly released global, annually updated gridded GDP series at 0.25-degree resolution (about 800 square kilometers [km] at the equator) covering 2012–21. Built through a machine learning method that integrates conventional GDP accounts with fine-grained ancillary indicators—population density, nighttime luminosity, land use, emissions, and net primary productivity—the data set delivers markedly finer subnational estimates of economic activity, thereby enhancing the capacity to evaluate local investments and policy interventions (Rossi-Hansberg and Zhang 2025).

Road network information draws on OpenStreetMap (OSM), the crowdsourced platform that provides a fully digitized inventory of highways, arterial roads, and local streets.[2] According to OSM, total road length increased almost twofold from 2014 to 2025, surpassing 50 million km worldwide (figure S7.1.1). The regions of East Asia and Pacific, South Asia, and Sub-Saharan Africa have driven this expansion. Highways—which account for only roughly 12 percent of total road length—constitute the structural backbone of the networks.[3] Their cumulative length in the data reached just under 6 million km by 2025.

FIGURE S7.1.1 Trends of roads and highways, by region, 2014–25

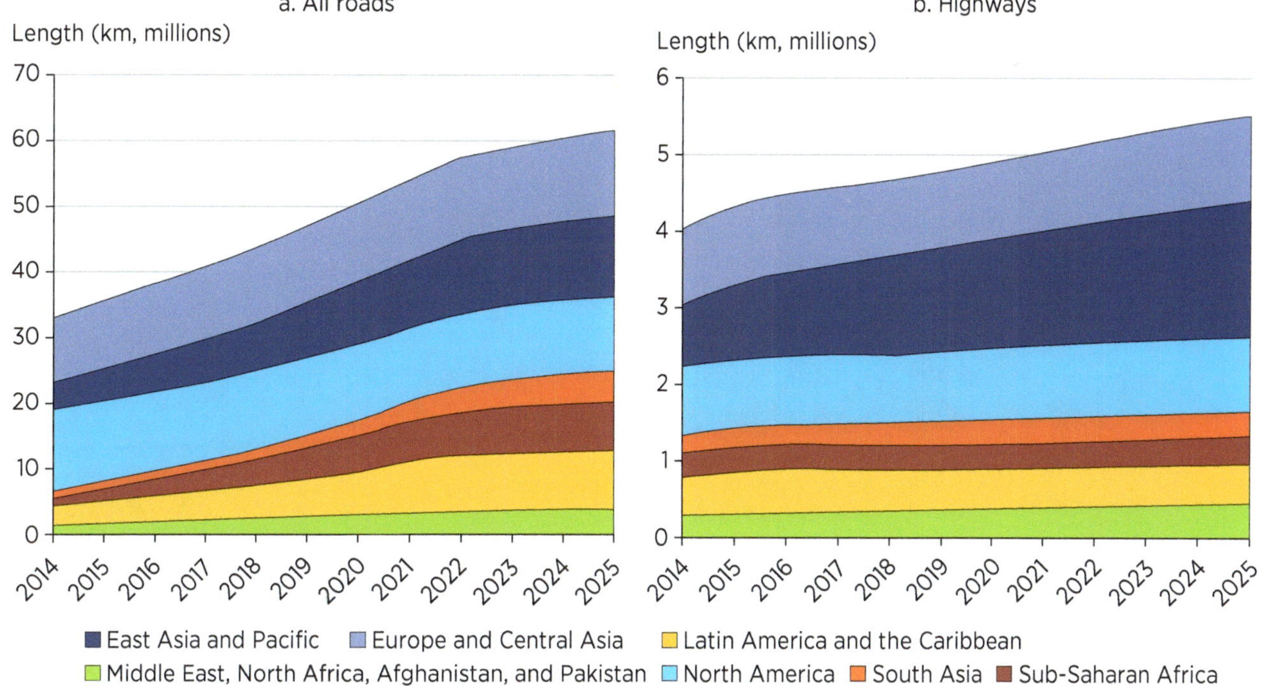

Source: Original calculation based on Gerrits et al. 2025.
Note: km = kilometer.

Empirical work on advanced economies and a select set of developing nations
has consistently documented the pivotal role of highways in reshaping the spatial
configuration of economic activity and spurring growth through various mechanisms
(Berg et al. 2017; Redding and Turner 2015). Consequently, the background study chose
highways as the focus of its empirical analysis. Because previous work has shown that
OSM coverage is sufficiently reliable from 2014 onward, the OSM highway layer spanning
from 2014 to 2021 is overlaid onto the 0.25-degree GDP grid, allocating highway length to
the intersecting cells.[4] Map S7.1.1 displays the globally consistent highway distribution at
0.25-degree resolution for 2025.

The identification of highway impact is achieved by comparing grid cells that transition
from no highway access to significant highway expansion with cells that remain without
access throughout the observation period. A cell is deemed to have highway access
once its cumulative highway length exceeds 1 km in a given year, classified as "with
access," whereas cells below that threshold remain classified as "without access." To avoid
contamination from longstanding infrastructure, any cell that already satisfied the 1 km
criterion in the initial year (2014) is labeled "always with access" and excluded from the
main estimation sample.

MAP S7.1.1 Map of gridded global highways, 0.25-degree resolution, 2025

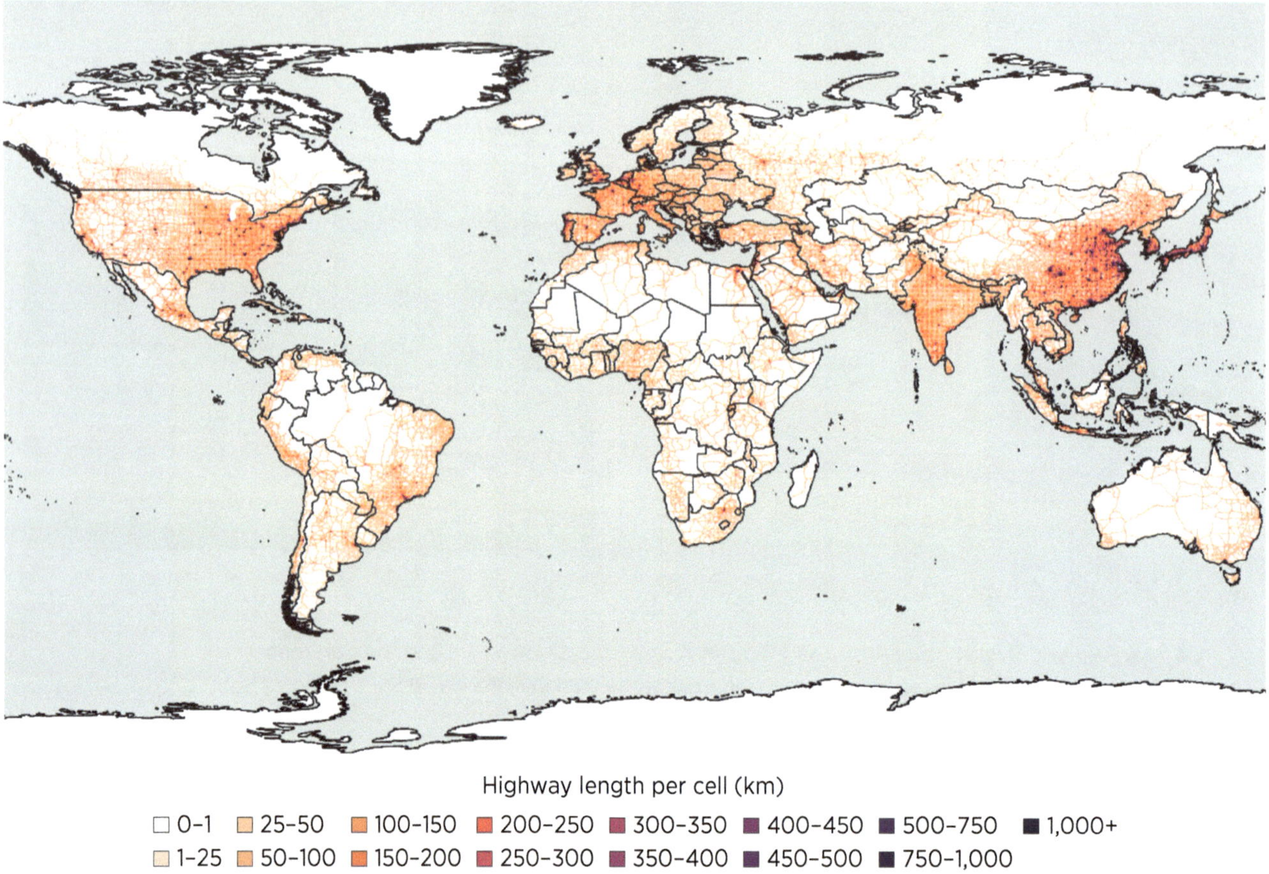

Source: Original calculation based on Gerrits et al. 2025.
Note: This map represents total kilometers of highways in 2025 at 0.25-degree resolution. km = kilometer.

The basis econometric specification is the following:

$$Y_{it} = \alpha + \beta\,WithAccess_i \times Highway_{it} + \theta Z_{it} + D_i + D_t + \varepsilon_{it},$$

where Y_{it} is the logarithm of GDP in grid cell i in year t; $WithAccess_i$ is a dummy variable that equals 1 if cell i ever changed status regarding highway access and 0 otherwise; $Highway_{it}$ is a dummy variable that equals 1 the year the cell gained highway access and all subsequent years; Z_{it} represents the set of control variables, particularly the presence of railways; and D_i and D_t denote cell-level and year fixed effects. β captures the average treatment effect on the treated (ATT) in this setting, indicating the estimated impact of having access to highways.

To accommodate staggered adoption and improve robustness, the analysis employs the SDID estimator (Arkhangelsky et al. 2021; Baker et al. 2022). Specifically, the SDID estimator addresses the reliance on parallel trend types of assumptions by constructing an optimal synthetic control group out of all cells with no highway access such that the group follows the parallel trend. Compared with the standard synthetic control method, SDID can also accommodate scenarios with multiple treated cities and multiple treatment times, and allows for level differences. Furthermore, the approach not only weighs cells without highway access but also weighs pre-highway time periods when estimating counterfactual outcomes.

This spotlight focuses on four countries as examples, whereas the ongoing research covers a broader set of developing countries. Figure S7.1.2 presents the event study analysis for the four selected countries: China, India, Indonesia, and Kenya. The panels plot the estimated effects of highway access (ATTs derived from the SDID estimation) against the number of years relative to the onset of highway access for each cell. Before treatment, the estimates hover around 0 and lack statistical significance, confirming the validity of the pretrend condition. Following the introduction of highway access, the estimates turn positive, become statistically significant, and generally increase in magnitude over subsequent years. Overall, the event study satisfies the pretreatment parallel trend condition, reducing concerns about omitted variable bias or endogenous placement of highways. The SDID-based estimates therefore provide credible evidence of the causal contribution of highway expansion to local economic growth across diverse developing country contexts.

FIGURE S7.1.2 **Illustration of the event study based on SDID estimation, selected countries**

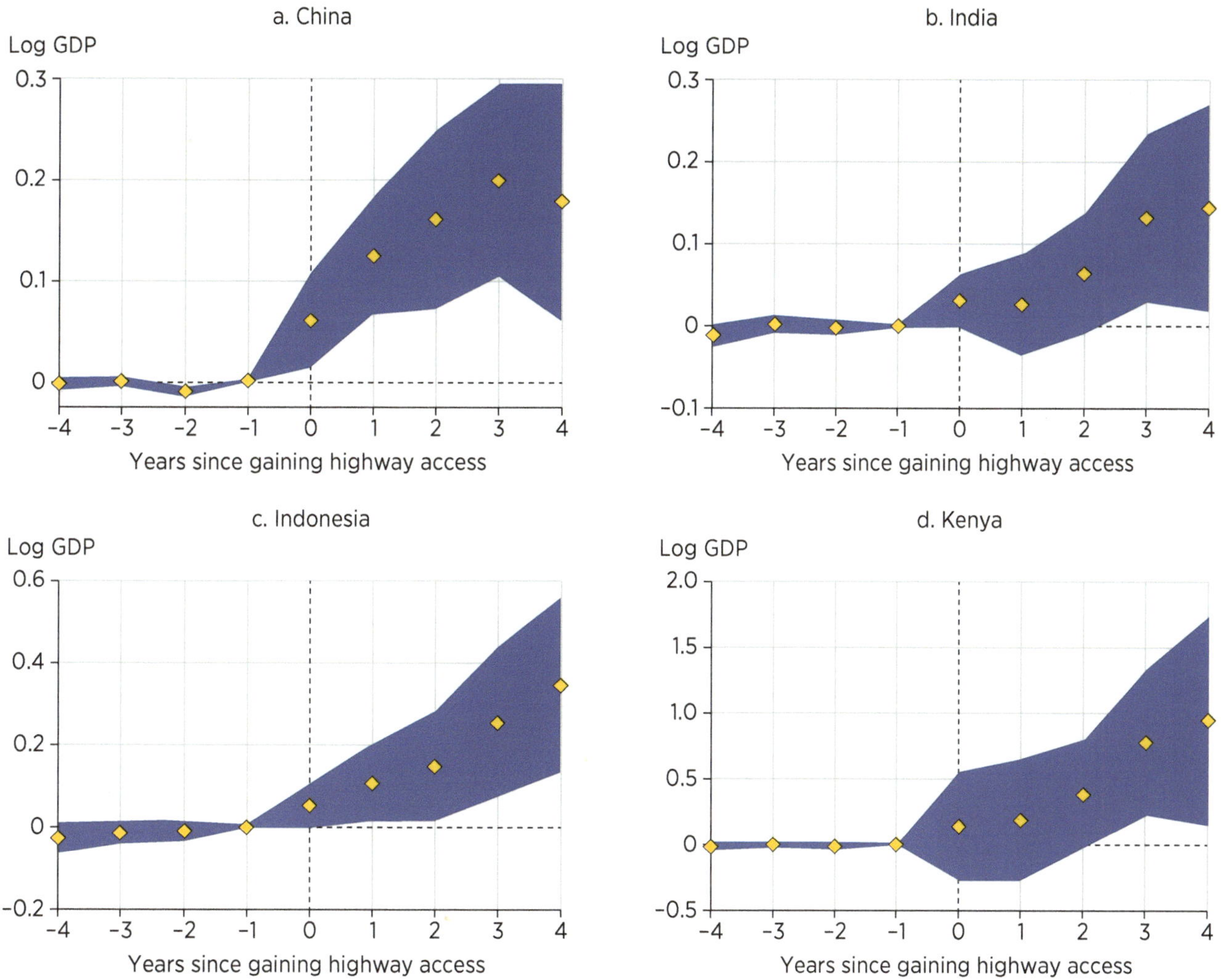

Source: Original calculation based on Gerrits et al. 2025.
Note: The figure plots estimates of ATTs relative to the year when a cell gained access to a highway. The y axis measures the logarithm of cell GDP in constant 2017 US dollars. An arbitrary increment of 1 was added to all GDP measures before taking the logarithm. ATT = average treatment effect on the treated; SDID = synthetic difference in differences.

The ATTs of highway access can be calculated as a weighted average of the estimates presented in figure S7.1.2, accounting for the length of treatment time. The average effects can also be transformed to elasticities such that they are comparable to the meta-analysis findings presented in the main body of chapter 7. The first type of semi-elasticity shows the percent increase in local GDP when the locality (grid cell) gains access to a highway; the second type, also a semi-elasticity, indicates the percent increase in local GDP when the total length of highways in the locality increases by 1 km; the third type is the elasticity representing the percent increase in local GDP associated with an increase of 1 percent in the total length of highways in the locality.[5]

Table S7.1.1 assembles the ATTs of gaining highway access together with the implied semi-elasticities and elasticity of GDP for the four selected countries. In Indonesia, for instance, providing highway access increases local GDP by approximately 7 percent (column 2). In Kenya, adding an additional kilometer of road to a cell increases its GDP by 1.9–4.4 percent (columns 4 and 7). Focusing on elasticity (columns 5 and 8), increasing total highway length by 1 percent in the locality increases local GDP by close to 0.05 percent in Indonesia, above 0.10 percent in India, 0.10–0.20 percent in China, and about 0.40 percent in Kenya.

These country-specific elasticities are comparable with the broader patterns identified in the meta-analysis. In that analysis, the average elasticity is estimated at about 0.021, and in South Asia it rises slightly to about 0.047; economies in Sub-Saharan Africa exhibit a markedly higher mean elasticity of roughly 0.264. The pronounced regional disparity signals that the growth gains from highway expansion are far from uniform; instead, they are mediated by a constellation of complementary factors— potentially including the quantity of existing transportation investment and quality of ancillary transportation services, institutional effectiveness, and the degree of market integration—that shape how efficiently additional road capacity can be translated into economic growth.[6]

TABLE S7.1.1 Highway impact elasticities, selected countries

	ATT of SDID estimation	Semi-elasticity with regard to highway access	Average highway length of cells with access at time of treatment	Semi-elasticity (following an additional km of highway)	Elasticity (following an increase in km of roads by 1 percent)	Average highway length in 2021 of cells defined as with access	Semi-elasticity (following an additional km of highway)	Elasticity (following an increase in km of roads by 1 percent)
	(1) β	(2) $\exp(\beta)-1$	(3) L	(4) $\exp(\beta/L)-1$	(5) $\beta/\ln(L)$	(6) L	(7) $\exp(\beta/L)-1$	(8) $\beta/\ln(L)$
China	0.251***	0.285	29.777	0.008	0.171	80.557	0.003	0.132
India	0.193***	0.213	25.820	0.008	0.137	46.139	0.004	0.116
Indonesia	0.070*	0.073	23.925	0.003	0.051	38.592	0.002	0.044
Kenya	0.517**	0.677	11.951	0.044	0.480	27.409	0.019	0.360

Source: Gerrits et al. 2025.
Note: Significance for the β coefficient, shown in column (1): * =10 percent, ** = 5 percent, *** = 1 percent. ATT = average treatment effect on the treated; km = kilometer; SDID = synthetic difference in differences.

NOTES

1. As described earlier, this three-step process begins with the Funnel Asymmetry Test (FAT), which visually and econometrically assesses publication bias by examining the relationship between effect sizes and their precision (standard errors). The Precision-Effect Test (PET) then evaluates whether a genuine effect exists beyond publication bias, and the Precision-Effect Estimate with Standard Error (PEESE) refines the estimate by accounting for a quadratic relationship between effect sizes and their variance.
2. OpenStreetMap, "Planet OSM," https://planet.openstreetmap.org.
3. Following the standard proposed by the Mapzen platform (https://mapzen.com/blog/osmlr-2nd-technical-preview/), highways include OSM segments tagged "motorway," "motorway_link," "trunk" and "trunk_link," "primary," and "primary_link."
4. To allow for country-level heterogeneity of road coding in OSM, the empirical analysis excludes primary roads when doing so provides a better correlation at the country level with the verified road network, using 2015 data from Garmin, *Digital Atlas of the Earth*, https://developer.garmin.com/datasets/digital-atlas/.
5. More specifically, the semi-elasticity with regard to highway access is $\exp(\beta)-1$, the semi-elasticity following an additional km of highway is $\exp(\beta/L)-1$, and the elasticity following an increase in km of roads by 1 percent is $\beta/\ln(L)$, where L is the is the average number of kilometers of highways in cells with highway access. L can be calculated as the average highway length of all cells with highway access in the year they gain access to a highway or as average highway length of these cells in 2021, the end year of the analysis.
6. Note that, given the data mobilized and methodology for the analysis, the estimates are based on recent investments, local impacts, and a focus on the extensive margin.

REFERENCES

Arkhangelsky, Dmitry, Susan Athey, David A. Hirshberg, Guido W. Imbens, and Stefan Wager. 2021. "Synthetic Difference-in-Differences." *American Economic Review* 111 (12): 4088–118.

Baker, Andrew C., David F. Larcker, and Charles C. Y. Wang. 2022. "How Much Should We Trust Staggered Difference-in-Differences Estimates?" *Journal of Financial Economics* 144 (2): 370–95.

Berg, Claudia N., Uwe Deichmann, Yishan Liu, and Harris Selod. 2017. "Transport Policies and Development." *Journal of Development Studies* 53 (4): 465–80.

Gerrits, Petrus, Yue Li, Harris Selod, Stéphane Straub, and Yawen Zheng. 2025. "Highway Investments and Local Growth: A Comparative Perspective." Unpublished background paper for this report, World Bank.

Redding, Stephen J., and Matthew A. Turner. 2015. "Transportation Costs and the Spatial Organization of Economic Activity." In *Handbook of Regional and Urban Economics*, Vol. 5, edited by Gilles Duranton, J. Vernon Henderson, and William C. Strange, 1339–98. Elsevier.

Rossi-Hansberg, Esteban, and Jialing Zhang. 2025. "Local GDP Estimates around the World." NBER Working Paper 33458, National Bureau of Economic Research.

Spotlight 7.2. Keeping the Lights On: A Direct Measure of the Benefits of Power Sector Investment

The core of this chapter measures the benefits of infrastructure by asking how much additional output is associated with higher stocks of energy, transportation, and digital infrastructure. In practice, however, policy makers, investors, and utilities also care about a different, more immediate question: what is the economic payoff from actually building the next power plant or transmission line that keeps the system from running short of electricity?

This spotlight presents a complementary direct approach to valuing energy investments. Rather than inferring benefits from the long-run causal link between power infrastructure and gross domestic product (GDP), it looks at what happens to system costs and unserved demand when countries implement their planned power sector expansion. The analysis combines the World Bank's Electricity Planning Model (EPM) with new cross-country estimates of the Value of Lost Load (VoLL) to quantify the direct benefits of planned investments for 76 countries up to 2040.

EPM, a power system planning model that integrates capacity expansion and production cost modeling in a single framework, is widely used to inform the operational work of the World Bank's staff and clients on a range of policy questions related to optimal power system expansion and dispatch. For this spotlight, the analysis uses the EPM "Base Scenario," which relies on a least-cost optimization to meet projected demand under existing policies and constraints, up to 2040. This scenario approximates what each country is effectively on track to build if it follows its current plans.

Consider two types of direct benefits of power infrastructure investment. The first benefit is the *changes in system costs,* calculated as annualized capital expenditure for new generation and transmission projects, fixed and variable operating costs, fuel for fossil plants, and reserve costs. For each country, the analysis tracks how the unit cost of providing capacity (total system cost divided by total capacity) evolves with implementation of the expansion plan. A reduction in unit cost signals that the new investment makes the system more efficient; an increase indicates that the system becomes more expensive to operate, often because of rising fuel prices, higher reserve needs, or the up-front cost of integrating renewables.

The second benefit is the *avoided economic losses from unmet electricity demand.* If investment fails to keep up with demand, electricity shortages force firms and households to curtail production and consumption. The resulting economic damage is approximated using VoLL, the monetary value that electricity consumers place on avoiding an interruption of supply. A meta-analysis by Jin (2025) assembles outage costs from 56 studies covering 47 countries and shows that VoLL is higher when incomes and electricity prices are higher and lower in countries with large populations and high total electricity demand. The results of the meta-analysis are extended to predict VoLL for countries not covered in the original set of studies by inputting each country's observable characteristics (residential electricity consumption, population, GDP, total electricity demand, and average residential tariffs) into the estimated model. The opportunity cost of unserved demand is estimated by multiplying the country-specific VoLL by the additional electricity generated by the expansion plan, assuming that this extra supply corresponds to demand that would otherwise have gone unmet or been met by very costly alternatives such as diesel generators.

To achieve a valid comparison across countries, the analysis then backs out an implied output elasticity based on estimated direct energy benefits that can be set alongside the energy output elasticities from the meta-analysis in the chapter 7 section titled "Meta-analysis Results." The implied elasticity is estimated using existing capital estimates from the EPM model alongside the additional annualized investment expenditures required to meet the plan. The analysis assumes that the direct benefit represents additional household consumption that contributes to GDP. Under this assumption, the implied elasticity indicates how much GDP would change, in percentage terms, for each percentage increase in power sector investment.

All in all, this measure of the benefits of power sector investment yields consistent, but not identical, results. A clear upward relationship exists between income per capita and the implied output elasticity of electricity: poorer countries cluster at low elasticities, whereas richer economies tend to exhibit higher values, albeit with substantial variation within each region (figure S7.2.1). This pattern suggests that, as economies develop and become more electricity intensive, the direct growth payoff from additional reliable supply rises.

FIGURE S7.2.1 Direct benefit implied output elasticities versus income, by region

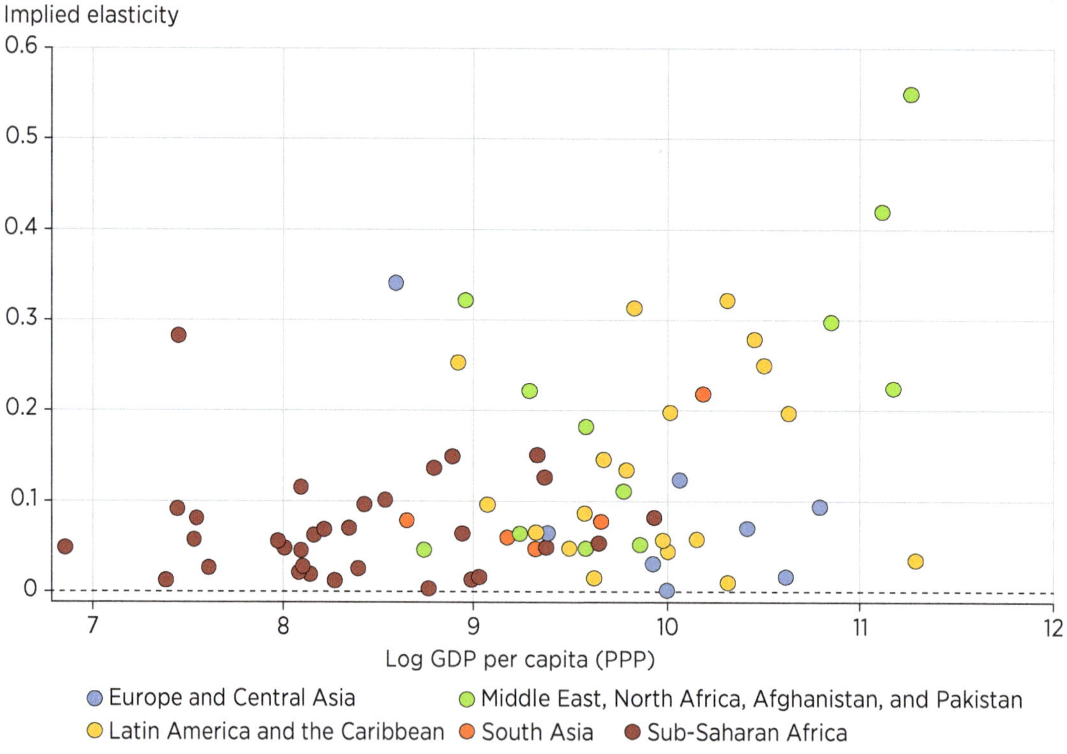

Source: Original figure for this publication.
Note: Because of data limitations, the figure does not show a comparison for the East Asia and Pacific region. PPP = purchasing power parity.

However, the levels and dispersion of benefits differ. For most countries, the direct benefit method yields substantially higher returns than those implied by the indirect, elasticity-based approach, because VoLL captures immediate production losses, damage to equipment, food spoilage, lost working hours, and other short-term costs of outages, many of which are only partially reflected in macroeconomic indicators that take longer to absorb impacts of energy infrastructure investment. Moreover, the dispersion of direct benefits across countries is larger than that of indirect benefits. Because the direct approach embeds detailed, country-specific information on demand growth, technology mixes, fuel prices, reliability constraints, and policy targets from EPM, it picks up heterogeneity that broad cross-country elasticities necessarily smooth out.

Finally, when the implied elasticities from this direct benefit approach are aggregated by region and weighted by generation capacity, they are broadly consistent in magnitude with the regional elasticities obtained from the meta-analysis discussed in the meta-analysis results section in chapter 7 (figure S7.2.2). At a broad regional level, for Europe and Central Asia and Latin America and the Caribbean, the elasticity obtained from the meta-analysis lies within and toward the lower end of the regional distribution of implied elasticities. For the Middle East, North Africa, Afghanistan, and Pakistan region and the South Asia region, the elasticity likewise lies below but just slightly out of bound of regional distribution of implied elasticities. By contrast, for African countries, the elasticity obtained from the meta-analysis

FIGURE S7.2.2 Direct benefit implied output elasticities versus meta-analysis estimates, by region

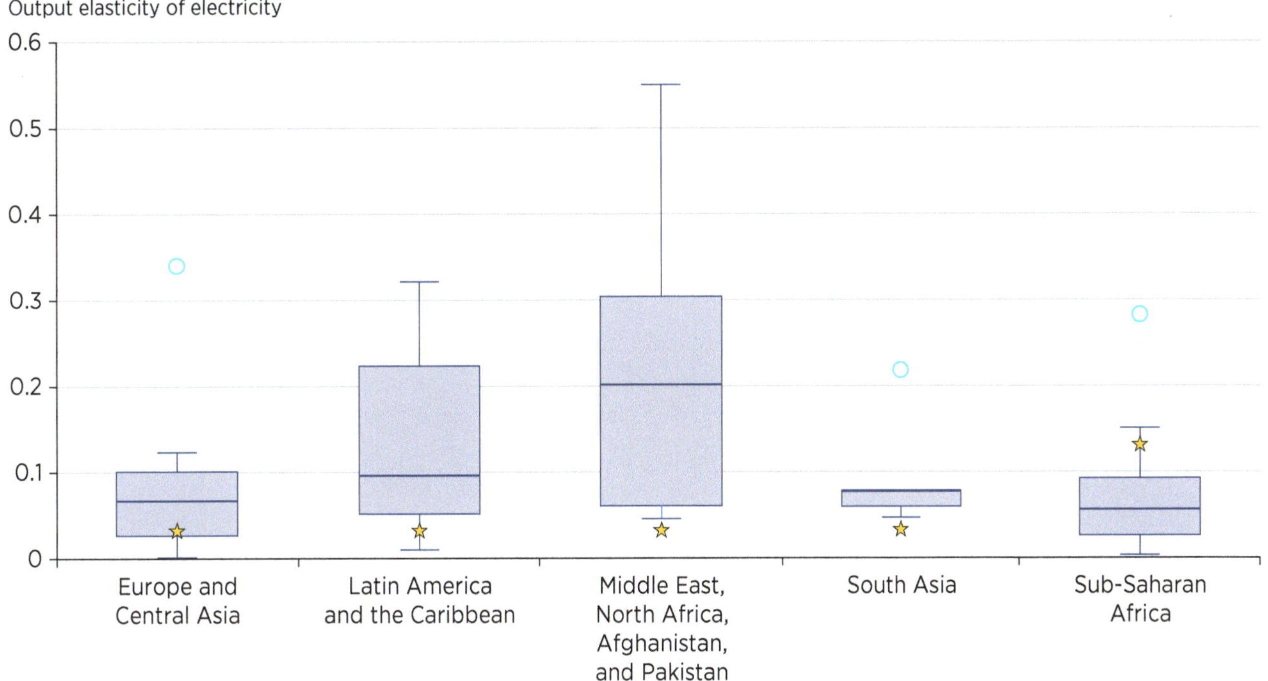

Source: Original figure for this publication.
Note: The boxplots show the distribution of implied output elasticities of electricity obtained from the direct benefit (EPM + VoLL) approach for countries in each region; the yellow star marks the single elasticity estimate from the meta-analysis. The energy elasticity is set to 0.0325 for all regions except those with reported regional estimates. For South Asia, the reported elasticity is 0.0333, and for Africa it is 0.1314. In this figure, Africa includes Sub-Saharan and North African countries. Because of data limitations, the figure does not show a comparison for the East Asia and Pacific region. EPM = Electricity Planning Model; VoLL = Value of Lost Load.

is situated in the upper end of the regional distribution, because lower incomes and power consumption levels mean that many African countries exhibit lower VoLL. This convergence increases confidence that both methods capture underlying economic relationships rather than artifacts of specific data sets or modeling choices.

REFERENCE

Jin, Taeyoung. 2025. "A Meta-Analysis of Outage Cost for Value-Based Reliability Planning." *Energy Strategy Reviews* 62: 101975.

www.ingramcontent.com/pod-product-compliance
Lightning Source LLC
Chambersburg PA
CBHW040130240726
48664CB00002B/432